ONSLOW COUNTY
A BRIEF HISTORY

ONSLOW COUNTY
A BRIEF HISTORY

Alan D. Watson

Division of Archives and History
North Carolina Department of Cultural Resources
Raleigh
1995

© Copyright, 1995, by the North Carolina Division of Archives and History

ISBN 0-86526-263-2 ▪

Contents

Maps and Illustrations

Foreword

Onslow County:A Brief History is the fourteenth volume to appear in a series of county histories published by the Historical Publications Section since 1963.Just as significantly, it is the fourth county history written for the series by Alan D.Watson. Dr.Watson has also prepared histories for Edgecombe, Bertie, and Perquimans Counties. In addition to his county histories and several other titles published by the Historical Publications Section, Dr. Watson has written numerous articles for the *North Carolina Historical Review* as well as other journals, published major histories of New Bern and Wilmington, and offered his counsel and advice to a generation of historians, students, and citizens interested in the history of North Carolina. He is currently a professor of history at the University of North Carolina at Wilmington. He received his doctorate from the University of South Carolina.

Onslow County holds a unique place in North Carolina history. In 1524 it was the first point of contact between Native Americans and European explorers. Giovanni da Verrazzano, sailing for France, furnished the occasion when one of his crewmen was swept ashore by heavy seas.The sailor carried gifts for the Indians, who greeted him warmly—evidence perhaps that southern hospitality began in North Carolina. With typical thoroughness and skill, Dr.Watson guides the reader through the social, economic, and political history of Onslow from the colonial era to the twentieth century. Unlike previous county histories in this series, *Onslow County* includes footnotes to help those researchers willing to delve deeper into the coastal county's rich history.

Publishing is a highly collaborative enterprise, and Dr.Watson had the able assistance of members of the Historical Publications Staff. Lang Baradell edited the manuscript, compiled the index, and saw the volume through press. Lisa D. Bailey contributed her proofreading skills.To them and to Dr. Watson, students of North Carolina history extend their hearty thanks.

Jeffrey J. Crow
Historical Publications Administrator

February 1995

Chapter One
Native Americans and European Settlement

Current Onslow County, lying along the south Atlantic coast of North Carolina, evidenced its earliest prehistoric human occupation during the cultural tradition called Paleo-Indian. Population was sparse, and the nomadic aboriginals depended mainly upon large game, which they hunted with spears. About 9,000-8,000 B.C. the Paleo-Indian period yielded to the Archaic. Changing climatic conditions and the passing of large animals forced a dependence upon smaller game. The aboriginals restricted their habitation to defined regions, though they moved occasionally within those bounds. At that time, however, the Atlantic coast extended twenty-five to forty miles farther east, and the subsequent rise in the sea level inundated much of the evidence of Paleo-Indian and Archaic presence in Onslow.[1]

During the succeeding Woodland period, beginning about 2,000-1,000 B.C. and characterized by the use of various types of pottery and the replacement of the spear by the bow and arrow, the Native Americans may have inhabited semipermanent villages along various watercourses. Fishing was productive in the early spring. During the late spring and early summer, when food became scarce, the villagers probably broke into small bands and dispersed to seek shellfish and gather other available food. In the fall, villagers recongregated to harvest cultivated as well as wild crops and remained together throughout the winter, subsisting on game and stored plant foods.[2]

Coastal North Carolina remains perhaps the state's most poorly understood archaeological area, but several archaeological investigations conducted in current Onslow by Thomas C. Loftfield of the University of North Carolina at Wilmington have added significantly to knowledge of the aboriginals of the Woodland period. Areas of Camp Lejeune, Permuda Island, and a site near Hammocks Beach State Park, among others, have been explored productively. Although Onslow occupies a geographic region often associated with the Siouan linguistic group of aboriginals at the time of European contact, Loftfield identified a common ceramic ware of the late Woodland period at Permuda as a product of Algonquian-speaking Indians living along the littoral coast and a much rarer ceramic as representative of Iroquoian Native Americans residing just west of the tidewater.[3]

Modern European contact with the Native Americans in Onslow may have originated with the exploratory voyage of Giovanni da Verrazzano in 1524. Sailing on behalf of France to reconnoiter the Atlantic coast, Verrazzano anchored off the southern coast of current North Carolina, perhaps between Bogue and New River Inlets. When the navigator sent sailors ashore in a small boat to seek water, aboriginals appeared. The Indians as well as the flora and fauna of the region greatly impressed Verrazzano, who wrote appreciatively of his visit to the Carolina coast.[4]

Subsequently the French failed to take advantage of Verrazzano's discovery and the Spanish confined their colonizing efforts mainly to Florida, leaving the North Carolina coast open to settlement efforts directed by Walter Raleigh in the 1580s. John White, an artist from the first Raleigh colony on Roanoke Island, participated in a coastal exploration as far as present Onslow. The second Raleigh expedition in 1587, or the "Lost Colony," and White's voyage in 1590 to seek the abandoned settlement may also have brought the English into contact with the Onslow coast.[5]

After the failure of the Raleigh settlements, the first permanent English colony was established in present Virginia in 1607. A half century later the Virginians moved into the present Albemarle region of North Carolina, just before King Charles II of England granted Carolina to the eight lords proprietors in 1663. Settlement gradually moved southward along the coast, reaching the Pamlico before the end of the century and the Neuse-Trent area by the first decade of the eighteenth century. However, only the defeat of the Native Americans in the Tuscarora War (1711-1714) allowed Europeans to extend appreciably their presence.

Onslow originated in the wake of the eighteenth century expansion of North Carolina's southern coastal frontier. Bath County, created in 1696 and subdivided in 1705, subsumed future Onslow in Archdale Precinct, which was later renamed Craven Precinct. A decade later the defeat of the Tuscarora Indians and allied tribes opened the way for white settlement to the south of the Neuse and Trent Rivers. From Craven

Precinct the General Assembly erected Carteret Precinct in 1722 and seven years later, New Hanover Precinct. During the succeeding decade Onslow Precinct was formed from Carteret and New Hanover.[6]

The actual settlement of the area that became Onslow, and certainly the New River region, began during the second decade of the eighteenth century, probably 1711-1714. Habitation proceeded along the water-courses—first the sounds, then the rivers and major creeks—which provided easy access to the interior and constituted the only feasible arteries of early transportation. Residents and nonresidents alike obtained land grants in future Onslow. Among the earliest permanent settlers were three brothers from Massachusetts—Phillip, Ebenezer, and Hope Dexter, whose lands were located on Bear and Mittum's (Mittam's) Creeks. However, between 1713/14 and 1730, as many as half of the land grants in the Onslow area were issued to nonresidents, perhaps for speculation. Among the nonresident grantees presumably was Thomas Brown Sr., whose eponym apparently endowed Browns Inlet, Browns Swamp or Creek, Brown's Sound, and Brown's Island.[7]

From the inception of Carteret Precinct, the White Oak and New River regions, future centers of Onslow settlement, were focuses of attention. A precinct court order in 1723 directed the construction of a road from the vicinity of Beaufort to White Oak River. By 1726 a road extended from the Neuse (in the vicinity of New Bern) to New River, with an intersecting highway to White Oak River, and continued below New River to the Cape Fear. During that year the establishment of a ferry over New River evidenced increasing overland traffic to southern Carteret.[8] The growing population of lower Carteret presaged the creation of a new precinct in 1731.

3

Chapter Two
Colonial Onslow

Onslow emerged amid controversy and bore dubious legal status after its formation as a political entity in 1731. As the growing number of residents of southern Carteret Precinct found themselves far removed from the center of public business, principally the court at Beaufort, they sought the establishment of a new precinct to lessen the burden of travel. Inhabitants along White Oak River, New River, and New Topsail Inlet petitioned Governor George Burrington, complaining of the "great hardships and expences [*sic*]" of attending the Carteret court. On November 13, 1731, the governor and a majority of his royal council responded by creating Onslow Precinct, named for Sir Arthur Onslow, the esteemed Speaker of the British House of Commons.[1]

Burrington's action, however, precipitated heated controversy. The hot-tempered, domineering governor had already antagonized many of the prominent men in the colony. In this instance, his chief opponents, Councilors John Ashe and Nathaniel Rice, charged that the formation of a precinct without the approval of the lower house of the General Assembly upset the constitutional balance of power within the government and violated the governor's royal instructions. When the legislature convened, the house of commons agreed with Ashe and Rice. The result was an impasse: the Onslow Precinct court organized and conducted business, but the lower house of the legislature refused to seat the elected representatives of the precinct.[2]

By 1734, however, the governor and council had relented and had agreed in principle to the statutory formation of precincts. In the November legislative session of that year the commons accepted John Starkey and John Williams, the elected representatives of the precinct, and

The Honble *ARTHUR ONSLOW.*

Onslow County was named for Sir Arthur Onslow, Speaker of the British House of Commons from 1728 to 1761. He also served as a member of the privy council, chancellor to Queen Caroline, and treasurer of the navy. Photograph of Onslow's portrait from the files of the Division of Archives and History.

readily approved the first reading of a bill to erect the precinct of Onslow. Although the arrival of newly appointed governor Gabriel Johnston abruptly ended the legislative session, a subsequent assembly in January 1734/35 quickly passed legislation to establish formally Onslow Precinct and to validate the proceedings of the court that had been meeting under the authority of Burrington's commission. According to the statute, the precinct was bounded on the north by White Oak River and on the south by Beasleys Creek, located a few miles below New River.[3]

Overshadowed by the more populous and wealthier counties along the coast, Onslow rarely figured prominently in provincial affairs before the Revolution. Only during military conflict did the county become an object of substantive attention. When agreeing to raise troops in 1743 for British service in the war against Spain, Governor Johnston and the council exempted men from Onslow, New Hanover, and Bladen from enlistment because those counties were too "thinly peopled" and "so much exposed [to invasion by] an Enemy." Indeed, Spanish vessels menaced the North Carolina coast in 1747-1748, prompting the General Assembly to appropriate funds to build four forts, including one at Bear Inlet, to protect the colony from a marauding enemy.[4]

In succeeding decades the French and Indian War and the Regulator movement again drew North Carolina into a military posture. Four companies of Onslow militia under the command of Colonel John Starkey stood ready for service against the French in 1754, though no record exists of their active participation in the hostilities. During the Regulator campaign of 1771, Onslow contributed one company, which was led by Colonel William Cray, a prominent figure in Governor William Tryon's western expedition. Three members of the Onslow company were wounded at the Battle of Alamance.[5]

Despite its inconspicuousness, Onslow exerted a significant voice in provincial politics throughout most of the colonial era, for representing the county in the General Assembly were Samuel Swann, from 1739 to 1762, and John Starkey, from 1739 to 1764. Swann, a surveyor and lawyer, had been active in the Albemarle region before moving to New Hanover Precinct to become one of the early developers of the Lower Cape Fear. By virtue of his ownership of land in Onslow, Swann qualified for political office in the county and acceded to the wishes of Onslow inhabitants by representing the county in the General Assembly. He became Speaker of the lower house in 1743 and retained that position, with the exception of two legislative sessions, until poor health forced his resignation from the commons. At mid-eighteenth century Swann, strongly seconded by

Starkey, was perhaps North Carolina's leading legislative opponent of the royal prerogative.[6]

Due to Swann's absentee residence, John Starkey emerged as Onslow's "first citizen," exercising unquestioned dominance in county, parish, and provincial affairs for more than thirty years. A member of the first commission of the peace in Onslow upon the erection of the precinct in 1735, Starkey sat continuously as a justice of the peace and fulfilled innumerable public responsibilities for the county until his death in 1765. During Starkey's quarter-century tenure in the General Assembly, he assumed increasingly important legislative assignments, eventually becoming one of the most influential legislators to serve in the North Carolina House of Commons before the Revolution. And, in 1750, he succeeded Eleazar Allen as the politically powerful public treasurer of the southern counties.[7]

Governor Arthur Dobbs accounted Starkey among his most formidable opponents in the commons. A leading republican, Starkey, along with Swann, spearheaded a junto in the lower house in opposition to royal government in North Carolina. According to the governor, by "wearing shoe strings[,] a plain coat[,] and having a bald head," Starkey seemed humble and self-denying, but actually he was the most scheming man in the province. "Not less in appearance than in principles, . . . [he was] a declared Republican, and by professing those principles . . . gained a great share of popular applause," reported Dobbs. As treasurer, Starkey could advance or delay payments to members of the assembly; as a result, the poorer legislators "follow[ed] him like Chickens." Although Dobbs retaliated by depriving Starkey of his commissions as justice of the peace and colonel of the Onslow County militia, such actions only heightened Starkey's prestige in the colony. According to historian Jack P. Greene, "it was not until Arthur Dobbs's tenure in the 1750s and 1760s that the Lower House . . . asserted its primacy in North Carolina politics under the guidance of Speaker Samuel Swann and Treasurers John Starkey and Thomas Barker."[8]

A succession of county luminaries followed Swann and Starkey to the assembly, most prominent of whom was William Cray Sr., who served with the exception of one session from 1764 to 1775. A merchant living on a plantation at the junction of Duck Creek and New River, Cray was active in county affairs for a quarter century before his death in 1778. In an era when holding multiple offices was common, he was clerk of the county court, registrar, and coroner. He also succeeded Starkey as colonel of the county militia.[9] In addition to Cray, Onslow sent Richard Ward, Henry Rhodes, John Spicer, Edward Starkey, and Ezekiel Hunter to the house of commons before the Revolution. All were active in local affairs. Ward served as chairman of the Onslow County court following Starkey's death, Rhodes was a longtime sheriff of the county, and Hunter helped to organize and minister to the New River Baptist Church.[10]

Local government in Onslow was controlled by the justices of the county court. Appointed by the governor, fewer than sixty men were magistrates in Onslow in the forty years prior to the Revolution, a clear indication of the restricted nature of county governance. Three justices comprised a quorum for the court, which met quarterly, though at any session as many as ten sometimes appeared. Death or removal from the county occasioned the termination of most magistrates' appointments, but Governor Dobbs dismissed Starkey in the course of their political conflict and in 1763 struck William Williams Sr. from the commission after unspecified charges brought against him by fellow magistrate James Howard were "fully proved."[11]

The most important officer of the court was the sheriff, who wielded extensive financial and administrative powers, especially by means of his authority to collect taxes and conduct elections. Although early North Carolina sheriffs have been accused of grossly abusing their authority, Onslow enjoyed an able set of officials, with one exception. Enoch Ward was summarily dismissed from office in 1763 by the governor, but the other nine men who acted as sheriff from 1739 to 1775 served conscientiously. Thomas Johnston, nominated ten times for the sheriffalty, and Henry Rhodes, appointed for eight, possibly nine, terms to that office, had the distinction of being nominated more often and serving more terms, respectively, than any other individuals in the colonial era, according to extant records.[12]

Whereas most counties depended solely upon the sheriff to collect and disburse public funds, some utilized a "treasurer," who was entrusted with the ultimate receipt and expenditures of tax moneys. Craven, Hyde, and Tyrrell, among other counties, experimented with the office of treasurer, but the position was most extensively and successfully used in Onslow, where John Starkey served in that capacity from 1749 until his death in 1765. Upon the collection of taxes the sheriff turned the funds over to the treasurer, who in turn assumed the responsibility for the payment of county obligations. The office worked extremely well under Starkey's command. Sheriffs reported promptly to him, the county quickly satisfied its creditors, and Starkey maintained a balance in his hands to meet unexpected demands upon the county. By providing continuity in office and overarching supervision of the county fiscal system, Starkey brought a measure of probity and efficiency to Onslow finances that generally was lacking elsewhere in provincial North Carolina.[13]

Assisting the justices and sheriff in an inadequate colonial law enforcement system were the constables. Although required to serve annual terms, many remained in office for several years, and some rose to eminence as magistrates and sheriffs. Yet others proved loath to accept their demanding positions. After his appointment Stephen Williams refused to qualify for the post, incurring a fine of fifty shillings. Joseph Lloyd, however, offered a satisfactory excuse—he could not write. Rather than risk a fine, others accepted their appointments but failed to fulfill their duties. In January 1752, Peter Perry was brought before the court for allowing a prisoner to escape; fifteen months later Perry was charged with failing to serve an attachment. Other constables were charged with failing to appear for court and grand jury duty, for treating the justices contemptuously, and for filing false returns on warrants.[14]

Other than the sheriff, the clerk was the most distinguished officer of the court. His copious duties ranged from keeping the minutes of the court to recording tavern keepers' fees and executing sundry orders of the justices. In the 1740s a succession of men occupied the office, including William Hodges, appointed in 1746. The following year several complaints were lodged against Hodges for nonattendance and for demanding exorbitant fees, charges that presaged later accusations against county clerks by the Regulators in the western counties of the province. When the court investigated Hodges, the clerk treated the justices "in a Very Indecent Manner" and was promptly dismissed. Not until 1753 (perhaps earlier), when William Cray Sr. assumed the clerkship, did the Onslow court find a trustworthy and able individual who brought longevity to the office. Cray remained clerk until 1774, when he was replaced by his son, William Cray Jr.[15]

Public buildings—courthouse and jail, plus accompanying stocks, pillory, and whipping post—occupied the attention of the justices and absorbed a large percentage of county expenditures. Onslow's first courthouse was located on Jarrett's Point at Court House Bay and was donated by John Williams, one of the principal promoters of the New River settlement. Beginning in 1735, however, the precinct abandoned Williams's proffered structure and held its court in the private residences of Christian Heidelberg and Joseph Howard.[16]

Meanwhile, the magistrates quickly took advantage of the 1735 legislation that not only established the precinct but also permitted the justices to select a site for a courthouse and to levy a tax for its construction. After Williams reneged on a contract to build a courthouse, the justices extended a slightly altered agreement to Joseph Howard. In April 1737 the justices convened "at the [new] court house on New River" at Paradise Point, a thirty-by-eighteen-foot structure accompanied by a prison, stocks, and whipping post.[17]

The General Assembly intended to relocate the seat of government in 1741 when the legislature incorporated the town of Johnston, named in honor of incumbent governor Gabriel Johnston and located on the south side of New River at Mittam's (Town) Point. Designating the town as the location of meetings of the court, general musters, and all other public business of the county, the legislature directed the magistrates to move the old courthouse to Johnston or to dismantle the building, sell it at auction, and use the proceeds to finance the construction of a new courthouse. The justices, however, continued to meet at the old courthouse at Paradise Point until April 1744, when they discovered that "some Malushious & evil dispos'd persons" had burned the building.[18]

That act of arson compelled the justices to hold court in private dwellings in Johnston beginning in July 1744. Although the magistrates soon assessed taxes and appropriated other funds to build a courthouse in Johnston, construction was not undertaken until 1751. When the justices apparently first occupied the courthouse, in July 1752, the building remained unfinished. Thus they appropriated funds to secure carpenters to complete the interior of the structure.[19]

The best efforts of the county magistrates were negated by a hurricane in September 1752, which not only destroyed the public buildings in Johnston but eventuated in the abandonment of the town. According to a report of the catastrophe, "At Johnston the Court House [was] blown to pieces, and all the public records were lost. Several other houses were also blown down, many trees tore up by the roots, and corn thrown down, much of it destroyed, and seven or eight persons killed." In 1753 the General Assembly provided for the reconstitution or replacement of the destroyed documents and required the construction of a new courthouse in Johnston within two years. In 1755, however, the legislature decided to move the seat of county affairs to Wantland's Ferry (present Jacksonville) on New River, declaring that Johnston was not centrally located in the county, that the wide ferry crossing at the town was inconvenient, if not often impassable, and that the town was virtually deserted.[20]

Upon the move to Wantland's Ferry, the county court again undertook the arduous task of erecting a courthouse. Securing land from James Wantland that was convenient to the river and a spring, the justices ordered the construction of a courthouse with the dimensions of that of

Johnston County. They occupied the new structure in July 1757, though William Gibson, the carpenter, did not complete the interior of the building, which included inserting glass window sashes and painting, until 1761. Thereafter the county incurred only minor expenses in caring for the courthouse—cutting the bushes in the courthouse yard, tarring the roof, and erecting steps.[21]

The jail or prison proved as difficult to secure and maintain as the courthouse. In 1735 Joseph Howard also agreed to construct a sixteen-by-twelve-foot jail and stocks to accompany the first courthouse. When the Onslow justices began to hold court in Johnston in 1744, they contracted with James Wright to erect a new jail, which was virtually finished in 1746 but badly damaged by the hurricane in 1752. Since no one lived nearby to serve as jailer, the court allowed the sheriffs thereafter to use their own homes or plantations for the detention of prisoners. In 1763 the court finally advertised for the construction of a "strong prison," and a jail was built by 1764. Nonetheless, sheriffs from that time to the Revolution regularly complained to the court about the "insufficiency" of the jail in order to absolve themselves of the responsibility for jailbreaks.[22]

In addition to underwriting the construction of public buildings, county funds sustained a variety of public services, including payments to jurors and the purchase of law books. In 1748 the General Assembly determined that jurors selected from the counties to attend district courts were entitled to three shillings per diem for attendance at such courts, in addition to reimbursement for ferriage charges when traveling to and from the courts. Juror expenses subsequently proved to be an annual burden for the counties, amounting to 8 percent of the total expenditures of Onslow in 1774-1775.[23]

In 1751 the provincial legislature authorized the county courts to purchase specified law books to assist the justices of the peace in the execution of their duties. The Onslow court entrusted John Starkey with the task of obtaining the volumes in the "most frugal" and "cheapest manner" possible. Starkey reported to the court the following year, having secured Henry Swinburne's *A Brief Treatise of Testaments and Last Wills*, William Nelson's *The Office and Authority of a Justice of the Peace*, and Giles Jacob's *The Law-Dictionary*, all for £7.16.4.[24]

Another expense for the county involved the purchase of weights and measures to serve as the county standard. Legislation in 1741 enumerated the particular items as well as the stamps and brands that the counties needed. Starkey, commissioned by the court, went to Boston to obtain the weights and measures. Upon their receipt in 1742, the justices appointed James Foyle standard keeper of the county. Seven years later the iron, brass, and copper weights were "greatly damaged" when Foyle's house accidentally burned. Thereafter the weights and measures were entrusted to Richard Ward, but upon his death in 1757, the court ordered William Cray, clerk, to take possession of the standard and to repair the weights. The order was redirected to John Starkey in 1761 in what appears to be the last reference by the justices to the county standard.[25]

A singular outlay for the county occurred in the early 1740s during King George's War when reports of a possible Spanish invasion caused the General Assembly to try to rectify the "Defenceless state" of the province. Legislation in 1742 empowered the justices of each county to levy a per capita tax to obtain a storehouse or powder magazine and to purchase powder, shot, and gunflints. The Onslow magistrates selected Starkey to acquire the supplies, which consisted of 50 pounds of powder, 200 pounds of swan shot or bullets, and 480 gunflints. Starkey was instructed to deliver the materiel to James Foyle, who for an annual stipend agreed to be the keeper of the magazine. Few counties used their military stores, and Onslow lost its powder, shot, and flints in the fire that destroyed Foyle's house in 1749.[26]

In the latter part of the colonial era the counties assumed the responsibility for paying bounties on animal scalps. Trying to rid the province of "vermin" or dangerous and destructive animals, the legislature established a system of bounty payments to encourage killing the animals. First paid by the parishes, the financial burden was shifted to some of the counties in 1762 and to the remaining counties, including Onslow, in 1764. The statutes called for payments for wolf, panther, and wildcat scalps. The laws remained in force for several counties until the Revolution. In 1774-1775 Onslow paid bounties on twenty-seven wolves, four panthers, and twenty-eight wildcats.[27]

Onslow was the scene of North Carolina's first effort to provide transportation facilities subsidized by public funds. When creating the town of Johnston in 1741, the General Assembly instituted a system of free ferriage for persons crossing New River from Whitehouse (Whitehurst) Point to Johnston. County residents who crossed the river to transact business at the courthouse passed without charge, and the ferry keepers presented a list of the fees to the court, which then paid them from county tax revenues. Before the first court convened in Johnston in July 1744, the justices appointed ferry keepers and instructed them "to have boats in order & [to give proper] attendance to transport people to & from Court." The free ferry proved so advantageous that the legislature continued its operation after the county seat was moved to Wantland's Ferry. Moreover, the General

Assembly applied the same approach to ferriage to Pasquotank and Perquimans Counties in 1754 and 1758, respectively, and extended the scope of free ferriage to additional counties in 1769.[28]

Onslow derived its revenue from a capitation tax, the most popular and remunerative levy in the province. It was imposed on all those designated as taxables: white males sixteen years of age and older; all blacks or mulattoes, male and female, twelve years of age or older; and white women married to blacks or mulattoes. Although North Carolinians bore a relatively onerous tax burden, Onslow County justices were less demanding, particularly after 1765. Before that date, the construction of three courthouse-and-prison complexes occasioned temporarily high levies in some years. The magistrates also responded with special taxes to fund the magazine in 1743 and to purchase law books in 1751. Otherwise, the county contended primarily with the annual charges of the sheriff's commission, the clerk's salary, juror compensation, bounty payments, and free ferriage fees, all of which accounted for 99 percent of the county's indebtedness in 1774. During the decade preceding the Revolution, Onslow's average annual tax was among the lowest in North Carolina.[29]

Onslow County's economy was based on agriculture, forest products, fishing, and limited, rudimentary manufacturing. The overwhelming majority of American colonials wrested a living from the soil and activities ancillary to farming. Onslow inhabitants were no exception. Constituting the foundations of agriculture in the county were Indian corn, because it was easy to raise and versatile, and livestock, which grazed readily on the marsh grasses, natural meadows, and upland wire grass ridges. Many persons raised flax, cotton, and a little tobacco for home consumption. Some of the wealthier residents, such as Samuel Johnston Jr., dabbled in indigo production. Vegetables, particularly peas, and fruits were also popular. Commercially, however, corn, peas, and livestock were the county's principal agricultural exports.[30]

The sea and forest attracted many. Proximity to the ocean offered opportunities for fishing and whaling.[31] Inhabitants of Onslow quickly turned to their extensive pine forests for the production of naval stores— crude and distilled turpentine, tar, pitch—for which North Carolina was so famous and which the English encouraged by means of a parliamentary bounty. Crude turpentine was resin extracted from the living tree by means of boxing; distilled turpentine was derived from the crude, the residue being rosin. Tar was resin forced from pinewood (green or preferably dead wood) by burning in kilns. Pitch was obtained by burning tar. The provincials also availed themselves of timber as well as the animal skins and hides of the abundant wildlife that roamed the woods.[32]

Other than the household production of food, drink, clothing, and other necessaries, which characterized all of colonial America, Onslow's principal manufacturing industry was milling. Difficult to identify but certainly evident in the county were the sawmills, which converted timber into finished wood products. The more numerous gristmills are easier to document because their construction had to be approved by the county court. Although the justices entertained scattered petitions for gristmills during the first years of the county's existence, they approved an average of two such requests per year from 1764 to 1775. The gristmills dotted the rivers of the county and virtually all of their principal tributaries.[33]

The General Assembly's attempt to improve the quality of North Carolina's exports by providing for the inspection of numerous merchantable commodities produced in the colony was advantageous to Onslow's economy. Responding to an inspection statute in 1740, the Onslow court appointed Sheriff James Foyle as the inspector for Bogue Inlet and rented his warehouse in order to save the county the expense of constructing a shelter to house the inspected commodities. The legislature broadened the inspection system in 1755, requiring Onslow to maintain inspectors at Bear and New River Inlets as well as at Bogue Inlet. In 1770 Weeks' Landing, Todd's Landing, and French's Landing were added to the list of inspection sites.[34]

As the population of Onslow increased, the county sought to improve its transportation facilities. From the inception of Onslow through January 1735, the precinct court supervised the road system. According to legislation passed in 1715, the precinct courts were allowed to authorize the construction of roads and bridges; to establish road companies, consisting of male taxables who would build and maintain the roads and bridges; to appoint overseers to direct the road companies; and to fine those who failed to comply with the law. Upon the erection of the precinct in 1731, the court designated overseers and approved several new roads to accommodate the populace.[35]

In 1734, however, the assembly replaced the 1715 legislation with two statutes. One retained the old approach to roads and bridges for the precincts of Albemarle County; the other originated the commissioner system for controlling road and bridge construction in the precincts of Bath County, which included Onslow. Under the commissioner system, each precinct was divided into geographic districts over which three to five men called commissioners were given virtually plenary powers to authorize, construct, and repair roads and bridges. The precinct court could only prosecute road commissioners for malfeasance and assist them in replacing commissioners who died or moved from the districts.[36]

14

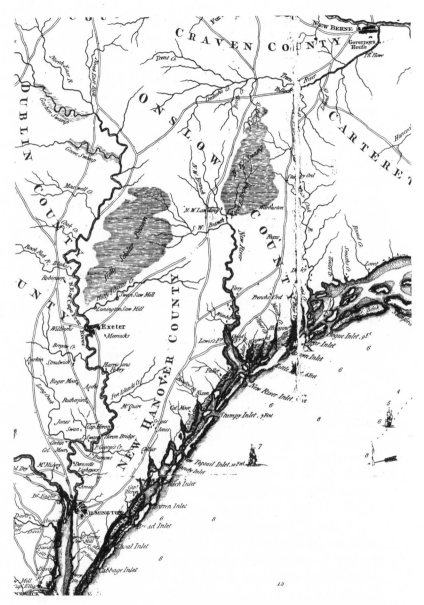

Onslow County as shown on "An Accurate Map of North and South Carolina . . . by Henry Mouzon and others," published in London in 1775 and in Paris in 1777.

Onslow switched to the commissioner system but found it to be inadequate. "In order to remove so great a nuisance," the court, in 1744, concluded that the "late law" appointing commissioners had expired and decided to adopt the overseer method used by the northern counties. Hence, Onslow appointed overseers to supplant the commissioners in what proved to be a short-lived experiment. The following year the assembly rectified its oversight by reinstating the commissioner system in the southern counties. Onslow was partitioned into four districts, over which five commissioners per district, named by the law, exercised jurisdiction.[37]

Onslow obligingly renewed the commissioner system but still considered it unsatisfactory. In 1758 the legislature, noting that the commissioner approach was "found inconvenient, and not so agreeable to the Inhabitants" of many of the southern counties, including Onslow, placed the regulation of roads and bridges under the control of the county courts. The Onslow justices immediately confronted the manifold demands that had befuddled the commissioners. Road companies alleged that more men were needed to repair the roads in the districts. Overseers complained that the taxables under their command refused to work. Christian Free, for example, listed eighteen men in his road company as delinquent in their work, some for as many as seven days.[38]

Nevertheless, by the end of the colonial period a network of roads served Onslow. In addition to the King's Highway, part of the principal thoroughfare that ran from Virginia along the North Carolina coast into South Carolina, numerous local and county roads fulfilled the needs of the people. From 1758 to the Revolution, the county justices approved the construction of approximately one road per year. However, despite provincial legislation and an Onslow court directive in 1764 to mark the major roads, traveler Johann David Schoepf later remarked that from New Bern to Wilmington nothing was written on the guideposts and that the "many paths and roads intercrossing . . . [the] woods often bring travelers to confusion." Still, the roads provided at least minimally adequate transport facilities for county residents.[39]

The ferries used to cross the county's numerous rivers and streams complemented the road system. At the inception of Onslow the county was served by the ferry over New River (later Sneads Ferry) that had been authorized by the Carteret Precinct court. The Onslow justices licensed at least two more ferries—at Joseph Howard's plantation on the Northeast Branch of New River and at Thurrell's Bluff on White Oak River—in addition to those mandated by provincial legislation at the town of Johnston and at Wantland's Ferry. Although traveler William Logan remarked in 1745 that he crossed at Sneads Ferry in "the most ordinary Bawble of a Boat [that] did not float above two or three inches above the surface of the Water," the paucity of complaints to the county court suggests that Onslow enjoyed reasonably satisfactory ferriage service.[40]

Water transport proved crucial to the development of Onslow's economy throughout the colonial era. County inhabitants plied their watercourses and traded beyond the county in various craft. In 1736 a canoe was seized and sold at public auction to pay the taxes of John and Moses Crosby. Perriaugers, versatile vessels propelled by oar or sail and capable of carrying more than fifty barrels of tar, were popular and valuable. At his death in 1751, Robert Courtney bequeathed a perriauger to his two sons. Sloops, shallops, and schooners, sailing craft of ten to sixty tons, were used in the coastal and West Indian trade. John Oldfield owned a twenty-ton schooner, the *Bedford*, which regularly brought cargoes of sugar, rum, and molasses from New England and the West Indies to the Cape Fear.[41]

Onslow was the scene of one of North Carolina's earliest efforts to improve navigation by artificial means. Legislation in 1741 directed the deepening of New River Inlet. Although some progress was realized, the paucity of funds and the death of those commissioned to supervise the work prompted the General Assembly in 1761 to reconstitute the project, appoint new commissioners, and finance the venture by means of a lottery. The use of the lottery, however, evoked strident criticism from the Board of Trade in England, which categorically rejected that means of raising money because there were insufficient regulations "to prevent fraud and abuse in a matter so peculiarly liable" to corruption. The law relating to Onslow was not repealed, but Governor Arthur Dobbs was strictly forbidden to assent to similar legislation in the future.[42]

Actually the best entree to the county was Bear Inlet, the depth of which ranged from eight to eleven feet throughout the eighteenth century. New River and other inlets offered far less satisfactory ingress. Only three to five feet of water were reported on the bar at low tide at New River. Hence it is not surprising that the General Assembly passed legislation in 1760 to improve navigation from Howards Bay in New River to Bear Inlet, funding the effort by a tonnage duty on vessels trading in Onslow County.[43]

The early attention devoted to New River Inlet may have reflected the pressure of merchants in that area who desired an improvement of local shipping facilities. Among many, including Gibbin Jennings, Edward Ward Jr., and James Howard, was Richard Farr, agent for the vessel *St. Andrews*, which arrived in Beaufort in 1759, bringing from London a cargo of clothes and dinnerware. Robert Hogg, who emigrated from Scotland to Wilmington, opened a store on New River in 1774, where he bartered bread, sugar, medicine, and clothes in exchange for naval stores.[44]

Shipping along the coast and in the sounds was often perilous. A shallop wrecked in 1729 about a mile west of Bogue Inlet. Eight years later four whites and six blacks drowned when their boat, anchored at the mouth of New River, capsized; however, five on board managed to escape. Four crewmen of the sloop *Sarah*, coming from Rhode Island in 1747, drowned when the vessel was wrecked off Bear Inlet. In 1752 a sloop bound for Boston with a cargo of tar was lost at the same place. Two craft from Wilmington overturned in 1765, one at Bear Inlet and the other at New River Inlet.[45]

Beginning as the southern frontier of Carteret Precinct, Onslow boasted relatively few people in its incipiency. Indeed, Ashe and Rice had charged in 1731 that the area did not warrant precinct status because so few people inhabited the region. Nevertheless, by 1734 the Reverend John LaPierre wrote that the "New River" settlement contained more than a hundred families. It was "a thriving place," he opined, "and likely in [a] few years to become a flourishing parish." Approximately the same number of people may have clustered along White Oak River to the north.[46]

In any case, the absence of a census before the Revolution compels a reliance upon the number of taxables in the county as an indicator of population. From 565 in 1743, the number of taxables rose to 695 in 1754, to 1,129 in 1765, and to 1,405 in 1774, which roughly translated into a population of 4,900 on the eve of the Revolution. Although its number of taxables steadily increased, Onslow failed to keep pace with the rest of the colony, particularly the backcountry, which experienced phenomenal population growth. In 1765 twenty counties reported more taxables than Onslow. Only six—Anson, Beaufort, Duplin, Hyde, Pasquotank, and Tyrrell—contained fewer taxables.[47]

Contributing to the burgeoning population in Onslow was the increasing number of slaves in the county. During the 1740s bondsmen approximated 15 percent of the county's inhabitants. By 1754 they represented 36 percent of the taxables, a figure that rose to 45 percent by 1771. While noteworthy, the institution of slavery in Onslow paled into insignificance compared to the Lower Cape Fear counties of New Hanover and Brunswick. In 1771 slave taxables were found in 32 percent of Onslow's households, but they numbered fewer than five in 79 percent of those families. Only eight persons listed more than ten slave taxables in that year: James Howard, Elizabeth Jameson, Stephen Lee, Henry Rhodes, Edward Starkey, John Starkey, Peter Starkey, and Richard Ward.[48]

By malingering, stealing, running away, or engaging in rebellion, slaves presented a constant threat to white society. In 1765 Simon, who belonged to magistrate Alexander Grant, and Mingo, who belonged to ferry keeper John Warburton, were accused of stealing a large sum of money. In a special trial Simon was found guilty and sentenced to hang; Mingo was deemed innocent. Extant records of other slave trials reveal the execution of Titus in 1777 for rape and the indictment of Isaac in 1779 for the theft of a musket.[49]

Like most eastern and central counties with substantial slave populations, Onslow availed itself of the search or patrol law, passed by the General Assembly in 1753 to thwart potential slave insurrections. According to the legislation, the justices were permitted to divide their counties into districts and appoint searchers or patrollers for those areas who would examine black habitations at least four times a year for weapons. Although Onslow began to designate patrollers in 1758, a year later the magistrates suspended the patrol, claiming that it had "not answered the good end in this county as was intended." By 1761, however, the patrol had been reinstated and was continued to the Revolution, though its effectiveness was questionable.[50]

Less numerous than the slaves but constituting a significant segment of the population were the indentured servants, poor persons who bound themselves to labor for a stipulated number of years in order to pay their passage from Europe to America. Theirs was a harsh lot as evidenced by the many complaints to the county court about "misuse" and "Immoderate Correction" at the hands of their masters. In the case of Mabel Ryley in 1736, the court ordered her master not to correct her "for any Trivial offences" but only for such as were deemed culpable by the nearest magistrate. In their vulnerable status a number of servant women bore illegitimate children, for which "crime" their term of indenture was lengthened. And at the end of their indenture many servants, like George Still in 1754, encountered difficulty in obtaining their "freedom dues."[51]

Free blacks constituted another element of Onslow's population. Originating as manumitted bondsmen, illegitimate children of free women, and successful runaway slaves, the number of free blacks was always small. The 1768 tax list contained none as heads of households; that of 1771 included but one, plus Jack Ransom, a mulatto living with a white family. One of the first free black residents of Onslow was Negro Dick, freed by the will of his master, Samuel Jones, in 1742. Eleven years later Negro Dick or Black Dick died, and his "small effects" were sold by his principal creditor, John Starkey, to pay his debts. In the mid-1760s, Andrew Fuller, a mulatto carpenter, accumulated a substantial debt to the mercantile firm of Nash and McNair by purchasing, among other things, shot and powder, numerous pieces of cloth, and a set of cobbler's tools.[52]

Also inhabiting Onslow was a vagrant, poor population. These migrants, who became increasingly numerous in early North Carolina, were occasionally recognized by the General Assembly in legislation, but the counties had to contend with the actual supervision of those who claimed no permanent home or regular employment. Among those unfortunates was Caleb Hermitage, a traveler, who became ill and died in 1746 while staying at the plantation of Edward Ward Sr. Another was John Bennett, "a profligate Wretch," who was indicted in 1761 for profane swearing and ordered put in the stocks for two hours since he had no money with which to pay his fine.[53]

Not only the vagrants but much of the Onslow populace seemed mobile in the colonial era. Only 68 percent of the heads of households in 1769 appeared two years later in the 1771 tax list. However, many of those missing in the latter year may have succumbed to the myriad diseases that beset the provincials. "Ague and fever," doubtless malaria, was common; smallpox, the scourge of the eighteenth century, was devastating. An outbreak of smallpox forced the Onslow County court to move in December 1765 from Wantland's Ferry to the site of the old courthouse on New River. Physicians were scarce in early North Carolina, particularly in Onslow, and those who practiced were called upon to care for humans and animals alike. When Robert Orme dispatched his slave, Caesar, to Dr. William Gibson in 1777, he also sent a sickly mare in order that the doctor might "Attend both Patients together."[54]

Life in colonial Onslow centered around four basic institutions: the family, the church, the county court, and the ordinary or tavern. Males dominated the family, though increasingly in the eighteenth century, women began to assume direction of their own lives. According to tax lists, fifteen women in 1769 and seven women in 1771 headed households in Onslow. During the colonial era at least three women in the county followed their deceased husbands into the ferry keeping business. Mary Leary kept the public ferry at Johnston; Mrs. (James) Wantland and later Mary Pounds operated the public ferry at Wantland's. Wantland and Pounds also kept ordinaries in the county, as did Ann Hurley and Mary Pitts.[55]

Children greatly swelled the size of families and occupied an integral place in Onslow society. In 1734 the Reverend John LaPierre observed "a vast number of children" among the county's early inhabitants. While young ones in the eighteenth century increasingly became objects of parental affection and delight rather than a necessary expansion of the labor force in an agrarian society, some offspring nevertheless found life difficult. This was true in part because parental deaths left so many orphaned, and in part because illicit liaisons produced so many illegitimates. Those children who possessed sufficient property were placed under guardianship; those without estates were apprenticed until they reached their legal majority.[56]

Provincial law directed guardians to raise their wards "according to their Rank & degree." Apprentices supposedly received training in a trade or handicraft. At the expiration of their servitude, apprentices, like servants, were given "freedom dues," which in the case of John Mixon in 1734 consisted of "one new suite of good apparrel . . . and one new Set of Coopers tools and one new set of Truss Hoops." Guardians and masters also bore the responsibility for providing the rudiments of education for their charges. Because they possessed some wealth, wards presumably obtained more extensive instruction. In the case of apprentices, the county court generally required their masters to teach the orphans to read in the Bible and to write legibly.[57]

In the two decades preceding the Revolution more children in Onslow warranted guardianship than apprenticeship. In both cases, however, the county court experienced difficulty in providing appropriate supervision for the orphans. The county grand jury in March 1764 found that the orphans of Thomas Cummings failed to receive proper care and that the orphans of Philip Morris had not been educated. Two years later Edward Roberts complained to the court of ill treatment at the hands of his guardian; the following year Grace Edge lodged a similar complaint against her master.[58]

The average colonial household in which the children and their families reposed contained a vast array of furnishings. Feather beds and accompanying "bed furniture" were prominent and valuable. Richard Ward, justice of the peace, churchwarden, and one of the wealthiest men in the county, owned 6 feather beds and bedsteads, 5 coverlets, 5 blankets, 1 bed rug, 7 pairs of sheets, 3 pillows, and 3 pillow cases. Other large furniture was minimal except in the more spacious homes. Ward enjoyed the use of an oval table, tea table, 2 square tables, 9 chairs, a desk, 3 trunks, and a buffet. His and most households reflected basic colonial industries by the presence of woolen and linen spinning wheels and a loom. Assorted kitchen and eating utensils also consumed considerable space. William Wells possessed 3 iron pots, 1 iron kettle, 2 frying pans, a pair of fire tongs, a tin colander, 4 pewter dishes, 12 pewter plates, 6 pewter basins, and 7 pewter porringers, among other cooking and serving items, including wooden and earthenware that supplemented the oft-used pewter.[59]

A number of more personal possessions complemented the furniture and kitchenware. Firearms—rifles, smoothbore guns, and handguns—rested beside most hearths; swords were also common. An occasional musical instrument, the violin of James Ambrose for example, helped to while away the hours. Razors and looking glasses improved personal attractiveness. Exemplifying clothing was the wardrobe of Joseph Ward, which included a greatcoat, 3 close-bodied coats, 5 waistcoats, 5 pairs of breeches, 9 shirts, 7 caps, 4 pairs of stockings, 2 pairs of shoes, and 2 beaver hats. Jewelry, such as Ambrose's pair of silver sleeve buttons, Joseph Ward's silver watch, James Glenn's silver snuffbox, and James Gray's silver-headed cane, enhanced the attire.[60]

The clutter outside the house, under sheds and lean-tos, and in other outbuildings was as great as that found inside the home. Saddles, bridles, and halters hung on the walls. Various tubs, pails, baskets, and casks awaited use. Steelyards were indispensable for weighing agricultural produce, and most men owned an ax and a pair of iron wedges for splitting wood. Agricultural implements—hoes, plows, harrows, and flax brakes—absorbed space. Exceedingly valuable were the short-bodied, two-wheeled horse and ox carts that were used on many farms.

The colonials' most valuable assets, other than land and slaves, were livestock and poultry. At his death in 1764, James Glenn owned 12 horses, 20 cattle, 19 hogs, 9 sheep, and 22 geese. Richard Ward had 62 cattle at his Sound plantation, 12 cattle and 30 hogs at his Rich Lands plantation, and an unknown number of horses, cattle, hogs, and sheep running loose on Topsail Banks. Relying upon oxen as much as horses for draft animals, many farmers owned one or more yoke of oxen plus ox chains and other necessary accoutrements.[61]

Mitigating the harsh life and rough manner of the people was organized religion. Although religion often rested lightly upon North Carolinians, the Church of England, or Anglican Church, became the established church in the colony early. In 1732 the Reverend Richard Marsden, Anglican itinerant, officiated gratis in Onslow, some forty miles from his residence in the Cape Fear. Two years later the Reverend John LaPierre stated that the inhabitants of Onslow were "very desirous to have the holy worship set up amongst them." And in 1735 the legislation that formally erected Onslow Precinct also established St. John's Parish, which was coterminous with the bounds of the precinct.[62]

Parish government organized within the year. Subsequently John Starkey, James Foyle, and Richard Ward, among county luminaries, served as churchwardens of St. John's Parish. The parish, however, never enjoyed its own minister. It utilized lay readers and relied upon visits by ministers of neighboring parishes, including those of the Reverend Alexander Stewart from St. Thomas Parish in Beaufort County and the Reverend James Moir from St. James Parish in New Hanover County. According to Moir, who came between 1742 and 1747, Onslow residents were unable financially to support a minister and unwilling to build a church. Still as many as three Anglican chapels may have served the populace before the Revolution.[63]

The presence of numerous dissenters was at least partially responsible for the limited appeal of the Anglican Church in North Carolina and in Onslow County. A few Quakers and Presbyterians inhabited the county, but the principal competition emanated from the Baptists. The General Baptists had assembled in the New River area as early as 1740; the Separates followed after midcentury. When the Sandy Creek Association was instituted in 1758, the New River congregation of Separate Baptists became a charter member. In 1761 the Reverend Stewart observed that Onslow was "the present seat of [Baptist] enthusiasm in this Province." Ezekiel Hunter and Robert Nixon, who spread the gospel beyond the bounds of Onslow to the Lower Cape Fear, stand out among New River Baptist ministers.[64]

The county court supplemented the church as a center of sociability and a guardian of morality. Many persons from all strata of society intermingled during the quarterly sessions of court. For their part, the justices, in addition to their administrative duties, imposed fines for offenses that ranged from profane utterances to adultery. Particularly active in 1736, the magistrates arraigned four men for swearing, one for drunkenness, and one for violating the Sabbath. They also disposed of four cases of illegitimate births, fining the responsible mothers and charging the fathers to provide monetary support for the maintenance of the children. Constantly appearing before the court at that time was Edward Howard, who not only had transgressed the Sabbath and mistreated his servant woman in 1736, but had been declared the father of an illegitimate child and had been involved in a neighborly altercation during the previous year.[65]

While the county court provided an opportunity for convivial association only four times a year, the ordinaries, or taverns, that dotted the countryside of Onslow offered constant entertainment. Licensed by the court, which also set the prices that the proprietors charged for food, drink, and lodging, the ordinaries served as centers of conversation, gaming, drinking, recreation, political discussions, and public auctions. The fare varied widely. Available were hot and cold meals, West Indian or New England rum, summer and winter cider, beer, wine, brandy, punches, and toddies. Depending upon the number of boarders, a lodger might enjoy a bed to himself or face the prospect of sharing a bed. Horses were stabled or pastured and fed oats, corn, hay, or marsh grass. While many travelers were extremely critical of North Carolina ordinaries, postal official Ebenezer Hazard commented favorably upon those public houses in Onslow at which he stopped in 1778.[66]

By the end of the colonial period Onslow claimed as many ordinaries as any county in the province. During the 1740s the court approved an average of five petitions a year for ordinary licenses. That number dipped to four in the 1750s but rose to six in the 1760s. On the eve of the Revolution, however, the average reached fourteen, including eighteen licenses granted in 1775, a remarkable number in light of the absence of an urban center, such as New Bern or Wilmington, where ordinaries tended to cluster. Onslow also benefited from the General Assembly's experimental effort in 1741, when, upon the creating of Johnston, the legislature mandated the establishment of two ordinaries "fit for the accommodation of Travellers," one in the town and one on the opposite side of New River. Although the assembly did not extend the requirement to Wantland's Ferry in 1755, it later utilized the Johnston precedent to enjoin the maintenance of ordinaries at the longer ferry crossings in the province.[67]

While all classes mingled and relaxed in the tavern atmosphere, by the 1770s the public houses began to assume a political significance. North Carolina taverns may not have been the nurseries of revolution that such institutions became in Boston under the leadership of Samuel Adams, but political discussions must have been commonplace as relations between England and the colonies deteriorated. Heightening the significance of taverns was the opportunity they presented for men in an essentially aural-oral society, particularly in a time of great stress and uncertainty, to cajole, argue, and declaim. The American Revolution was not undertaken lightly, and many colonials still remained loyal to England after 1776.

Chapter Three
From Revolution to Civil War

More than a century and a half after the permanent settlement of English colonies in America, thirteen provinces along the North American coast broke the bonds of empire to declare their independence and create a nation. Restiveness under British control mounted in the eighteenth century as the colonials chafed under exactions of the mother country that seemed to threaten popular government and economic development in America. So momentous an upheaval as the American Revolution stemmed from myriad causes, all culminating in a desire for American autonomy, which was announced in 1776 but achieved only after a protracted struggle that ended in the formal British recognition of American independence in 1783.

The years following the French and Indian War found North Carolinians joining the chorus of colonial objections to British legislation and royal policy decisions that jeopardized colonial welfare. The Regulator movement, beginning in the mid-1760s and concluding with the Battle of Alamance in 1771, briefly distracted the Carolinians. But events beyond the colony—the Boston Tea Party, the Intolerable Acts, military actions in neighboring provinces—combined with controversial internal issues, such as the extent of gubernatorial authority, currency shortages, and the proper jurisdiction of colonial courts, to place North Carolina squarely on the road to revolution.

Reacting to the punitive British legislation that followed the Boston Tea Party, the American provincials held a Continental Congress in Philadelphia in September 1774 to consider a united response. North Carolinians, in a provincial congress that met in New Bern in August 1774, selected delegates to represent the colony in Philadelphia.

nting Onslow in the First Provincial Congress were William Cray, in Harvey, and John Harvey, though the last lived in Perquimans John Harvey had been one of the most vocal critics of the British, ____ ___ was chosen moderator of the congress. In the ensuing four provincial congresses, which carried the colony into statehood, Cray appeared once more. Local notables Henry Rhodes, Edward Starkey, and John Spicer each appeared three times; John King and Benajah Doty twice.[1]

At the behest of the First Provincial Congress and the Continental Congress, incipient revolutionaries in most towns and counties in North Carolina organized "committees of safety" to disseminate information, repress loyalists, and implement retaliatory measures against the British. The Onslow Committee of Safety included William Cray, Seth Ward, Joseph French, Edward Ward, Robert Snead, John Ashe, and John Gibbs. News of the April 19, 1775, confrontation at Lexington and Concord in Massachusetts reached Cray on May 7, who hurriedly forwarded the information to the Wilmington-New Hanover Safety Committee. Meanwhile, the Onslow committee doubtlessly exemplified royal governor Josiah Martin's contention that "Usurping some new authority every day," the powers of the committees "soon became practically unlimited." The safety committees were the engines of revolution.[2]

By the summer of 1775 the revolutionary movement in North Carolina had progressed sufficiently that Governor Martin had been deposed and a provisional government erected. At a district meeting of safety committees, which convened in Wilmington on June 20, 1775, delegates from Onslow joined those from New Hanover, Brunswick, Bladen, and Duplin Counties in denouncing Martin and British Prime Minister Lord North. In late 1776 North Carolina's Fifth Provincial Congress drafted a constitution by which to establish a state government. County government made the transition from colony to statehood almost imperceptibly. Civil and military officers in Onslow took the oath of allegiance to the United States at the July 1777 meeting of the county court.[3]

Following Lexington and Concord the Americans prepared militarily to secure their freedom against a much vaunted British army. Although the militia composed the backbone of the military force in North Carolina and Onslow, some Onslow soldiers joined the Continental Army. Most probably served in the First Regiment of North Carolina Troops. They participated in numerous battles beyond the state, including Brandywine and Germantown in Pennsylvania in 1777 and the surrender of Savannah in 1778. Contrarily, Obed Scott spent nine months in the Continental Army but participated "in no particular engagements."[4]

Colonel William Cray Sr. was the ranking militia officer of the county until his death in 1778. He was succeeded by Henry Rhodes, who died in 1780. Rhodes was followed by George Mitchell, who served until his resignation in 1787. Field returns for the Onslow militia in 1777 revealed eight companies totaling 684 men. An unprotected seaboard had convinced North Carolina's Fourth Provincial Congress in 1776 to raise five independent military companies to patrol the coast. One of the companies, captained by Seth Harvey, guarded the area from Bogue Inlet to New River. The company, however, disbanded before the end of the year. Five years later the General Assembly ordered another company of militia raised and stationed at the mouth of White Oak River to defend the Onslow coast.[5]

The Atlantic provided an unexpected visitor to Onslow in December 1778, when a French vessel, the *Conquerant*, sailed through New Inlet and anchored near the mouth of Gilletts Creek at William Hadnot's saltworks. The ship had been a British prize, and British sailors had been left on board to hold the vessel. A storm separated the ship from the British fleet, however, and left the men without adequate rations. Thus the prize crew turned the *Conquerant* over to its French navigator who brought the vessel safely to shore in Onslow. A decision by a local admiralty court, upheld upon appeal to the Continental Congress, returned the *Conquerant* to its French owner.[6]

The revolutionaries encountered resistance from those who remained loyal to the Crown and Great Britain. The county grand jury declared one Demsey Jones an "Enemy" of the public for uttering "many things very disrespectful to the Liberties" of the state. The same body also found the actions of Captain Archibald Chase "inimical to the American Cause" after Chase had rendezvoused his vessel with an armed British craft outside New Inlet and apparently obtained permission from the enemy to trade.[7]

The British occupation of Wilmington throughout most of 1781 elicited the sympathies of loyalists and threatened Onslow. Under Major James Craig the British not only interdicted trade at the port but also raided and foraged in the surrounding countryside. In late June and early July a British party from Wilmington plundered the property of some of the inhabitants in the vicinity of the New River Chapel and collected cattle from the area between Holly Shelter and New River. Onslow men were embodied but never engaged the enemy.[8]

In August Craig took 250 British regulars and 80 loyalists on a northern foray through Duplin County that reached New Bern before returning to the Cape Fear. Brigadier General Alexander Lillington, with troops from Onslow, Jones, Craven, and Dobbs Counties, was unable to stop the British who penetrated the Rich Lands area of Onslow along the way and ravaged several farms. The British, however, failed to carry out a threat to destroy valuable saltworks in the county.[9] Though only a raid, the British action graphically revealed the helplessness of the patriots in the face of even a limited number of enemy soldiers and cooperative loyalists.

Although the Americans talked bravely of engaging the enemy, they generally confined themselves to watching the British. The British presence not only encouraged the loyalists but so dampened the ardor of the revolutionaries that General Richard Caswell reported confusion within the ranks of the Onslow militia and a loss of confidence in its officers.[10] After a three-day occupation of New Bern the British returned to Wilmington. They evacuated the port in November after learning of Cornwallis's defeat at Yorktown, Virginia. The war virtually concluded at that juncture for Onslow, though a formal peace settlement ending the conflict and recognizing American independence did not occur until 1783.

Dominating local politics after independence were such pre-Revolutionary luminaries as William Cray Sr., Henry Rhodes, Thomas Johnston, George Mitchell, John Spicer, and Edward Starkey. Cray presided over the Council of State in 1777 and 1778. Spicer served on the Council of State in 1780 and represented Onslow in the state senate in 1777, 1783, 1785, and 1794-1796. Rhodes, Johnston, and Mitchell sat in both houses of the legislature between 1777 and 1789. Starkey, a member of the state house of commons for several terms, became Speaker in 1783, the only Onslow legislator to act in that capacity after the Revolution.[11]

As the American revolutionaries achieved success, they erected a formal government in 1781 based on the Articles of Confederation. Reflecting the colonial fear of centralized power and executive authority, that constitution created a loose alliance of the thirteen states. However, in the estimation of many throughout the country, events quickly showed that the national government was unable to cope with exigencies abroad and demands at home. A movement to broaden the authority of the government culminated in the 1787 convention at Philadelphia, from which emerged the federal Constitution, a plan for a potentially powerful national government that threatened to subordinate the states.

In the ensuing battle over the ratification of the proposed federal Constitution, proponents of the document, called Federalists, found relatively little support in North Carolina and Onslow. Opponents of the Constitution, or Antifederalists, seemed satisfied with the status quo. The state laggardly called for a convention at Hillsborough in 1788 to consider ratification. At Hillsborough the Antifederalists commanded a large majority, including the Onslow delegates—Thomas Johnston, John Spicer, and Daniel Yates.[12] The Hillsborough Convention neither ratified nor rejected the Constitution. Instead it offered amendments and proposed a bill of rights to protect the states and individuals from national authority. It was an audacious move, for already enough states had ratified to institute the new nation in 1789.

The Federalists in North Carolina fought back, conducting an intensive "educational" campaign to propagandize the public on the necessity of joining the new nation. The state legislature called for a second convention to meet in Fayetteville in November 1789 to reconsider the Constitution. By that time sentiment had changed radically. Although Onslow delegate George Mitchell opposed ratification, Robert Whitehurst Snead and John Spicer joined the majority at the convention in approving the document by a vote of 194 to 77.[13] North Carolina entered the Union before the end of the year.

During the late eighteenth and nineteenth centuries, Onslow's geographic dimensions and seat of government remained virtually unaltered from the colonial era. The General Assembly in 1819 mandated a survey of the Duplin–Onslow line to settle disputes between the counties over their common boundary, and the Onslow court directed the county surveyor to assist in running lines between New Hanover, Jones, and Duplin, but the boundaries of Onslow changed little. The county court continued to convene at Wantland's Ferry, the name of which was changed in 1819 to Onslow Court House and in 1842 to Jacksonville.[14]

County government in Onslow changed little from that of the colonial era. The governing body was the county court composed of the justices of the peace, who were appointed for good behavior by the governor of the state. Meeting quarterly, a quorum of three magistrates exercised judicial and administrative jurisdiction within the county. State law in 1851 instructed Onslow voters in each militia district to select one of the justices of the peace to be a "special magistrate" in the district to supplement the county court in handling minor civil and criminal cases. Functionally, however, the judicial powers of the county court waned in the nineteenth century as its administrative responsibilities became paramount.[15]

As an administrative agency the county court controlled the fiscal system, registered deeds, probated estates, cared for orphans, and regulated transportation, which included roads, bridges, and ferriage. The county court, among other responsibilities, also appointed various local officials, including a clerk of court, coroner, register, entry takers, surveyor, inspectors of naval stores, wardens of the poor, county attorneys, tax listers, election officials, sheriff, trustee of the taxes, and treasurer of public buildings. Periodically the justices ordered the construction of new courthouses, often accompanied by jails, to replace buildings that had succumbed to the elements and neglect.

The county obtained its operating revenues from fees, fines, and taxes. The last, consisting of a poll tax and property tax on the value of land, both farms and town lots, was the most remunerative source of income. For example, fees and fines from the October 1814 term of court to the November 1819 term of court amounted to $132.05. Taxes in 1814 totaled $691.28; in 1818, $394.65. The tax burden climbed sharply, however, reaching $3,665 at midcentury. The state received one-third of that sum. The poor and the public schools absorbed 31 and 16 percent, respectively. The remainder was used for general county purposes.[16]

Onslow, like other counties, experienced some difficulty in holding public officials accountable for funds entrusted to them. Legislation in 1819 appointed a county finance committee to ascertain indebtedness to the public and to settle with officials responsible for the moneys. In its report the committee found several delinquencies, mainly for funds due to St. John's Parish to support the poor in the county. Although legislation in 1835, effective in August 1836, abolished the offices of county trustee and treasurer of public buildings, difficulties continued. In 1839 former sheriff Peter Harrell left the county without making provision for collecting taxes, and in 1863 the estate of deceased sheriff White D. Humphrey owed the county more than one hundred dollars in tax collections for the year 1860.[17]

Economically, as measured by the value of its landed property, Onslow's relative position among the counties improved during the antebellum era, though it was an improvement qualified by the creation of several additional counties during those years. In 1827 the state tax on Onslow land amounted to $267.55. Twenty counties among the sixty-three paid less. In 1837 the state-assessed land tax on the county was $239.17. Ten of the remaining sixty-five counties paid less than Onslow. Two decades later, in 1855, net state taxes derived from Onslow amounted to $268.27. Of a total of eighty-five counties, thirty-five, mostly in the west, paid less.[18]

The population of Onslow County grew slowly from 1790 to 1860. While that of the state increased by 150 percent, the population of the county rose 64 percent, from 5,387 to 8,856 (See table 1). Actual losses, primarily due to out-migration, occurred in the second decade of the nineteenth century, when the white population declined by 250, and during the fourth decade of the century, when the slave population declined and the number of whites rose but slightly. Onslow, like other eastern counties, including neighboring Jones and Duplin, suffered from the departure of those trying to escape the limited economic opportunities, one-party politics, and cultural stagnation in what many perceived to be the "Rip Van Winkle" state—North Carolina.

Table 1

Population in Onslow County

	1790	1800	1810	1820	1830	1840	1850	1860
Whites	3,555	3,809	4,329	4,179	4,569	4,675	5,003	5,195
Free Blacks	84	--	41	60	101	113	172	162
Slaves	1,748	1,814	2,299	2,777	3,144	2,739	3,108	3,499
Total	5,387	5,623	6,669	7,016	7,814	7,527	8,283	8,856

SOURCE: Guion Griffis Johnson, "Antebellum Onslow County: A Social History," 3, a paper presented to the Seminar on Onslow County History, Swansboro, N.C., 1982.

White emigrants from Onslow found homes in Georgia, Tennessee, and the Gulf Coast states where land was plentiful, fertile, and cheap, and the hiring out of slaves brought several times the compensation obtained in North Carolina. In 1843, at the age of 22, James Buckner went to Texas, returned to Onslow, married in 1847, and went back to Texas with his wife, her brother, and two slaves. Meanwhile, Joseph M. French, postmaster at French's Mill in Onslow, wrote that he was "depressed in consequence of many of my neighbors removing from this county to the West."[19]

Those who remained in Onslow worked mostly in agriculture and naval stores. However, the 1850 census for the Swansboro District revealed additional occupations: 24 coopers, 7 turpentine workers, 5 merchants, 5 mechanics, 4 clerks, 3 pilots, 16 sailors, 2 tailors, 2 shoemakers, 2 millers, 1 tavern keeper, and 31 day laborers. Whites were predominantly English in origin, interspersed with a scattering of French, Germans, Scots, Welsh, and Irish. Most were natives of the state—in 1820, all but three (unnaturalized foreigners) hailed from North Carolina; in 1850, all but thirteen.[20]

Amid the predominantly agrarian populace of Onslow appeared clusters of people in sufficient proximity to constitute villages or towns. Small neighborhoods included French's Mill, Foy's Store, Stones Bay,

Aman's Store, and Wolf Pit. The first incorporated town to appear in the county was Swansborough, chartered by the General Assembly in 1783. Located on a bluff at the mouth of White Oak River and known formerly as Weeks' Wharf, Bogue, and New Town, Swansborough was named for Samuel Swann, the colonial politician.[21]

As was customary for most North Carolina towns, the governance of Swansborough (hereafter, Swansboro, according to the modern spelling) reposed in a self-perpetuating board of trustees named by the act of incorporation. The legislation directed the trustees to compel the residents of Swansboro to meet annually to clear and maintain the streets of the town. The law also empowered the trustees to enact regulations for removing rubbish, clearing lots, and pulling down wooden chimneys that were deemed a fire hazard. Within four years tax reports showed that Swansboro contained thirty lots, half of which were "improved" or utilized beneficially for some purpose.[22]

By the mid-nineteenth century Swansboro had achieved respectable size by North Carolina standards. Its population, which had risen from 149 in 1800 to 801 in 1850, may not have challenged Wilmington's 7,264 in 1850, but it surpassed that of most "urban" areas in the state. Swansboro's 1850 population included 569 whites and 4 free blacks. Slaves, often comprising a significant percentage of the urban populace in North Carolina, numbered 228, or 28 percent of the total.[23]

On the eve of the Civil War Swansboro generated ambivalent emotions among visitors. A correspondent to the Newbern *Weekly Progress* felt that the town, unlike the state, justly deserved the appellation "Rip Van Winkle," for its citizens had "not the energy possessed by [those in] other small villages of North Carolina" to avail themselves of the "natural advantages" of the area. Education and religion languished in Swansboro, according to the writer. Yet the town remained a small port, the outlet annually for some one hundred thousand dollars of county produce. The Swansboro Academy employed three teachers and could accommodate more than a hundred students.[24]

During the nineteenth century the General Assembly often addressed the governance of Swansboro. Legislation in 1806, reinforced in 1810, allowed the freeholders of the town to elect commissioners to regulate municipal affairs. But in 1816 the General Assembly returned to the practice of legislative appointment of commissioners. A statute of the 1848-1849 session of the legislature, reincorporating Swansboro, denominated six self-perpetuating commissioners, who in turn appointed a magistrate of the police and a town treasurer, passed ordinances for the benefit of the town, and, subject to limitations, imposed poll and ad valorem property taxes.[25]

Jacksonville, Onslow's only other incorporated town before the Civil War, evolved at the site of the county courthouse at Wantland's Ferry. John Spicer, representing Onslow in the state house of commons in 1785, introduced legislation to create a town at the courthouse, but the bill was rejected on its first reading. Thus the area remained known as Wantland's Ferry until 1819, when it was renamed Onslow Court House. Not until 1842 did the General Assembly incorporate the site as Jacksonville, named for Andrew Jackson, the Hero of New Orleans and former president of the United States. However, no action was taken under the 1842 law, and the commissioners named in the act failed to qualify. Subsequent legislation in the 1848-1849 session of the General Assembly revived the earlier act and appointed a five-member, self-perpetuating board of commissioners to govern the town.[26]

Despite North Carolina's long-standing reputation for democracy, a hierarchical social system led by the slave-owning planter elite prevailed in Onslow. According to the son of prominent planter John A. Averitt, "It was a long, long way socially from the front piazza of the planter to

Palo Alto was one of the largest plantations in antebellum Onslow County. The owner, David W. Sanders, was an active community leader who served as justice of the peace, sheriff, member of the Council of State, and delegate to the 1835 convention to revise the state constitution. From the files of the Division of Archives and History.

the cabin door of either the overseer or the 'poor white trash' element." Averitt was one of thirteen individuals in the county in 1850 who possessed realty worth at least $10,000. Heading the list were David W. Sanders ($28,000), owner of Palo Alto plantation on White Oak River; Averitt ($25,000), owner of Rich Lands plantation on New River; Edwin W. Montford ($23,800); and nonresident Edward B. Dudley ($20,000), who owned plantations in the Half Moon District.[27]

Magnificent houses obviously and immediately distinguished the planters. Rich Lands plantation, encompassing over 22,500 acres and 125 slaves, stood on the west side of New River on the stage road that led from Wilmington to New Bern. A four-hundred-yard avenue, forty feet wide, led from the highway to the manor house. Inclusive of the piazzas, the three-story house with attic, built of Carolina pine and weatherboarded with poplar, was sixty feet square. Twelve-foot-wide piazzas ringed the first and second stories. Large windows opened to the floor. The house sat on brick pillars, five feet off the ground, to avoid unhealthful dampness.[28]

Below the landed gentry in the social order appeared the small farmers, merchants, learned professionals, and artisans. There were few yeoman, a circumstance which constituted "our greatest weakness," admitted one of the planter elite, though he hastened to add that there were advantages under the "old regime" that more than compensated for that weak thread in the social fabric. Middle and lower class dwellings likely followed a vernacular style of building emanating from the earliest settlement of Onslow. One or two room houses of log or plank construction with mud and stick chimneys were popular, as were homes of plank construction with clapboard overlay. Porches and sheds offered additional space.[29]

Many Onslow residents possessed little or no realty. Forty-six percent of the heads of households in the county in 1850, including 65 of 109 in the Richlands District, were landless. These were the shopkeepers' clerks, day laborers, overseers, and an impoverished element called "poor white trash." Averitt employed the last to guard his turpentine orchards against fire, salt his livestock, care for his stocks of bees, and work on the plantation roads. The poor white families may well have herded livestock on the open range in the county, hunted, fished, and raised corn and poultry on land offered to them by planters like Averitt in exchange for their labor.[30]

Many at the lower end of the socioeconomic scale were destitute and desperate. In seeking a pension for his Revolutionary War service, Fabin Gilgo, a shoemaker, claimed that an injured wrist left him incapacitated. An older daughter could spin "a little," a younger daughter was "too Small to do any thing," and his son, "a poor [sickly] boy," was barely able to cut firewood.[31] Those unable to care for themselves suffered the ignominious fate of being designated as poor and placed upon the charge of the county.

The Revolution witnessed a shift in the philosophy of poor relief whereby the public shouldered the burden originally borne by private care or by the Anglican Church. Statutes in 1785 and 1797 authorized Onslow to build a poorhouse. Eventually such an institution was erected at Alum Spring. But the poor were not simply boarded by the county; the able-bodied were annually hired out to reduce the expense of ministering to the less fortunate. In 1850 the county maintained thirty-eight paupers at an annual cost of $1,076.[32]

The male head of the household dominated family life among all classes. The role of women in society varied according to their marital status. In marriage a woman legally merged her identity with that of her husband unless she arranged for a prenuptial agreement, a relatively rare occurrence even among those of upper class status. Generally married women retained charge of the domestic sphere of the home, though husbands and fathers were mindful of their parental responsibility. In an emotional, yet didactic, letter to his daughter at her boarding school, Marcus LaFayette Redd recalled nursing and loving her as a baby, listening to her first attempts to talk, and helping her up and drying her tears as she stumbled in taking her first steps. But Redd did not lose the opportunity to admonish his daughter to obey her parents, to study assiduously, and to maintain the strictest integrity in dealing with others.[33]

Single women, spinsters, and widows enjoyed far greater latitude in their social and commercial relationships. They comprised 13 percent of the heads of households in Onslow in 1790 and 11 percent in 1850. In rural Onslow independent females operated farms with the assistance of sons or other kinspeople. Nancy Ambrose kept the public ferry at Onslow Court House. Catherine Hawkins ran a boarding house in Swansboro in 1850 and claimed property valued at sixteen hundred dollars, which placed her wealth above that of most of the men in the county.[34]

Free blacks in North Carolina were insignificant in number before the Revolution but increased sixfold, from 5,041 to 30,463, between 1790 and 1860. In Onslow, however, the free black populace rose erratically to a peak of 172 in 1850, then declined to 162 in 1860 (See table 1). Most lived in the Richlands (Upper and Lower) and Southwest (Upper and Lower) Districts. Altogether free blacks never accounted for more than 2 percent of the total residents of Onslow.[35]

Several factors accounted for the paucity of free blacks in Onslow, including determined white opposition to their presence, legislative discouragement of the emancipation of slaves, and particularly, the rising value of bondsmen during the antebellum era. Nevertheless, whites in the county occasionally liberated their bondsmen. Edward Starkey by his will sought to free eight slaves in order to reward their "faithful and meritorious services." He urged his executors to make such provision for them as would enable them "to maintain themselves in a respectable though humble station in life."[36]

Free blacks occupied an unenviable position in Onslow, existing on the periphery of the social and economic order. They suffered from numerous legal disabilities as whites attempted to discourage their presence and control their actions. A free black "code," instituted by legislation in 1830-1831, was followed by disfranchisement and restrictions on their right to bear firearms in later years. Legislation in 1831 demanded that slaves emancipated after that date leave the state within ninety days and never return.[37]

Hostility toward free blacks continued to mount, particularly in the 1850s, when friction between the North and South reached a fever pitch. Onslow state senator Lott W. Humphrey unsuccessfully sought to reenslave David Jarman, who had lived as a free man for more than thirty-five years in the Lower Southwest community. Jarman had been purchased and manumitted by his own father, a free black, in 1822. The state supreme court denied Humphrey's contention that Jarman's father was a bondsman at the time he purchased his son, and therefore did not own and could not liberate the young man.[38]

Humphrey's opposition to free blacks did not abate. Indeed, a petition in 1858, signed by fifty-eight inhabitants of Richlands, urged the senator to consider the "alleged evils" of the county's free black populace. Humphrey responded by cosponsoring a bill in the legislative session of that year to prohibit the immigration of free blacks to North Carolina and to enslave those who remained after two years had elapsed. At the same session Humphrey also proposed legislation to permit free blacks to enslave themselves under masters of their own choosing. Although both bills failed to pass, Humphrey and Onslow reflected the growing white animus in eastern North Carolina toward free blacks.[39]

Support in Onslow for Humphrey's position waxed on the eve of the Civil War. Early in 1860 one white contended that there was "no one curse" more "calculated to immoralize and injure a community in a more vital and serious manner than that malignant and despicable race called free negroes." Five months later a public meeting of whites in Swansboro, purporting to represent the sentiment of the town, denounced the marriage of a reportedly free black to a white woman. The citizenry expressed their "horror of amalgamation and its disgusting associate vices." Whether or not the man was black, he left Swansboro hurriedly, according to a townsman, "feeling that these quarters might get too warm for him."[40]

Against these odds free blacks attempted with difficulty to carve a life for themselves in the county. Of the seventy-four free blacks listed by occupation in the 1860 census, twenty-nine were domestic servants and sixteen were farmhands. Others were engaged in crafts—bakers, carpenters, coopers, masons. Twenty-four owned personal property; seven, six of whom were farmers, owned realty. The aggregate value of the property of the free blacks in the county was $5,210. Only one free black was a denizen of the county poorhouse at the time.[41]

Free blacks occasionally owned slaves. Jemboy and Virgil Dry were among twenty-five free blacks in 1790 who reported bondsmen. The 1830 census listed five free blacks among Onslow's slave owners. But none in the 1860 census claimed slaves. Most free blacks who owned slaves probably purchased relatives and friends in order to liberate them. For example, Benjamin Jarman, farmer, cartwheel maker, and former slave himself, bought his wife, oldest son David, and at least two other blacks, Rebecca and Ben. At the time of Jarman's death, only Rebecca and Ben remained enslaved, but by his will Jarman directed his son to free them.[42]

The institution of slavery survived the Revolution to become an increasingly integral part of Onslow's society and economy. The slave populace increased steadily, declining only between 1830 and 1840 in consequence of white planter emigration to the south and west. Not only did the number of slaves double from 1790 to 1860 (See table 2), but their proportion of the population climbed from 32 to 40 percent. However, the number of slave owners did not rise commensurately. Only one-third of the families in Onslow owned slaves on the eve of the Civil War. Thus the average slave holding in 1790 was 6.3; in 1860, 11.2.

Throughout the years of slavery blacks and whites attempted to adjust to the institution of bondage, in the process greatly affecting each other and producing a way of life that blended elements of the African and European cultures. Whites, like Rich Lands plantation owner John A. Averitt, might look upon blacks as "overgrown children," but they treated their slaves with a measure of respect. The black-white relationship was reciprocal, and each race struggled to define the limits within which it could live with, or endure, the other.[43]

Slaves perpetuated and developed their own culture within the predominantly white society. They followed an extended family system that was recognized and respected by some whites (within the confines of bondage). Averitt utilized slave preachers to solemnize wedding ceremonies on Rich Lands plantation. The bride and groom, their families, and the Averitts gathered in the dining room of the plantation house. Others stood on the veranda or in the yard. After the ceremony the married couple dined in the kitchen. Ample refreshment was provided for the others, and a dance in the slave quarters concluded the festivities.[44]

Table 2

Size of Slaveholdings, 1790 and 1860

Number of Slaves Held	Number of Slaveholders	
	1790	1860
1	60	50
2 to 4	89	96
5 to 9	83	73
10 to 19	31	49
20 to 49	14	34
50 to 99	1	6
100 and over	0	5
Total slaves	1,748	3,499
Slaveholders	278	313
Average size of slaveholding	6.3	11.2

SOURCE: Guion Griffis Johnson, "Antebellum Onslow County: A Social History," 8, a paper presented to the Seminar on Onslow County History, Swansboro, N.C., 1982.

The lot of the slave was harsh. On the plantation the workday began before sunrise for many, who rose at an early hour to feed the stock and draw water. An assembly bell rang at sunrise. An overseer or foreman issued work orders for the day. After a meager breakfast men left for the fields, drivers of mule teams headed toward the turpentine orchards, women departed for the dairy, and carpenters, smiths, and other artisans began work at their respective trades. From noon to two o'clock slaves consumed a dinner of pork, perhaps with gravy and cornmeal, and molasses or sorghum. Afterward men and women enjoyed their pipes, a "chaw," or snuff. Recalcitrant bondsmen were subject to a curtailment of their weekend privileges, corporal punishment (mainly whippings), or solitary confinement. Incorrigibles ultimately might be sold, perhaps to the Deep South.[45]

The number of slaves in a household often determined relationships with whites, privacy, and lodging. When the number was small, slaves and masters or mistresses lived and worked in close proximity. Slaves might lodge in the main house, kitchen, or barn. On the plantations most slaves were relegated to separate quarters, slave cabins, which were constructed especially for that purpose. In some instances the bondsmen were allowed to keep poultry and to maintain garden plots in which to grow corn, peas, or cotton. In Onslow in 1860, the average slave cabin housed four to six bondsmen. Slaves criticized their cabins as overcrowded, filthy, and drafty, though at Rich Lands plantation cabins were given two coats of whitewash once a year and inspected weekly to maintain at least minimal sanitary conditions.[46]

Slaves in Onslow, as elsewhere, manifested their opposition to bondage in many ways—malingering, feigning sickness, breaking agricultural implements, abusing animals, and engaging in such criminal behavior as theft, poisoning, arson, and murder. As early as 1715 the North Carolina legislature provided for the creation of special courts, operating beyond the bounds of the system of traditional judicature, to deal summarily with alleged transgressions of bondsmen. In Onslow trials, slaves faced charges stemming mainly from theft. Some were found innocent; others, deemed guilty, received punishments ranging from fifty lashes to execution by hanging.[47]

Many slaves ran away, taking advantage of the county's lowlands and swamps for protection. Josiah Howard of New River exemplified the problems faced by slave owners when he advertised for two runaways in 1796. Some slaves merely wanted a respite from the rigors of work. Others refused to return to the farm or plantation. The latter sometimes committed acts of depredation and were outlawed, as was Cuff in 1807, who belonged to John Fullwood. A slave belonging to Christopher Dudley was outlawed and killed in 1827. A few may have even conspired to engage in rebellion. The slave patrol, instituted in the colonial era, proved an imperfect mechanism by which to maintain control over the subject portion of the population, however.[48]

In addition to those who ran away alone or in small groups, large bands of blacks threatened the tranquillity of white society on occasion. Amid rumors that slaves along the coast from Washington to Wilmington planned a rebellion, Colonel William L. Hill of the Onslow militia reported in 1821 that a large number of bondsmen had taken refuge in a swamp in the county. Hill contended that their ranks "were filled with the most daring runaways, who well armed and equipped had long defied civil authority, and in open day had ravaged farms, burnt houses, and ravished a number of females." County magistrates called out two detachments of militia, numbering two hundred men, who spent twenty-six days under arms during the proclaimed "Negro hunt." The only confrontation occurred when the two militia units, thinking that they had discovered the runaways, unwittingly fired upon one another. The crisis concluded by the middle of September when the band of slaves dispersed.[49]

Eight years later, the publication of David Walker's *Appeal*, a tract encouraging slaves to seek their freedom by rising against their masters, unnerved Onslow magistrates. The county court ordered slave patrols to kill all dogs and take all stock that belonged to blacks, to accept no passes that did not specify destinations, to prevent slaves from gathering except for funerals, to confiscate all weapons, and "to use all diligence to keep . . . [slaves] obedient and in good order." Two years later, in the aftermath of the Nat Turner Insurrection in Virginia, Onslow justices believed that they had found evidence of a potential slave rebellion in the county, though the episode was probably a reflection of white paranoia.[50]

The swamps and low-lying areas that served as refuges for runaway slaves also gave rise to concerns about health. Malaria and respiratory illness were ongoing threats as reflected in the 1833 petition of Harvey Cox, protesting the erection of a gristmill and pond. He contended that an earlier mill on the same site occasioned death, "considerable sickness," and "large Doctors['] Bills" for the family that lived in the vicinity. The wealthy attempted to escape seasonal illness by building summer homes farther inland, going to Nags Head or Beaufort, or frequenting spas or watering places in the west, particularly in Warren County.[51]

For those who remained in the county, several physicians provided medical services. At the turn of the nineteenth century Drs. Nathaniel Loomis and William French tempered their practices by engaging in politics; in 1846 Samuel Langdon and William D. Cowan announced the formation of a medical partnership in Jacksonville; at midcentury the Averitt family used the services of Drs. Christopher Whitehead and Charles Duffy. The latter was also one of the larger turpentine producers in the county. Surely the most public-spirited antebellum physician was Dr. Edward W. Ward, who moved to Onslow, the home of his parents, about 1850 and successfully farmed Cedar Point plantation. Ward served as a county magistrate, superintendent of county education, and chairman of the county medical board. He was in the forefront of the secession movement in the county, representing Onslow in the state secession convention in May 1861 and captaining a cavalry company.[52]

The educational attainments of Onslow residents reflected the hierarchical nature of county society. Educational opportunities for most children in Onslow remained restricted, particularly for those of limited means, until the advent of free public schools in the nineteenth century. Beyond the family, old field schools usually sufficed for institutionalized instruction. James Howard of New River advertised in 1787 for a schoolmaster to keep a "country" school.[53] Parents were eager to secure proper training for their children, and through the apprenticeship system even the poor presumably were exposed to the fundamentals of learning.

The General Assembly's establishment of a public school system in 1839 reflected the long-standing belief of many in the state and in Onslow that at least the rudiments of education ought to be made available to all. According to an Onslow correspondent to the Newbern *Weekly Progress* in 1860, those of moderate means more zealously sought an education, because they realized its value, having "no time to idle and no money to spend." True or not, public education could only help in Onslow, where, in 1850, 45 percent of the adult white population (37 percent of the males and 53 percent of the females) was illiterate.[54]

Upon the passage of the public school legislation in 1839, the Onslow County court divided the county into school districts, each controlled by a superintendent. By 1858 the county contained twenty districts, though students were taught in only seventeen. The school year averaged five months, a figure enhanced by District 16, which held forth for a reported twelve months during the previous year. Among the teachers were but three females, who were paid less on the average than their male counterparts.[55]

The public school system failed to reach the majority of Onslow's eligible children—those from ages six through twenty. While all the children in District 1 attended classes in 1858, only 11 of 65 eligible in District 15 appeared in school. In the fall session of 1859 in District 4, the 23 boys in attendance averaged twenty-eight days in class. Nine girls averaged seventeen days. A major impediment to instruction was the lack of schoolhouses. District 5 reported a finished structure only in 1855; a report for 1858 suggested that the 114 children in District 7 failed to attend school due to the lack of a building.[56]

As Americans established their independence but groped for a sense of national identity in the Revolutionary era, an appropriate education for citizens of the young republic seemed basic to many lawmakers. Accordingly, the North Carolina legislature chartered the state university and numerous private academies at the end of the eighteenth century and during the nineteenth century. The academy, a forerunner perhaps of the modern high school, was a finishing institution for most students, though a preparatory school for college for a fortunate few. Onslow joined the academy movement in 1783, when the General Assembly approved legislation sponsored by Edward Starkey to charter one such school at the newly incorporated town of Swansboro and another at Richlands. The statute listed self-perpetuating boards of trustees for both institutions.[57]

Like so many of North Carolina's academies, those in Onslow enjoyed a checkered existence, not achieving stability and continuity until the end of the antebellum era. The legislature rechartered the academy at Richlands in 1791 and again in 1809, naming the latter school Onslow Academy. In 1810 the General Assembly rechartered Swansboro Academy and authorized the trustees to raise as much as four thousand dollars by lottery to support the institution. A similar enactment in 1824 again chartered Swansboro Academy and permitted the utilization of a lottery to raise funds.[58]

By the mid-nineteenth century three academies had emerged in Onslow to enjoy a more permanent status. Led by Methodist ministers William Closs and E. E. Perkins, residents of the Richlands area organized Richlands Academy in 1848, designed as a preparatory school for Randolph-Macon College in Virginia. With the exception of the Civil War years, the school operated until 1904, when it was replaced by a graded public school, the first erected in Onslow by popular vote.[59]

Supplementing Richlands Academy were schools in Swansboro and Jacksonville. In April 1848, J. C. McDonald advertised the beginning of a new term at Swansboro Academy. Subsequently the institution was incorporated under the direction of a board of trustees and expanded to include male and female departments. The Jacksonville academy, begun as early as 1851 as a female seminary, added a course of study for boys the following year to become the Jacksonville Male and Female Seminary.[60]

The length of the terms and the courses of study in Onslow's academies approximated those in schools throughout the state. The Richlands, Swansboro, and Jacksonville institutions offered five-month terms. The Jacksonville Seminary in 1852 divided its male department into several classes: English, spelling, and reading; advanced English, grammar, and arithmetic; algebra, Latin, and Greek; and "Lectures on all the higher branches" of study. The female department comprised three classes: spelling and reading; writing and mathematics; and advanced study, including philosophy, with options to take music (piano or guitar), painting and drawing, and needlework. Students at Swansboro in 1858 might have taken courses in natural and moral philosophy, rhetoric, logic, Latin, Greek, classical literature, and a rigorous regimen of mathematics, encompassing algebra, geometry, and differential and integral calculus. Also available were French, navigation, and astronomy.[61]

Yet not all were pleased with the available instructional opportunities. According to one visitor in 1860, Swansboro suffered "more the want of educational facilities than for anything else." Dr. Charles Duffy of Catharine Lake found "our school systems here, are very imperfect." He sent his son, Lawrence, to New York for tutelage in order to qualify the boy for admission to West Point. A rigid disciplinarian, perhaps Dr. Duffy was satisfied with Richlands Academy, which sent monthly progress reports to parents or guardians and advertised that "discipline is mild but firm, and a strict regard will always be had for the morals and mannerly conduct of the students."[62]

Duffy exemplified the efforts of the county's elite to send their children to finishing schools and colleges beyond Onslow. Planter John A. Averitt enrolled his daughter in St. Mary's in Raleigh, one of the finest schools for young women in the state during the antebellum era. One of Averitt's sons went to Princeton. The other studied at William I. Bingham's school near Hillsborough before enrolling at the University of North Carolina.[63]

Despite the relentless demands of farming, naval stores production, and household tasks, people of all classes enjoyed leisure time, though their activities may have differed. Common pastimes were hunting, fishing, riding, and dancing. As one remarked, dancing and riding came "Under the laws of heredity." Informal dances, with their hops and reels, as well as formal cotillions, "greatly embellished by a . . . brilliant Appearance of most charming Ladies," proved irresistible.[64]

Southerners prided themselves on their horses and both bred and raced their animals to great satisfaction. Unlike Halifax and some other areas in the state, Onslow was not a center of horse breeding. Still, Jesse Ward in 1797 advertised Young Mouse-Trap, a chestnut sorrel with an impressive lineage, for stud service. Tax records for 1856 reveal two stud horses in the county. Racing was prominent everywhere. Most towns, even the unincorporated village of Bogue before it became Swansboro, boasted "rasepaths."[65]

Hunting and fishing put food on the table as well as whiled away leisure hours. Fox hunting combined a love for horse and dog and was therefore popular with Onslow residents. Chasing the fox was far more exhilarating than the search for deer and bear. However, while fox hunting in 1860, E. W. Fonville's dogs had to expel the bountiful deer before they could search for the fox. Other prey beckoned, including opossum and raccoon, though a distinction had to be made between the two: opossum was sought mainly for food; raccoon, for sport.[66]

Members of the planter class lived an almost idyllic life, judging from the memoirs of one planter's son. James Averitt recalled a day's excursion from Rich Lands plantation to the sulphur springs about three miles distant. Couples in carriages and on horseback were accompanied by two wagons carrying food for dinner, which included such cold meats as ham, lamb, beef, chicken, and venison, among other edibles. Slave minstrels with fiddle, flute, banjo, triangle, and castanets provided music for dancing in the morning and afternoon. On buffalo robes and afghans laid on the ground, the young people played whist, old maid, seven-up, cribbage, and backgammon.[67]

On other occasions members of the Averitt family and guests went to Beaufort to enjoy a pony-penning or roundup of wild ponies on the coastal islands. They traveled first to Swansboro to stay with innkeeper Robert McClane, who prepared sailing vessels for the company to make their way along Bogue Sound to Beaufort. In addition to witnessing the pony-penning, some of the party visited Fort Macon and swam in the ocean. Returning home via Swansboro and taking carriages to the plantation, the party sang "Home Again From a Foreign Shore."[68]

Oyster roasts provided "royal entertainment" for Onslow inhabitants, who took full advantage of the seafood to be found in the ocean, sounds, and rivers, including trout, flounder, sheephead, and croaker, plus the waterfowl that inhabited the area. New River oysters were especially prized. Preparation for oyster roasts entailed setting up tables on which each plate was accompanied by an oyster knife and fork and a napkin with which to hold the hot shells. Accompanying the oysters might be bread and butter and cucumber pickles, all to be enjoyed with hot coffee.[69]

At the other end of the social scale slaves engaged in some of the same activities as whites. On the Averitt plantation they did not work after noon on Saturday except during the harvest season. The bondsmen hunted for raccoon, opossum, and squirrel, fished, and rode the draft animals they commanded on the plantations. On Sundays they might visit among themselves on the plantations or travel (with passes) to neighboring plantations. Slaves sang and danced to the accompaniment of fiddles. They ran footraces, pitched quoits, played ball, and enjoyed such games as mumblety-peg and "five corns," a variation of dice in which grains of corn were substituted for the cubes.[70]

County residents eagerly anticipated holidays ranging from New Year's to Christmas. A May Day party in Swansboro in 1860 featured a military parade, an excursion to the banks, and dancing. Two months later the town celebrated the Fourth of July with the usual firing of cannons and display of flags. A procession headed by a band from New Bern formed at 10:30 A.M. at the flag pole on Front Street. Led by Capt. George T. Duffy, marshal of the day, it marched to the academy where music was followed by readings of the "Mecklenburg Declaration of Independence" and the national Declaration of Independence, and a speech by the Reverend John F. Mattocks. At four o'clock in the afternoon the ladies of Swansboro presented a flag to the local cadet corps, who then paraded thorough the streets. A dance in the evening concluded the festivities.[71]

Christmas was the "queen of plantation high days and holidays." The Averitt family celebrated noel for a week in the great house and in the cabins, though preparations began as early as mid-November with hog-killings. Wagons brought pine and lightwood to the house for "cheerful fires, so essential to a well kept Christmas." Eight to ten days before Christmas, wagons took lard, poultry, eggs, butter, roasting pigs, and items made by the slaves to New Bern and Wilmington where they were exchanged for nuts, fruits, candies, and other holiday treats.[72]

Additional entertainment was derived from traveling shows that occasionally visited the county. Although the principal eastern thoroughfare connecting the two largest towns in the state, New Bern and Wilmington, passed through Onslow, the county lacked urban centers that might attract such entertainment. Moreover, Swansboro, the largest town in Onslow, lay rather isolated on the coast. However, the popular Eldred and Robinson Circus visited the county in the 1840s. And, in 1860, one Dr. Barker, a phrenologist, lectured in Jacksonville. According to a report, Dr. Barker was "coining money after a fashion that would make a miser's fingers etch[sic]."[73]

Also offering a respite from the cares of everyday life and an opportunity to socialize in an often isolated rural existence was the church. The evangelicalism of the Second Great Awakening, camp meetings, and exhortations of itinerant preachers continually reinforced the spirit among the people. The prevailing denominations were Baptist and Methodist, though county residents benefited from free chapels at Richlands, Swansboro, and Jacksonville. The first free chapel, organized near present Richlands in the 1730s, eventually became Union Chapel, then Union Chapel Christian Church. A chapel near Swansboro, dating from the colonial era, and one in Jacksonville, dating from 1850, were supplemented by those established by planters who sought religious services for their families.[74]

The Baptists continued to thrive and expand from their pre-Revolutionary roots in the New River area. Under Robert Nixon the New River Baptists gained a reputation throughout southeastern North Carolina. Eventually, three divisions of Baptists emerged: Primitive, Free Will, and Regular. Baptists claimed five organized congregations in 1850 and seven in 1860. Among them was Ward's Will Church, reputedly begun in 1832 on the basis of a bequest of five hundred dollars by General Edward Ward. In his will Ward, who died in 1834, stipulated that the church building should be available to all Christians, but eventually the Primitive Baptists used it exclusively.[75]

After its introduction to North Carolina just before the Revolution, Methodism flourished in the state and in Onslow. The efforts of the great circuit rider Bishop Francis Asbury, who visited Onslow numerous times, were partially responsible. Asbury found his task formidable. When he preached at Swansboro in April 1785, he found "a wicked people indeed," though "a few had joined society." A decade and a half later Asbury preached to "a very serious but unaffected" congregation at Richlands on New River. By 1803 Asbury despaired—"the people of Onslow. . . *please not God and are contrary to all men.*" Two years later he passed through the county without preaching, though he lodged with Lot Ballard, whose family had long supported Methodism in Onslow.[76]

Bishop Asbury fervently promoted the incorporation of blacks into the religious communities of the Methodists, and indeed the Methodists and Baptists accepted slaves within their respective churches. Most Africans had been animists before their arrival in America, and many retained that approach to religion. Planters, however, encouraged slaves to accept Christianity, fostered religion, and accepted the presence of slave preachers, though perhaps less so after 1830, when the threat of slave insurrections seemingly loomed larger. The membership of South West Primitive Baptist Church in 1850 comprised fifty-two whites and twenty-one blacks.[77]

Beyond the church men gathered at taverns and mercantile stores for camaraderie as well as for business. In 1847-1848, there were sixteen taverns and ten stores in Onslow. Nine men operated taverns, three ran stores, and seven maintained stores and taverns jointly. Some stores occasionally catered illegally to slaves, exchanging whiskey and other items for corn, poultry, pigs, and merchantable items. As a result area slave owners usually combined to buy out the proprietor, a more palatable alternative for the owner than risking a coat of tar and feathers or the rope of "Judge Lynch."[78]

In a rural area where one might travel for miles without seeing a person or house, social interaction centered on the household. Opportunities beyond the home for organized activity were few. Among them were the very popular military companies, which not only served to protect the community but also paraded for regimental reviews at the courthouse and on such festive occasions as holidays. Each of Onslow's two battalions of militia at the turn of the nineteenth century comprised five companies. The number of companies increased during the nineteenth century. The General Assembly incorporated the Onslow Troopers in 1832-1833, and additional companies, including the Onslow Cavalry, captained by Dr.

Edward W. Ward, and the Onslow Greys, captained by Marcus L. F. Redd, appeared in the burst of martial enthusiasm on the eve of the Civil War.[79]

Endemic to the organizational structure of the nation and state was the Masonic Order, which had appeared in North Carolina by the mid-eighteenth century. The North Carolina legislature incorporated the LaFayette Lodge No. 83 in Onslow in 1825, not coincidentally the year of a visit to North Carolina and other parts of the United States by the popular Frenchman, the Marquis de LaFayette. By 1850 the LaFayette Lodge actively supported another organizational effort, when the Masons celebrated June 24, St. John's Day, in Jacksonville in conjunction with a gathering of the Sons of Temperance.[80]

During the second quarter of the nineteenth century the temperance movement gained momentum in the United States. At midcentury the Sons of Temperance, founded in New York in 1842 and organized in North Carolina in 1843, boasted divisions in Jacksonville and Richlands. When the Sons and Masons rallied on June 24, 1850, the temperance advocates were joined by divisions from Richlands and from Tuckahoe in Jones County and by a "Committee of Ladies," who claimed to be "your humble co-laborers in this noble cause." The next month the annual examination of the students of Richlands Academy was followed by the assemblage of the Richlands Division of the Sons of Temperance, who marched in full regalia to the Methodist Church, sang a temperance ode, and listened to declamations against alcoholic beverages.[81]

Agriculture and naval stores remained the pillars of the Onslow economy during the antebellum era. Large and small farms often combined both operations. Dominant, but unrepresentative, were plantations such as that of Edward B. Dudley, which lay along New River about five miles from Jacksonville. When advertised for sale in 1855, the Dudley plantation contained four thousand acres, half cleared and half timbered. A two-story house was accompanied by various outbuildings, including the overseer's house, slave cabins, two large barns, a steam sawmill, and gristmill. Livestock encompassed 14 mules, 20 horses, 300 hogs, 100 cattle, and 150 sheep. Three landings along the river facilitated market transportation.[82]

Slave labor on the Dudley plantation and other farms provided an inestimable contribution to the Onslow economy. While many planters used white overseers to supervise field slaves, John A. Averitt of Rich Lands plantation viewed such managers with disdain, declaring that they came from that element of the population that lacked integrity and the ability to provide "discipline and good, wholesome government" for the slaves. Averitt felt that he obtained better results from a system of black foremen, headed by "Uncle Philip" who was literate and commanded the respect of the other "servants," as they were called. Subordinate foremen directed other aspects of plantation endeavor: hoeing, ditching, turpentine boxing, and gristmilling. That approach, according to Averitt, produced better management, larger crops, and more harmonious relations among slaves than might be obtained under white control.[83]

On the eve of the Civil War farming flourished in Onslow and in eastern North Carolina. Improved acreage in the county rose by 20 percent from 1850 to 1860; the cash value of farms, from $536,676 to $2,141,690; and the value of farm implements and machinery, from $22,601 to $129,242. As was the case throughout the state and the South, Indian corn constituted the principal crop, followed by far less significant amounts of wheat, rye, and oats. Truck crops, such as peas, beans, and potatoes, like the grains, were consumed mostly on the farms. By midcentury Onslow farmers grew little tobacco but harvested significant amounts of rice, despite nettlesome ricebirds. An increased emphasis on cotton—53 and 336 ginned bales in 1850 and 1860, respectively— portended a bright future for that crop. With the exception of sheep, livestock (horses, mules, oxen, cattle, hogs) increased significantly; the value of livestock holdings almost doubled during the decade.[84]

While farmers contended with the vagaries of the market for their products, they also contended with the vagaries of nature in the form of destructive animals and storms. Legislation in the post-Revolutionary era continued the colonial practice of requiring the destruction of crows and squirrels and offering bounties for killing wild animals. Farmers also penned their livestock, particularly sheep, to protect them from wild dogs and foxes. Predators did not constitute the sole danger to agricultural operations, however. Three successive storms in July 1860 demolished the stables, poultry house, and five thousand panels of fencing belonging to Owen Huggins, one of the principal plantation owners in the county. The storms also destroyed 1,200 acres of corn, 120 acres of cotton, 23 acres of sweet potatoes, and left not a pea standing out of 400 bushels that had been planted.[85]

The more progressive farmers in the county joined those of the state in the first half of the nineteenth century in instigating an agricultural revolution in North Carolina. They sought to preserve the quality and vitality of the soil by allowing fields to lie fallow for a season, planting cover crops, and using marl, abundant at least along New River. Planters bred cattle (Durhams and Devons), hogs (Berkshires, Chester whites, and Jersey reds), and sheep (Marions and Southdowns). Ultimately the large planters sought self-sufficiency, particularly if they engaged in the naval stores industry in conjunction with farming, in order to realize the greatest possible profit from tar, turpentine, and resin production.[86]

Onslow residents were also interested in improved agricultural implements and practices. As early as 1799, Robert Whitehurst Snead owned a cotton gin, probably the first in the county. Ten years later there were eight gins in Onslow. In 1849 Dennis Aman announced his intention to patent a peanut picker that would pick two bushels in thirty minutes. In 1860 J. W. Mattocks of Swansboro advertised a "Chemical Apparatus" for examining soil to show its suitability for crops and its need for fertilizer, all at a cost "calculated [not] to frighten even the most tight-fisted."[87]

The 1850s found an upsurge of interest in the advancement of agriculture. Onslow farmers apparently formed a county agricultural society in 1852, some forty years after the first county agricultural societies appeared in the state. Under its auspices the first annual Onslow Agricultural Fair was held in Jacksonville in January 1860, during which "all was fun and frolic," according to one participant. A subsequent and probably more elaborate fair, supervised by Chief Marshal Dr. E. W. Ward, took place in the county seat in November 1860. The agricultural society offered premiums for outstanding farm crops, livestock, poultry, manufactures, "Ladies' Sewing Clothes," and "Ladies Eatables."[88]

Agrarian Onslow continued to display little industry during the antebellum era. Most such activity was small scale, household related or ancillary to farming, and immediately dependent upon the county's natural resources of forest and water. Saltworks dotted the coastline—at least three in 1815—and beckoned to the British during the Revolution and to the Federals during the Civil War. Gristmills remained a common sight. And, according to the census of 1810, some 703 looms in Onslow households annually produced seventy-two thousand yards of cloth valued at $28,300. Tanners, hatters, and distillers of whiskey and brandy added to the diversity of manufactures. Seafood—one reported shad and herring fishery and one reported oyster enterprise in 1860, together employing twenty-eight laborers and producing $19,100 in annual value—broadened the industrial base of Onslow.[89]

The premier industry in Onslow remained naval stores. A traveler in 1860 saw little but unbroken pine forest in the county where people engaged mostly in the production of tar, pitch, and turpentine. Eight turpentine distilleries in the county in 1820 produced an output valued at $16,675. Two decades later Onslow ranked fourth among North Carolina counties (behind Craven, Beaufort, and Pitt) in naval stores production. At mid-nineteenth century the county contained six steam turpentine distilleries—owned by David W. Sanders, John A. Averitt,

Robert White, Edward W. Montford, Cyrus B. Glover, and Ward Montford—and twenty-four tar and crude turpentine distilleries, four of which were also owned by Sanders, Averitt, White, and Edward W. Montford. Total annual output was valued at $219,000.[90]

The largest operations were those of Sanders and Averitt. The former produced twenty-five thousand barrels of resin and spirits of turpentine and five thousand barrels of crude turpentine, all valued at $63,300. Averitt trailed with twelve thousand barrels of resin and spirits of turpentine and ten thousand barrels of crude valued at $47,000. Averitt's turpentine "orchards" encompassed twenty-two thousand acres of pines surrounding Catharine Lake. "Uncle Philip" presided over fifty slaves in an operation that not only required boxers and dippers in the woods but drivers for the mules and wagons. In addition, slaves were used to man the cooperage shops, the glue house, the stables, and a windmill to drive the pump that provided water for the distilleries. Among the disadvantages of the naval stores operations were the lack of supervision of slaves in the forests and the ever present threat of fire, against which insurance was difficult to secure.[91]

Shipbuilding added greatly to the manufacturing output of Onslow after the Revolution. From the Revolution to the War of 1812 the county produced at least twenty-three vessels, including thirteen schooners, six brigantines, and two three-hundred-ton, ship-rigged craft. Two-thirds of the vessels, including all of the larger ones, were built in Swansboro shipyards. According to the United States government agent William Tatham in 1807, "The town of Swansborough seems to be chiefly employed in shipbuilding for the West India and coasting trade." Bear Banks, Bear Creek, White Oak River, Sneads Ferry, and New River also turned out ships, though a shifting, shallow bar at New River Inlet, "seldom admitting six feet of water," according to one observer, inhibited ship construction in that area.[92]

Shipbuilding proceeded apace in Onslow during and after the War of 1812. County shipwrights undertook three vessels—two schooners and a six-hundred-ton craft, ninety feet in length and thirty-five feet in the beam—during the war. From 1815 to 1861 an additional thirty-five oceangoing, sailing craft were constructed in the county—thirty two-masted schooners, four brigs, and one sloop. Swansboro remained the center of shipbuilding activity, followed by the New River district. A few vessels were built in the vicinity of White Oak River and Bogue Inlet.[93]

Onslow was also the site of the construction of two steamboats built during the antebellum period. The *Prometheus*, built at Swansboro in 1818 and financed by famed privateer and Onslow native Captain Otway Burns, was the first steamer constructed in the state. It was taken to

Wilmington for use on the Cape Fear River and generated much excitement upon its arrival in that port in June 1818. The *Prometheus* transported President James Monroe on his tour of the Wilmington harbor in 1819 but enjoyed a checkered career thereafter and was abandoned by 1825. The 199-ton side-wheeler, *David W. St. John*, built at New River in 1836, was taken to Savannah, Georgia, for the river trade and scrapped in 1844.[94]

Overland transportation improved little following the Revolution. Nonresidents of Onslow, unused to local conditions, almost uniformly agreed that travel through the county was "disagreeable." Summer heat was oppressive. Roads, mere beds of white sand sometimes hiding tree roots, fatigued and endangered horse and rider alike. Also threatening were the pines that lined the roads, which after years of boxing for turpentine and forest burning were apt to be "overset" by high winds. The landscape was uninviting, termed by President George Washington on his southern tour in 1791, "the most barren country . . . [that he] had ever beheld." Any tavern that broke the monotonous woods was likely to be "a dismal place surrounded with moccasins, wildcats, and wild human beings."[95]

Shipbuilding has a long history in Onslow County. The *Prometheus*, constructed in Swansboro in 1818, was the first steamboat built in North Carolina. The city in the background is Wilmington. Illustration from James Sprunt's *Tales and Traditions of the Lower Cape Fear, 1661-1896* (Wilmington, N.C.: LeGwin Brothers, 1896), 12. Reprint edition, The Reprint Company, Spartanburg, S.C., 1973.

Although the network of country roads became more complex, construction and maintenance of roads and bridges continued to depend upon the directions of the county court and the efforts of the road overseer-company system. Deficiencies were obvious. In 1779 overseer Christian Free submitted a list of more than twenty men who had failed to work on Queens Creek Bridge, some of whom had been delinquent for as many as six and seven days. In 1803 the county grand jury indicted one S. Shephard with failing to keep open the road from the Upper New River ferry to the South West Bridge. The county attorney also accused John Mumford of blocking the main road from the courthouse to Swansboro with fence rails.[96]

Wealthy planter John A. Averitt's decision in 1847 to alter the route of the public road running through his plantation evoked considerable excitement and resentment. That highway connected Limestone Road and Newbern Road. The latter linked New Bern and Wilmington and served not only travelers but also those seeking to market their turpentine, corn, and other produce. Averitt supplanted the old road, which was convenient, safe, dry, and "had existed as long as the oldest persons can remember," with a longer road beside New River that extended over an "exceedingly bad and hilly tract of land." Averitt prevailed upon the local overseer to accept the new road and obtained an order from the county court to confirm the replacement.[97]

Antebellum efforts in the nation and state to improve highway transport centered upon turnpikes and plank roads. The turnpike movement, spawned by the success of the Lancaster Turnpike in Pennsylvania in the 1790s, was embraced by North Carolina in the form of a number of private companies that sought to charge tolls for the use of properly constructed and maintained roadbeds. Onslow belatedly joined the turnpike mania when the General Assembly in its 1830-1831 session chartered the White Oak Turnpike Company. However, the White Oak Company doubtlessly became just another futile attempt in the state to instigate a private toll road, in this instance connecting Onslow Court House to the road on the northeast side of White Oak River in Jones County.[98]

An extension of the turnpike movement was the surge of interest in plank roads following Governor William A. Graham's suggestion to the legislature in 1848 that plank road construction might satisfy North Carolina's desperate need for cheap and improved transportation. The General Assembly chartered over eighty plank road companies between that time and the Civil War, including the Wilmington and Top Sail Sound Plank Road Company in 1851, which built a road that ran from the port approximately twenty miles to the New Hanover-Onslow county line. Encouraged by the apparent success of the company, residents of Onslow and New Hanover obtained an extension of the road in 1855, when the legislature incorporated the New River and Wilmington and Top Sail Plank Road Company to continue the plank road to Sneads Ferry or some other point on New River.[99]

Neither the New River plank road nor other such highways designed to connect Onslow ultimately with markets in Wilmington and New Bern proved successful. The General Assembly incorporated the Jacksonville and Trent River Plank Road Company in 1852 and the less ambitious Richlands and New River Plank Road Company (to connect Richlands and Tar Landing on New River) in 1855.[100] Yet neither of those roads seems to have been built. Not only were plank roads an expensive undertaking initially, but they faced competition from railroads and water transport. Ultimately the advent of the Civil War effectively ended the plank road experiment.

Onslow's interest in improving water transport facilities during the colonial era revived after the Revolution, focusing on the county's two principal rivers, the New and White Oak. After several leading citizens of the county had raised funds to clear shoals at the mouth of New River, the General Assembly in 1791 incorporated the Commissioners of New River Navigation to formalize and legitimate the undertaking. The effort resurfaced in variant form in 1811, when legislation named twelve "commissioners" to collect funds and appoint agents to supervise clearing the river from Sneads Ferry to its mouth, and again in 1816, when the General Assembly incorporated the New River Canal Company to cut a channel through the marsh at the mouth of the river and to clear the river from its source for proper navigation.[101]

The General Assembly also took cognizance of White Oak River. Legislation in 1800 appointed commissioners to divide the river into geographic districts and directed all persons living within four miles of each side of the river to assist in an effort to keep the watercourse open for the passage of boats, rafts, and fish. Although the legislature repealed that statute in 1801, an enactment in 1810 invested the Swansboro commissioners with the power to remove "any obstruction which may impede the free passage of vessels up and down" White Oak River. Almost a half century later, in its session of 1858-1859, the General Assembly incorporated the White Oak Navigation Company, capitalized at thirty thousand dollars, to improve the navigation of the river from Swansboro to Job Smith's plantation.[102]

Meanwhile, Onslow remained concerned about the New River. Congress appropriated funds in 1836, 1837, and 1838 to remove the "oyster shoal," an obstruction near the mouth of the river that had stymied efforts by the colonials to eradicate. A petition to Congress by Onslow residents in 1850 resulted in an appropriation to resurvey lower New River, upon which it was found that the stubborn oyster bed remained. Federal efforts were unavailing, and the state legislature in its 1854-1855 session incorporated the New River Navigation Company, capitalized at thirty thousand dollars and funded in part by the state, to clear the river from Sneads Ferry to the ocean.[103]

Like past attempts to improve navigation on New River, that of the New River Navigation Company failed. At its first meeting, in November 1855, Lott W. Humphrey, president of the board of directors, reported that the contracts had been let to hire a surveyor and to secure a dredging machine. But work proceeded slowly. At the July 1857 annual meeting, President Jasper Etheridge noted that work had lagged in 1856 due to the paucity of laborers, sickness of the available men, and lack of a dumping boat to carry off spoilage. Frequent breakdowns of the dredge, which had to be repaired in Wilmington, cost valuable time. Still, by May 1857, the company had opened a 25- to 60-foot-wide channel, 7 feet deep at low water and 1,975 yards in length. Work ceased by 1859, however, at which time the company's dredge and dumping boat lay on the bottom of the river.[104]

In addition to efforts to clear New River, several attempts were made to link the river with neighboring waters to facilitate the exportation of county produce. Legislation in 1800 appointed commissioners to supervise the construction of a canal between New River and Browns Inlet, the cost of which would be repaid by means of toll charges. The idea was revived in the 1852 incorporation of the New River Canal Company, capitalized at fifty thousand dollars and led by John A. Averitt, Lott W. Humphrey, and Owen Huggins, among others. However, a report by a civil engineer countered the original plan with a proposal to construct a canal to link New River and Swansboro. None of those efforts appears to have been successful, nor were the endeavors of the New River and Bear Creek Canal Company, incorporated in the legislative session of 1846-1847.[105]

As interest in internal improvements throughout North Carolina gained momentum in the aftermath of the War of 1812, particularly in light of Archibald D. Murphey's program to improve the state's transportation system and the advent of the railroad, many Onslow residents sought state support for such projects. When consideration was given to cutting a series of canals to connect the rivers of the state in order to focus their traffic upon a central outlet, one plan suggested Swansboro as the seaport hub. Subsequent surveys, however, proved that the proposal was too costly. Later, in 1833, in a meeting at Onslow Court House chaired by William Jones, a group of citizens called for "liberal" state aid for internal improvements and selected Edward Ward, David W. Sanders, and Edward S. Jones to represent the county in a forthcoming internal improvements meeting in Raleigh.[106]

The application of steam to travel in the United States during the antebellum era produced revolutionary results. When, after 1830, the railroad proved a viable means of transportation, North Carolina and Onslow showed interest. Railroad construction in the state, particularly the Wilmington and Raleigh (Weldon), proved rewarding. Onslow remained disappointed, however. Legislation passed in the 1854-1855 session of the General Assembly authorizing a railroad from Beaufort to Fayetteville via Onslow never came to fruition.[107]

Because of Onslow's coastal location and the increasing consequence of the port of Swansboro in the late eighteenth century, shipping in the county merited the attention of the state legislature after the Revolution. In 1787 the North Carolina legislature erected the port district of Swansboro to complement the existing districts of Brunswick (soon Wilmington), Beaufort, Bath, Roanoke, and Currituck. Trade through Port Swansboro proved relatively insignificant, however; tariff collections from shipping entering the port were minuscule compared to revenues obtained from other state ports. An examination of available shipping records for Port Swansboro reveals that twenty-two vessels entered the port from July 1, 1789, to March 10, 1790. All were small sloops and schooners, averaging forty tons. Port Swansboro's trade beyond the state was linked primarily to South Carolina, though a few vessels arrived from the West Indies and New England.[108]

The colony and state exported naval stores, wood products, and foodstuffs but failed to offer a broad market for foreign goods. Foodstuffs, such as corn, bacon, pork, chickens, eggs, and potatoes, followed distantly. Imports consisted of salt, molasses, rum, foodstuffs, and dry goods, which Onslow merchants began to obtain from certain northern ports, principally New York, as opposed to South Carolina, New England, and the West Indies. In 1807 Bazel Hawkins engaged Edward Ward's vessel, the *Two Sisters*, for two trips to New York. Nineteenth-century Onslow merchants, like so many in the state, depended upon New York goods to stock their shelves.[109]

Storms, shallow channels, and shifting sandbars wreaked havoc on North Carolina's coastal shipping, including that of Onslow. In 1795

Samuel Chadwick of Swansboro found a small vessel, bottom up, on Bogue Banks, from which he salvaged fifty-three firkins of butter, sixty-one firkins of lard, and eight broken barrels of flour. Four years later John Collier failed to navigate the New River bar safely, causing Christopher Dudley's schooner, the *Sally*, to beach on the coast. And, in 1833, William Ennett announced the sale of the schooner *Faithful* and her cargo, which had wrecked on Stump Sound Banks.[110]

On the eve of the Civil War, some forty years after the advent of steamboats on North Carolina waters, residents of Onslow began to advocate a steam connection with the neighboring ports of New Bern, Beaufort, and Wilmington. Trade between Swansboro and Beaufort, conducted in flatboats, might take four or five days; that between New River and Wilmington, two to three weeks by sailing craft. Speedier and more dependable steam transport possessed an undeniable appeal. However, proposals to run a steamer from New Bern via Beaufort to Swansboro or from New River to New Bern or Wilmington failed to materialize.[111]

Merchants continued to exercise considerable influence over the course of trade in Onslow. They served as factors for the planters, provided shipping facilities for the county's exports, and brought northern dry goods and fashions to Onslow. Among the approximately ten stores in the county in the mid-1840s was that of William P. Ferrand on Front Street in Swansboro. Ferrand also owned a fireproof storehouse for his merchandise and a distillery in or near the town from which he shipped turpentine to New York and the West Indies. A decade later Z. B. Barnum similarly claimed a brick store in the port as well as two ships, three turpentine distilleries, and several tracts of land in the county to supplement his mercantile trade. When Stern and Brother of Wilmington announced the opening of their mercantile store in Richlands in 1852, they advertised "Fancy and Staple" dry goods, clothing of the latest fashions, shoes, hats, hardware, groceries, and, "In fact, every article that is usually kept in a country store."[112]

While the nation accepted the Constitution as the working basis of a new government, political divisiveness in the 1790s gave rise to the first American party system. The Federalists seemed to represent an elitist conception of leadership in conjunction with a belief in a powerful, active national government and chief executive. The Jeffersonian Republicans found favor in North Carolina and in Onslow, however, with their espousal of limited government, a strict interpretation of the Constitution, an agrarian economy, and a democratic polity. In preparation for North Carolina's second congressional election in 1791, John Spicer and

Robert W. Snead, Onslow's representatives in th
announced their support for ardent Jeffersonian Ti
the Cape Fear District. Bloodworth lost the electio
a 199-vote majority in Onslow.[113]

Local politics in the early years of the Republi
emotions that sometimes resulted in physical viole
of Onslow's leading citizens, George Mitchell and R
for election to the state senate, Snead called Mitch
crowd that had gathered at the courthouse at New   ~~on a shot
was heard, and rushing to the area people found Mitchell dead and Snead
standing nearby. Snead was arrested but allowed to post bail. At his trial
for murder in the Superior Court of the Wilmington District, the jury
returned a verdict of manslaughter. Six months later, when Snead
appeared at the court for sentencing, he brought a pardon from Governor
Alexander Martin. Thereafter he resumed his active career in Onslow
politics.[114]

Perhaps a dozen or so families controlled local politics in Onslow at
the turn of the nineteenth century, highlighted, among others, by the
Dudleys. Christopher Dudley, often a member of the state senate from
1797 to 1820, was among the richest men in the county in 1800, owning
sixty slaves and engaging in shipping with his schooner, the *Sally*. His son,
Edward B. Dudley, born in 1789 near present Jacksonville, achieved
greater fame. By 1809 he was a second major in the Onslow militia; five
years later he was appointed colonel. In 1811, at the age of twenty-two,
Dudley represented Onslow in the state house of commons, a position
to which he was reelected in 1813. In 1814 he was elevated to the state
senate. Subsequently he moved to Wilmington and in 1836 became the
state's first popularly elected governor.[115]

Members of other elite families included Robert Whitehurst Snead,
who was active in local affairs in the 1780s, served in the senate from 1790
through 1794, and later became sheriff and county clerk. George Warren
Mitchell, son of George Mitchell, appeared in the house of commons
from 1801 to 1803, after which he served as sheriff of Onslow. Edward
Ward Sr. capped a distinguished career in local government with a stint
in the house of commons in 1806. About the same time, his son, Edward
Ward Jr., embarked upon his career of public service, serving in the
commons in 1810 and in the senate in 1811.[116]

Among the newcomers achieving political prominence were two
physicians. Dr. Nathaniel Loomis represented Onslow in the commons
from 1796 through 1799. Afterward he became clerk of the county and
superior courts until his death in 1814. Dr. William French entered the

Edward Bishop Dudley was an Onslow native who represented the county in the state house of commons in 1811 and 1813 and in the state senate in 1814. After moving to Wilmington, he served in the U.S. Congress, helped found North Carolina's Whig Party, and in 1836 became the state's first popularly elected governor. Photograph of Dudley's portrait from the files of the Division of Archives and History.

commons in 1804 and, after serving two terms, ended his career of public service with two years in the senate.[117]

The War of 1812, or Second War for American Independence, followed a quarter century of antagonistic relations between the United States and Great Britain. Fought specifically to redress violations of American neutral rights on the high seas and to protect western borders from British-incited Indians, the conflict ultimately was a test of the integrity of republican government. The United States fared poorly during the course of the war. Wracked by internal division, lacking financial resources, and fielding an inept army, the country was fortunate to conclude the war on the basis of status quo antebellum. That, however, did gain the respect desired by Americans for their experiment in republicanism.

The war had little effect on Onslow. The county's legislators, as Jeffersonians were wont to do, approved of the struggle against Britain but were unwilling to bear the monetary expense of the conflict. Opposing bills in the legislature to outfit the state's militia, Onslow lawmakers Lott Humphrey, William Jones, and Jason Gregory favored resolutions to seek federal assistance in the form of arms, troops, gunboats, and supplies.[118]

For its part, the federal government sought troops by recruiting for the regular army and by drawing upon the states for militia. Apparently the county produced its quota of men when President Madison called upon North Carolina for militia levies in 1812, 1814, and 1815, though Onslow troops saw little action during the war. Onslow militia, assigned to the

Third Brigade of the Sixth Division in 1812, helped to garrison Fort Hampton near Beaufort, North Carolina, but returned home by the end of the year. Onslow men were also among the five hundred militia called by Governor William Hawkins in 1814 to defend Wilmington.[119]

The success enjoyed by the United States during the war centered mainly upon naval actions and privateering. North Carolina supplied at least four privateers, one of which was the *Snap Dragon*, commanded by Otway Burns. A native of Onslow, Burns had been a sailing master before the war, commanding a merchant vessel that traded between New Bern and Portland, Maine. Burns and his vessel, backed by New Bern merchants, undertook three successful voyages before the *Snap Dragon*, under a different captaincy, was lost to the British.[120]

As had been the case during international conflicts of the eighteenth century, county and state residents feared for their exposed coast, which admitted easy incursion by the enemy. Although the British never attacked North Carolina, they periodically caused consternation by raiding coastal lands and taking supplies and sometimes slaves. In 1813 several Onslow residents beseeched Governor Hawkins to assist them. They observed the ease with which the British could penetrate White Oak and New Rivers and contended that only fifty infantry, fifty cavalry, and two mounted cannons would suffice for protection. The governor's reply, if any, was unreceptive. With a long coastline and little money, Hawkins had decided to concentrate the state's defensive efforts on Beaufort and the Cape Fear.[121]

Otway Burns, born near what is now Swansboro, was the legendary captain of the privateer *Snap Dragon* during the War of 1812. He was also a shipbuilder and financed the construction of the *Prometheus*, first steamer built in North Carolina. Photograph of Burns's portrait from the files of the Division of Archives and History.

Following the War of 1812, national politics generated little enthusiasm among North Carolinians. The Federalist Party disbanded as a national organization, leaving the field to the Republicans. When James Monroe sought reelection to the presidency in 1820, he had no opposition. Apathy characterized the contest in the state and in Onslow. Only sixty-one voters bothered to go to the polls in the county to cast ballots for Monroe.[122]

The splintering of the Republican Party in 1824, from which emerged several presidential hopefuls, revived interest in politics throughout the country. In North Carolina the contest centered on Andrew Jackson, the Hero of New Orleans, who headed the Peoples' Ticket, and William Crawford of Georgia, who had been secretary of the treasury in Monroe's cabinet. Like the state, Onslow preferred Jackson—295 to 225—in 1824, an election that was ultimately decided, however, in favor of John Quincy Adams, who was chosen by the House of Representatives in 1825.[123]

Two political parties emerged from the disputed election of 1824-1825. The Democrats championed Jackson, who began campaigning for the presidency in 1828. The national Republicans supported President Adams. Onslow emphasized its determination to support Jackson in a meeting in 1828 chaired by Christopher Dudley and attended by 205 "friends of General Jackson." Unanimously the group adopted resolutions denouncing the previous election of Adams by the Congress as "the result of intrigue and corruption," which exhibited "the most barefaced defiance of the public will, that has appeared in the history of our Government." Onslow backers of Jackson formed a Committee of Vigilance and Correspondence to cooperate with similar Jacksonian groups throughout the state in order to promote the election of the Tennessean.[124]

North Carolina and Onslow threw their full support to Jackson and the Democrats in 1828 and 1832, helping the Hero defeat Adams and Henry Clay, respectively, in those elections. In the aftermath of his defeat Clay formed the Whig Party, an anti-Jackson organization that appealed to the president's mounting antagonists. Among the many factors contributing to the dissatisfaction with Jackson was his selection of Martin Van Buren as his vice presidential candidate in the election of 1832. A New Yorker, Van Buren's position on the tariff and slavery did not necessarily coincide with the views of many in the South. In a positive sense, the Whigs found favor among those in North Carolina who perceived the state's backward condition and supported an activist government willing to promote internal improvements and education.[125]

Whiggery failed to take root in Onslow, though at the outset the appeal of internal improvements elicited the support of a few county residents. On behalf of the Whigs in 1835, Lewis Dishong, internal improvements

60

advocate, challenged Democrat James McKay for the district congress seat. Dishong carried Onslow 404 to 275 but lost the district cont. McKay. Dishong may have been encouraged by Onslow polit._____ Edward Ward, who had planned to challenge McKay in 1833 on a platform of "a liberal construction of the Constitution" and "justice to the manufacturer and all other branches and classes of industry." Shortly after his burst of enthusiasm, Ward reconsidered his prospects and withdrew from the race.[126]

The emergence of partisan politics led to the realization of constitutional reform in North Carolina. Almost from the state's inception demands for constitutional revision arose, but the revolutionary document lacked a mechanism for amendment, thus necessitating a convention for that purpose. By the 1820s the western counties, correctly contending that they were not adequately represented in the General Assembly, led an increasingly vociferous campaign for a convention. Although Democrats in the east generally opposed reform, pockets of Whigs—the Albemarle region and urban areas, who sought state support for internal improvements and commerce—aided the western cause.[127]

Yielding to western pressure and the realization that some reforms were needed, the General Assembly in 1834 approved the Convention Act, which submitted the question of holding a constitutional convention to the populace in a referendum. Numerically superior western voters emerged triumphant, carrying the referendum in the affirmative by a vote of 27,550 to 21,694. Onslow remained firmly loyal to its section and the Democratic Party, opposing the call for a convention by a vote of 496 to 31.[128]

The convention opened in Raleigh on June 4, 1835. The delegates chose as their president Warren County representative Nathaniel Macon, the respected elder statesman of the group who remembered many of the framers of the original constitution. Joseph D. Ward of Onslow was named assistant secretary. John A. Averitt and David W. Sanders, Onslow's delegates, arrived on June 5. Epitomizing the socioeconomic elite of the county, Averitt and Sanders owned two of the largest plantations in Onslow—Rich Lands and Palo Alto, respectively. Both participated actively in local government, serving in the capacities of justice of the peace and sheriff. Later they served on the Council of State. In their political sentiments they diverged: Averitt was a staunch Democrat; Sanders, probably a Whig, at least early in his career.[129]

Averitt and Sanders did not participate in the debates, listening instead to the oratory of Craven County politician and jurist William Gaston, among others. However, their votes recorded their assessment of the issues addressed and approved by the convention, mainly the disfranchisement of free blacks, the elimination of borough representation in the General Assembly, the inclusion of all Christians (particularly Roman Catholics) in the political process, the popular election of the governor, biennial meetings of the legislature, and apportionment of the General Assembly to grant western counties supremacy in the house of commons and eastern counties a majority in the senate. In essence Averitt and Sanders usually canceled Onslow's voice in the convention. The conservative Averitt voted to maintain the status quo except for disfranchising free blacks and eliminating borough representation, both of which he favored. Sanders opposed disfranchisement, favored borough representation, and supported the other religious and political reforms. Both, however, agreed to the changes in legislative apportionment.[130]

The package of amendments approved by the convention was submitted to the electorate in a referendum according to the stipulation of the Convention Act. Onslow remained loyal to the east, though the county's turnout was smaller and its pro-convention vote was greater than had been the case in the first referendum. By a vote of 357 to 97 Onslow rejected the labors of the convention. However, superior western numbers again carried the balloting, 26,711 to 21,066, to approve the amendments.[131]

Although the state divided fairly evenly in its political allegiance to the Democratic and Whig Parties after the Convention of 1835, Onslow proved overwhelmingly Democratic. While many North Carolinians, even Democrats, harbored reservations about Martin Van Buren, the party's presidential candidate in 1836, an Onslow meeting at Jacksonville fervently espoused the New Yorker. Resolutions adopted by the gathering praised Van Buren "as a man of the highest grade of talent, a profound Statesman, a sound Republican of the Jeffersonian School, and in every respect eminently qualified to discharge the duties of President of the United States." Between 1836 and 1856, the Democratic presidential candidates obtained from 76 to 83 percent of Onslow's votes.[132]

Likewise, in congressional and gubernatorial contests Democrats expected heavy turnouts in their favor. The congressional contest in 1835 proved an aberration in Onslow, for in subsequent elections Democratic candidates carried the county by lopsided majorities. James McKay defeated his opponent in 1837, 570 to 17. Twenty years later, in 1857, Thomas Ruffin received 600 Onslow votes; his opposition, 15. Democratic candidates for governor regularly received from 75 to 88 percent of the ballots between 1840 and 1858. The Whig candidate in 1836 and 1838, Edward B. Dudley, was a native of Onslow and resident of Wilmington, whose local popularity depressed Democratic victory margins in Onslow to 67 and 70 percent, respectively.[133]

Between the Convention of 1835 and secession in 1861, the Democrats in Onslow liberally shared the state legislative seats. From John A. Averitt (1836) through Christopher D. Foy (1848) representatives in the commons served but one term. In the 1850s Edward W. Fonville and Lott W. Humphrey each served two successive terms, followed by James H. Foy, who took his seat in 1858 and continued through most of the Civil War. A similar pattern occurred in the senate. Daniel Sanders (1836) was the first of a series of one-term senators that lasted until George H. McMillan, Edward W. Fonville, and Lott W. Humphrey each served two terms successively from 1850 through 1861.[134]

One-party politics did not always produce Democratic harmony, however. In 1846 Edward W. Sanders, who had represented the county in the commons in 1844-1845, had the temerity to announce his candidacy for the state senate in opposition to William Ferrand, who had been nominated by the party regulars. Worse, Sanders denounced the Sub-Treasury, a scheme to divorce the federal government from commercial banking and a cardinal plank in the national Democratic platform. While other instances of intraparty division occurred—in 1854 Edward W. Fonville defeated Sanders, 229 to 146, for the senate, and Lott W. Humphrey defeated Owen Huggins, 487 to 347, for the commons—they apparently did not involve a challenge to party integrity.[135]

Although the Democrats commanded a handsome majority in Onslow, occasionally they felt compelled to reproach their opposition. Demagogically appealing to the masses' disdain for privilege and the legal profession, they denounced the Whigs as "gentry" and "Federal lawyers" who harangued the people in a futile cause. Democrats voiced the hope in 1840 that victory would "consign to oblivion the modern Whig party." Whigs retaliated, at least in Raleigh, if not in Onslow. By a strict party vote in 1844 the house of commons expelled Onslow representative John Ennett on a charge of forgery. But Ennett returned to Onslow, stood for election to fill his vacant seat, and won. The house seated him before the conclusion of the 1844-1845 session.[136]

Whiggery in North Carolina declined precipitously in the early 1850s, largely due to the dissolution of the national party. Many Whigs temporarily took refuge in the American or Know-Nothing Party, a short-lived nativist organization. The Know-Nothings found no more support than the Whigs in Onslow, and their penchant for secrecy left them open to Democratic charges in the county that they were "dangerous" and "inimical to Republican institutions." Of the ten militia-voting districts in Onslow—Stump Sound, Lower South West, Upper South West, Lower Richlands, Upper Richlands, Half Moon, Northeast, White Oak, Swansboro, Wolf

Pit—only Half Moon and Lower South West offered more than nominal support for the Whig-Know-Nothings.[137]

As Know-Nothingism receded and Whiggery revived in North Carolina in the late 1850s, the nation was rent by the slavery question or, more broadly, "Southern Rights." Southerners viewed with grave suspicion the appearance in 1854 of the Republican Party, which seemed to represent antislavery interests. The presidential election of 1860 occurred against the backdrop of decades of increasing animosity between South and North and, more immediately, the scare occasioned by John Brown's raid in Virginia in October 1859. In Onslow the outlook was grave. According to a county correspondent to a New Bern newspaper in January 1860, the current course of events would lead inevitably to a "dissolution of the Union." "Civil war," he declared, was imminent.[138]

The same writer warned that "Party politics" would contribute to the destruction of "this glorious confederation." At the local level, county Democrats heeded his admonition about "party politics," for they broke with precedent by forgoing a convention to select party candidates for the state legislature. According to "Onslow," a correspondent to the *North Carolina Standard*, the county's Democratic leaders were well known. A convention might not only be construed as a sign of weakness by the opposition but could become "the engine of a few strategic, artful politicians" to support a friend or secure the nomination themselves.[139]

The gubernatorial contest in North Carolina in 1860 pitted Democrat John W. Ellis against John Pool, who represented a resurgent Whig Party that was denominated the "Opposition." The candidates indicated their intention to meet on the stump in Onslow but failed to appear at the appointed time. Although prominent Onslow planter A. J. Murrill offered his "elegant span of horses," family carriage, and a "cautious" driver to transport the men from New Bern to Jacksonville, perhaps neither candidate felt the trip would be worthwhile in light of Onslow's obvious political preference. Indeed the county delivered the usual majority to the Democrat, casting 841 ballots for Ellis and 133 for Pool.[140]

In perhaps the most momentous presidential election in American history, the national Republican Party in 1860 settled upon a dark horse nominee, Abraham Lincoln. The Democratic Party divided: the northern wing supported Senator Stephen A. Douglas of Illinois; the southern, prominent Kentuckian John C. Breckinridge. A compromise party, the Constitutional Union, offered John C. Bell, who drew heavily upon adherents of the former Whig Party. Onslow to a degree exemplified North Carolina in its voting behavior by ignoring the Republicans and casting a minimal number of ballots (24) for Douglas. Like other middle-eastern and southern counties in which slavery was prominent, Onslow overwhelmingly preferred Breckinridge to Bell, 781 to 153, though statewide Breckinridge received a bare majority of the votes.[141]

Responding to the election of Lincoln, residents of Onslow held a meeting at Jacksonville on December 8 to express their sentiments during the crisis. With Owen G. Huggins in the chair and Henry Cox and D.W. Simmons Jr. acting as secretaries, the gathering denounced northern infractions of the Constitution, personal liberty laws, and the triumph of a sectional party whose "avowed object was aggression upon the rights of the Southern people." Resolutions were adopted that called for determined resistance "at all hazards and to the last extremity" to encroachments upon the Constitution and for the repeal of personal liberty laws. The meeting also sought legislation to better organize the militia and to encourage the formation of volunteer military companies. Finally it called for a state convention and conference of southern states to consider southern rights and grievances.[142]

As South Carolina seceded from the Union in December 1860, followed by six additional southern states in early 1861, who together formed the Confederate States of America, North Carolinians debated the merits of disunion. In January 1861 the state legislature decided to place the issue before the electorate in a referendum. Voters would decide whether to hold a convention to consider secession. Voters would also elect delegates to represent their respective counties in the convention in the event of an affirmative ballot. Predictably Onslow favored the convention, 631 to 89, and overwhelmingly supported Dr. Edward W. Ward, a secessionist, as the county's representative. The result of the state referendum, however, was a narrow defeat for the convention, 47,323 to 46,672.[143]

Despite North Carolina's rejection of the convention, soon followed by the inauguration of Abraham Lincoln as president of the United States, the secessionists in the state remained active. After the fall of Fort Sumter, Lincoln's call for troops, and Virginia's secession, sentiment in North Carolina changed dramatically. Governor John Ellis convened the legislature in a special session on May 1. The lawmakers in turn called for an election on May 13 for delegates to assemble in a state convention on May 20. With Dr. Edward W. Ward representing Onslow, the convention adopted an ordinance of secession and ratified the Provisional Constitution of the Confederate States of America. Onslow and North Carolina prepared for war.[144]

Chapter Four
Civil War, Reconstruction, and the Late Nineteenth Century

As the nation, North and South, prepared for war in 1861, Onslow citizenry, like most throughout the country, expected a conflict of short duration. Fired by an initial burst of patriotism, excitement, and adventure, men on both sides volunteered with alacrity. They marched off to training camps with eager anticipation. But events soon revealed a protracted civil conflict replete with maiming and bloodshed for those at the front and, in the South, increasing distress and poverty for those at home. Although not overrun until the end of the war, Onslow County bordered Union-occupied territory in North Carolina for three years, and its inhabitants came to understand the agony of war better than most in the state.

Like North Carolina, in relation to its population Onslow contributed a disproportionately large number of soldiers to the war effort—five companies of infantry and two companies of cavalry, or almost one-fifth of the total white population of the county in 1860. Among the first to tender their services were the Onslow Greys, captained by Marcus L. F. Redd, who enlisted on May 13, 1861, and the Onslow Light Infantry, captained by Edward H. Rhodes, who enlisted on July 1. Both were sent to Camp Clarendon at Garysburg in Northampton County for training. The Onslow Greys and the Onslow Light Infantry became companies E and G, respectively, in the Third Regiment N.C. State Troops and remained with that regiment throughout the war.[1]

The Third Regiment saw extensive action. Sent to Aquia Creek in Virginia in August 1861, the Third was mustered into Confederate service. The following year the regiment went to New Bern to confront the Union invasion of that town in March but did not participate in the fighting. Returning to Virginia, however, the Third engaged Federal forces in the Seven Days' Battles around Richmond. As a part of the Army of Northern Virginia under the command of Robert E. Lee, the Third Regiment participated in the bloodiest confrontations of the war—Sharpsburg, Fredericksburg, Chancellorsville, Gettysburg, the Wilderness, Spotsylvania Court House, and Cold Harbor. Detached to aid Jubal Early's raid on Washington, D.C., in 1864, the Third remained in the Shenandoah Valley until December, when it rejoined the Army of Northern Virginia. Subsequently the Third followed Lee to Appomattox Court House, where the Confederate army was surrendered on April 9, 1865, and fifty-eight members of the Third Regiment were paroled on April 12.[2]

The Onslow Guards, captained by George T. Duffy, enlisted at Jacksonville on May 6, 1861. Ordered to Weldon for training, the Guards became Company B of the Fourteenth Regiment N.C. Volunteers. Subsequently the regiment went to Virginia to join General John B. Floyd's Army of the Kanawha and then the Army of Northern Virginia. The Volunteers were reorganized as the Twenty-fourth Regiment N.C. Troops in November 1861 while at Blue Sulphur Springs, Virginia. The Onslow Guards remained Company B. They returned to eastern North Carolina early in 1862 to guard the Petersburg and Weldon Railroad but were transferred back to Virginia during the summer. Duffy, deemed "the best Captain in the regiment," was wounded at Monocacy River, Maryland, in September 1862. That incident ended his active service; later he was assigned to the Invalid Corps.[3]

During the remainder of the war the Twenty-fourth divided its time between Virginia and North Carolina. After a brief sojourn in North Carolina early in 1863, the regiment returned to the Army of Northern Virginia in May to serve in the Richmond-Petersburg area. In January 1864, the Twenty-fourth joined General George E. Pickett in North Carolina, who unsuccessfully tried to retake New Bern. Later, however, the Twenty-fourth assisted General Robert F. Hoke in recapturing Plymouth and Washington and then returned to Virginia, where Lee needed troops to defend Richmond. The regiment, reduced to fifty-five in number, also yielded with Lee at Appomattox Court House.[4]

Late in 1861 and in 1862 Onslow offered another company of troops and two companies of cavalry. The Rough and Readys, mustered into service and ordered to Camp Crabtree west of Raleigh in October 1861, were assigned to the Thirty-fifth Regiment N.C. Troops as Company A. At the beginning of the next year the Rough and Readys were transferred to Confederate service and participated in the Battle of New Bern in March 1862. After spending time training in Kinston, the company brigaded with the Twenty-fourth Regiment N.C. Troops in Virginia. Subsequently it shared a history and fate similar to that of the Onslow Guards in the Twenty-fourth Regiment.[5]

Onslow's contribution to the Confederate cavalry consisted of Captain Edward W. Ward's Gatlin Dragoons and Captain Lott W. Humphrey's Humphrey Troop, both assigned to the Forty-first Regiment N.C. Troops (Third Cavalry) as Companies B and H, respectively. The Gatlin Dragoons were mustered into Confederate service in December 1861 but stayed in Onslow on picket duty. The Humphrey Troop was mustered into Confederate service in May 1862 and remained in the Cape Fear military district until 1863. By 1864 both companies had joined the Army of Northern Virginia, with which they remained for the duration of the war.[6]

The last company to enlist from Onslow, organized in 1862 and captained by F. D. Koonce, became Company K of the Sixty-first Regiment N.C. Troops. The company saw action at Kinston in December 1862, Charleston and Savannah in 1863, and Petersburg in 1864. Returning to Wilmington in December 1864, Company K evacuated the port after its fall in January-February 1865 and joined General Joseph E. Johnston's army to participate in the Battle of Bentonville in March. After Johnston's surrender to General William T. Sherman in April, the regiment was paroled at High Point early in May.[7]

In addition to constituting several companies in the Confederate service, Onslow men were scattered in other sections of the Confederate military. Election records in 1864 show that county residents served in the following North Carolina units: Companies G and H in the Tenth Regiment; Company I, Twenty-seventh Regiment; Company B, Thirty-sixth Regiment; Companies I and K, Forty-first Regiment; and Company H, Sixty-sixth Regiment. They were also stationed in the James River squadron in Virginia and aboard the steamer *Albemarle* in the Cape Fear River.[8]

Onslow remembered the soldiers at the front. Captain Marcus L. F. Redd of the Onslow Greys thanked Mrs. A. A. Freeman of Brown's Sound in 1861 for the "lot of wool socks" that she had sent to the men at Camp Howe in Virginia. Redd urged others in the county to send blankets and underclothing. Three years later the ladies of Swansboro and Wolf Pit Districts donated $360 for the care of sick and wounded Onslow soldiers. Others sent boxes of food and clothing to family members at the front. At the same time, those who remained at home became increasingly concerned about the enemy.[9]

Upon joining the Confederacy North Carolina confronted a threat faced in earlier wars against England—an unprotected coast. As early as May 1861 the state sank several vessels in Bear Inlet to stymie enemy incursions, but in September one E. L. Perkins pointedly observed to Governor Henry T. Clark that Bear, Bogue, and New River Inlets were defenseless. Lending credence to Perkins's claim was a Union landing of some fifty men at Bogue Inlet in October, followed in December by the appearance of a boatload of men from the Union barge *Gemsbok* on the banks just north of the mouth of New River. Neither party inflicted much damage, however.[10]

At the suggestion of Colonel James G. Martin, North Carolina adjutant general, a six-gun battery was constructed on the south side of Bogue Inlet during the winter of 1861-1862. Located on the tip of Huggins Island, the open-faced, thousand-foot earthwork contained six cannons, a powder magazine, and barracks. Captain Daniel Munn's artillery company, called the Bladen Stars, manned the fort from January 1862 until early March, when the company was summoned to defend New Bern. Presumably the cannons were removed and the fort abandoned at that time. On August 19, 1862, the Twenty-fourth Massachusetts Volunteers under Colonel Thomas G. Stevenson destroyed the magazine.[11]

Numerous saltworks, which seemed an open invitation to the enemy, added to the attractiveness of Onslow's exposed coast. Coastal residents manufactured salt by evaporating seawater to supplement that which was mined in the Confederacy or brought through the Union blockade. Among the many salt producers was Marcus L. F. Redd, who may have been detached from his company for that purpose. In 1863 Redd advertised the sale of salt at Stump Sound for two dollars below the prevailing price on the Wilmington market. During the war many of the Union forays into Onslow attempted to destroy the valuable saltworks.[12]

The war quickly affected Onslow. Union General Ambrose Burnside captured lightly defended Roanoke Island in August 1861 and overwhelmed New Bern in March 1862. From New Bern, Burnside extended Union influence to Newport, Morehead City, Beaufort, and Fort Macon. As the Federal occupation achieved permanence, White Oak River constituted the division between the Union-occupied area in eastern North Carolina and the Cape Fear defense district of the Confederacy. During the remainder of the war Union forces raided Onslow. Most of the Federal forays constituted attempts to gain information, destroy saltworks, and lower Confederate morale.

Following the fall of New Bern in 1862, Onslow received its first taste of military action. In April 1862 a detachment of the 103rd New York Volunteers visited Swansboro, encamping around the home of Thomas Gillette. The Union soldiers rebuffed a Confederate attack by the Nineteenth Regiment N.C. Troops (Second Regiment N.C. Cavalry).

The invaders allegedly carried off prominent men in "iron and ropes," plundered homes and stores, used "the most abusive language to all, particularly the women," and encouraged slaves to rise against their masters, all the while promising to return soon.[13]

Union troops twice menaced Swansboro in August 1862. Confederate artillery and small arms fire repulsed the first raid, though not before the Federal soldiers destroyed the barracks and powder magazine of the vacant fort on Huggins Island. The second Union effort, more formidable than the first, consisted of five steamboats and two gunboats carrying seven hundred soldiers, which anchored off Swansboro on August 17. Overawing three Confederate companies, the Federals plundered homes in the town and destroyed saltworks along the sound.[14]

Onslow citizens responded to the Federal raid by holding an open meeting at the courthouse in Jacksonville on September 1, at which they sought protection for their county. The gathering adopted a resolution requesting the services of eight thousand to ten thousand troops and appointed a committee to solicit Governor Zebulon Vance for aid. The governor forwarded the petition to Confederate President Jefferson Davis, who in turn ordered General S. G. French to send troops to the county. Any relief that may have materialized proved short-lived, for the Confederacy lacked the necessary manpower to maintain a large garrison in Onslow. Two companies of cavalry remained, however, to protect the county, though according to an Onslow correspondent to the *Wilmington Journal*, the Confederate pickets from Sneads Ferry to Wilmington served little useful purpose. Their posts were too widely scattered, and the men failed to ride their stations.[15]

Subsequently one of the more daring Federal incursions into Onslow occurred in November 1862. Led by Lieutenant William B. Cushing aboard the gunboat *Ellis*, the Union force entered New River on November 23 and steamed to Jacksonville, where it captured two small schooners, occupied the town for an hour and a half, and intercepted the Wilmington mail. Under constant Confederate fire on his return, Cushing had the misfortune of running the *Ellis* aground. The Confederates shelled the stranded vessel relentlessly on November 24-25. After the powder magazine of the *Ellis* exploded, Cushing set fire to the vessel and escaped in one of the prizes. Most of his crew had already departed safely in the other prize. It was an incredible effort on the part of Cushing, who gained a reputation for such exploits during the course of the war.[16]

Military activity in Onslow in 1863 and 1864 consisted mainly of reconnaissance expeditions by Federal cavalry. Union soldiers visited the county in January, March, June, and December 1863 and in April and

June 1864. Usually the Confederates retreated to safety beyond New River, and the invaders contented themselves with the military exercise and the destruction of saltworks. An expedition to Swansboro in April 1864, however, resulted in the capture of three boats and twelve Confederate soldiers and the destruction of much property. According to one resident, the Yankees arrived early in the morning, roused the citizenry from their beds, and broke open virtually every house in town. After staying for three hours the invaders fired a warehouse. Only the efforts of women and schoolchildren prevented the flames from spreading and engulfing the town.[17]

Throughout the war Onslow's open coast beckoned to enemy and friend alike. With their superior navy the Federals with impunity periodically raided Swansboro or, in the case of Cushing in 1862, New River and Jacksonville. Generating much excitement and offering Swansboro residents an opportunity for revenge was the capture of the Northern schooner *Alice Webb*, which put in at Swansboro in November 1863. The captain mistook the port for Beaufort, which was occupied by Federals. After running aground, the vessel became a prize of war. Crew and passengers surrendered at Swansboro.[18]

Occasionally blockade-runners, which probably intended to steam to New Inlet for an entree to Wilmington, entered Onslow waters. In mid-December 1863 the schooner *G. A. Bigelow* ran into Bear Inlet to avoid capture. Learning that the vessel had landed safely, Major General John L. Peck sent the USS *Daylight* and the USS *Howquah* to Bear Inlet, where they destroyed the *Bigelow*, its cargo, and four large saltworks along the coast. The following February the blockade-runner *Nutfield*, pursued by Union vessels, was deliberately stranded and burned at New River Inlet to avoid capture, and in June 1864, the 543-ton *Pevensey*, en route from Bermuda to Wilmington, was chased ashore and lost on Bogue Banks.[19]

The last major naval incursion by Union forces occurred in March 1864. Seeking to destroy two schooners near Swansboro and to capture a reputed Confederate force and battery on the south end of Bogue Banks, two hundred soldiers and forty-five sailors left Beaufort in the USS *Britannia* and several smaller craft. Confederate fire thwarted the expedition to Swansboro, but a Federal incursion into Bear Creek destroyed a schooner and brought back a large number of contrabands or slaves. Unable to return to their ship because of adverse weather, the Union force and contrabands made their way through Bogue Sound to Morehead City and Beaufort.[20]

Citizens who remained in Onslow waged a war of their own—a war against hunger, poverty, and inflation. The county court in 1861 took extraordinary measures to meet the anticipated crisis. The justices decided to issue ten thousand dollars worth of bonds and to add a military surtax to the usual county levy. Recognizing the burden that the war placed on the families of the county's soldiers, the justices not only exempted volunteers from the county poll tax but paid each volunteer five dollars as "a bounty or pocket money." The magistrates also organized a county committee to care for the families. The county committee collected and distributed supplies to the needy via subcommittees established in each of the county's militia districts.[21]

The foresight of the court was laudable, though wartime demands exceeded the capacity of public authorities. As one older woman in the county declared, "if the Lord don't provide for us," I "don't know what will become of us." In addition to local funds the county court utilized appropriations from the state for the support of the wives and children of soldiers; periodically it designated one of the justices to buy provisions for the needy. Private efforts, such as the attempt by inhabitants of the Wolf Pit District to raise money by subscription for the indigent, supplemented public exertions.[22]

As the war lengthened, the crisis on the home front intensified. The district relief committees and wardens of the poor remained active. The county magistrates in 1863 directed Justice Christopher Stephens to go to Raleigh to collect Onslow's share of the General Assembly appropriation that year for the wives and children of the soldiers. Locally, the court instructed Justice Henry Cox to purchase and store provisions (corn, pork, bacon, lard) for the soldiers' families and the poor and named Justice Andrew J. Murrill to deliver the provisions as needed. At the end of the year the court ordered the relief committees to ascertain the number of families, the ages of family members, and the condition of the families in their respective districts.[23]

When the county justices convened in March 1864, the relief committees reported a "great scarcity of Provisions" among families of the soldiers. Thus the court directed A. J. Murrill to purchase foodstuffs wherever they could be found and ordered the clerk of the court to petition the commandant of conscripts in Onslow's military district to send as many men as possible to help with seasonal agricultural work. For its part, the county court attempted, probably in vain, to borrow thirty thousand dollars to buy provisions for indigent families.[24]

Among the most critical shortages experienced by Onslow residents, and most other Southerners, was the scarcity of salt. Numerous saltworks appeared along the coast, and they became prime targets of Federal raids. In 1862 the county court appointed John Shepard salt commissioner for

Onslow and authorized the distribution of one-third of a bushel of salt a month to each indigent family in the county, an amount altered in 1864 to one peck per family member. However, the county probably was unable to procure sufficient salt to satisfy the needs of the poor.[25]

Despite the best efforts of the county authorities, by the close of 1864 Onslow residents experienced extreme deprivation. In December Dr. E. W. Ward chaired a public meeting that called for a statewide, cooperative effort to impose price restraints in order to relieve the distressed conditions. For their part Ward and other county physicians earlier had standardized charges for travel, visitations, and prescriptions. They also agreed to treat soldiers' families for half the usual fee.[26]

Despite the hardships and constant Federal threats, inhabitants of the county tried to maintain some semblance of normal life. Onslow residents still enjoyed picnics, fishing parties, and sailing excursions along New River and on the Banks. On one such outing, involving some forty men and women, the party spent the night at the home of Daniel L. Russell, whose wife was "one of those ladies who possessed that peculiar art of rendering all easy and happy around her, [and] had everything calculated to make one joyous and contented."[27]

The county school system maintained a skeletal existence throughout most of the war. From April 1863 through March 1864, teachers offered classes in three of Onslow's twenty-three school districts. One of the sessions lasted only a month, however, and enrolled only a third of the eligible children in the district. For advanced study Richlands Academy remained open as late as the fall and winter of 1862-1863.[28]

Beneficiaries of the war were the slaves who took advantage of the proximity of Federal troops to gain their freedom behind Union lines. In their forays into Onslow, Federal troops encouraged slaves to leave homes and plantations. The Union expedition in March 1864 to Bear Creek took a large number of blacks, only to abandon many due to a lack of boats to transport them to New Bern. Among the black troops fighting for the Union was John Everett of Sneads Ferry. He enlisted in the United States Colored Navy, serving in the rank of landsman for a year.[29]

After North Carolina seceded from the United States to join the Confederacy, Onslow's prewar political leadership continued to control politics. When Dr. Edward W. Ward resigned his seat in the secession convention, which convened from 1861 to 1862, he was replaced by Andrew J. Murrill. James H. Foy continued his antebellum service in the state house of commons until replaced by Murrill in 1864. John F. Murrill served in the state senate from 1862 to 1864; Isaac N. Sanders, from 1864 to 1865.[30]

Opposition to the war, though concentrated in the Mountains, existed throughout North Carolina. Approximately one-sixth of Onslow's voters opposed secession in 1861. Union sympathies manifested themselves early in the county when a Union party landed at Bogue Banks in October 1861 and armed a number of Onslow fishermen. However, the men were subsequently arrested and sent to Fort Macon. As the war continued, with the enemy entrenched in eastern North Carolina, news of Union military successes and the threat of Federal incursions disheartened some eastern Carolinians. They began to listen to William W. Holden, whose Raleigh newspaper, the *North Carolina Standard*, counseled peace.[31]

Onslow, located immediately adjacent to Union-held territory, proved particularly vulnerable. Although the county in 1862 supported the gubernatorial candidacy of Zebulon B. Vance, a former Unionist who quickly became a staunch advocate of the Confederacy upon the outbreak of war, an Onslow correspondent to the Wilmington *Journal* in 1863 noted that a few in the county were "a little tainted" by Holden and the peace party. Indeed, the *North Carolina Standard* had subscribers in Onslow. In the congressional race for the Third District in 1863, Onslow's vote went to James T. Leach, a "submissionist" aligned with the Holden party. The following year Onslow fully supported Vance's reelection as governor, but the county elected Isaac N. Sanders, a partisan of Holden, to the state senate.[32]

Despite the ever present Union threat county governance changed little during the Confederate experience. The county court sat regularly to continue its administrative functions—levying taxes, probating estates, licensing dealers of spirituous liquors, maintaining roads, supporting the public schools, and aiding the poor. Local notables who had not left the county dominated the court and county offices. Following Owen Huggins, Andrew J. Murrill chaired the court from 1862 through 1864. Most conspicuous among the justices of the peace were Joseph Ennett, Henry Cox, and Henry H. Sandlin. Elijah Murrill Jr. succeeded White D. Humphrey as sheriff in 1862. A. J. Johnston served as clerk of court throughout the war years. Only occasionally did the war disrupt proceedings. In its March 1862 session, following the fall of Roanoke Island and the advance of Federal troops toward New Bern, the Onslow justices directed the clerk to remove all county records to a place of safety.[33] The conclusion of the war and the transition to provisional government in Onslow were succinctly related by a note in a county deed book for the period:

There was not any court held on 1st Monday in June A.D. 1865 as was usual. Genl R. E. Lee's army had surrendered. So had Genl Johnston's. North Carolina was under Military Government, by the United States forces, and we had no civil law. Consequently, no right to hold any court. W. W. Holden, the military or provisional Governor of N.C., appointed magistrates, who met at Jacksonville, on the 18th day of July A.D. 1865 and qualified as such, whereupon a called court was held that day.[34]

In the aftermath of the Civil War the southern states attempted to rejoin the Union under a reconstruction plan proposed by President Andrew Johnson. North Carolina held a constitutional convention in 1866, to which Onslow sent J. H. Foy, and formed a new government (though Onslow voters rejected the constitution, 273 to 19). In the subsequent election for governor Onslow preferred Jonathan Worth to William W. Holden (190-5) and elected Jasper Etheridge (over Foy, 112-72) and Andrew J. Murrill (no opposition) to the state senate and house of commons, respectively. However, like its sister states of the former Confederacy, North Carolina found that a Republican-dominated Congress in Washington, D.C., rejected its request to reenter the Union.[35]

Instead Congress substituted its own plan of reconstruction for that of the president, in part at least because blacks had been excluded from the political process by the southern states under the Johnson plan. Congress demanded another reorganization of southern state governments, utilizing the black franchise and anticipating black officeholding, to be carried out under the auspices of the U.S. Army. Congress hoped that the organization of the Republican Party (termed the Radicals by the Democrats) in the South would provide a basis for stable politics and protection for black rights. Although some whites joined the Republicans—northern émigrés and southerners (former Whigs, fortune seekers, and humanitarians)—blacks comprised the bulk of the Republican Party adherents.

As a result of congressional reconstruction, North Carolina in 1868 held another constitutional convention, formed a government controlled briefly by the Republican Party, and returned to the Union in 1869. Although North Carolina voters ratified the 1868 constitution, Onslow presented a solid majority against the document, 724 to 417. And Onslow hardly seemed penitent. In the 1868 presidential campaign Democrats (termed Conservatives briefly during Reconstruction) called for the repeal of the "unconstitutional" Reconstruction acts of Congress and the denial of "negro equality and supremacy." Indeed, as registered whites outnumbered registered blacks by 954 to 481, or 66 to 34 percent, in 1868 (reflecting a total population that was 68 percent white), Onslow never fell under the sway of the Republican Party. The county did not experience the bitter political divisions occasioned by Republican control in nearby counties, such as Craven and New Hanover, where blacks formed a majority of the population.[36]

Thus the Conservatives or Democrats controlled Onslow politics. The party delivered majorities for the Democratic presidential and gubernatorial candidates from 1868 to 1888, though the Republicans produced a steady 26 to 42 percent of the vote in those elections. The Conservatives campaigned vigorously, holding meetings to select delegates to regional and state conventions, to nominate candidates, and to promote electioneering. In the presidential contests the party formed Seymour and Blair clubs in 1868 and Tilden and Vance clubs in 1876. Speakers renowned for their stump oratory regaled listeners for hours, while committees drafted resolutions to support the party and to denounce the Radical opposition. The Democratic Party stressed a strict construction of the Constitution, probity and economy in government, free speech and freedom of the press, and an able judiciary.[37]

Onslow also rewarded Democratic congressional candidates and state legislative hopefuls with large majorities. Prominent Democrats who represented Onslow included James G. Scott (senate, 1870-1872; commons, 1869-1870, 1872-1874) and John W. Shackelford (senate, 1872-1877; commons, 1879). Scott, born in Hillsborough in 1826, graduated by the University of North Carolina in 1844, and trained in the law, moved to Onslow about 1853. He first appeared in public service in Onslow in 1869, when he was elected county examiner of the public schools. Upon his election to the house of commons, Scott was accorded membership on the committee that directed impeachment proceedings against Governor William W. Holden.[38]

Shackelford, after his service in state government, represented North Carolina's Third District in the Forty-seventh Congress (1881-1883), "redeeming" the district from "Radicalism," according to Onslow Democrats in a reference to the displacement of erstwhile Republican and Greenbacker Daniel L. Russell. Shackelford, a native of the Rich Lands area, was born in 1844, attended Richlands Academy, and attained the rank of lieutenant during the Civil War. His service in Congress consisted mainly of presenting his constituents' petitions, most of which came from Onslow and dealt with improving the navigability of the watercourses, including New and White Oak Rivers and the sounds between Morehead City and New River. Illness plagued Shackelford during the second session of the Forty-seventh Congress, and he died in January 1883 before its conclusion.[39]

Although the Democrats controlled Onslow politics, the Republicans managed to entice some to change their party affiliation. Among them was Jasper Etheridge, elected to the state house of commons in 1867, but identified as a "Radical" by the following year when he represented the county in the 1868 constitutional convention. While Etheridge claimed the status of an "Independent" in 1872 when he was defeated for the state senate by James G. Scott, by 1875 he had accepted an appointment from Republican President Ulysses S. Grant as a federal revenue officer.[40]

The most outstanding Republican affiliated with Onslow was Daniel L. Russell, a native of Brunswick County but raised by his maternal grandfather, David W. Sanders, on Palo Alto plantation in Onslow. Russell married the daughter of Isaac N. Sanders, an anti-secessionist who refused to fight and subsequently represented Onslow in the state legislature in 1864-1865 as a supporter of Holden. Although Russell's public career was pursued from Brunswick County and Wilmington after the war, Onslow Democrats delightedly helped defeat his bid for reelection to the bench of the Fourth Judicial District in 1874. Narrowly beaten by Allmand A. McKay of Sampson in the district, Russell was swamped in Onslow, 1,004 to 497.[41]

Resorting to intimidation, fraud, and terrorism, white Democrats exerted every effort to discourage the Republicans, particularly blacks, during Reconstruction. In the contest over the ratification of the 1868 constitution, prominent Democrats James Spicer and Hill E. King reportedly threatened blacks in the Stump Sound District. When Governor William W. Holden sought federal troops in 1870 to counter the Ku Klux Klan, preserve order, and uphold the law in North Carolina, Onslow was among the counties in which disturbances allegedly occurred. Sheriff Elijah Murrill, a Democrat, hotly denied any wrongdoing in Onslow, however.[42]

Blacks participated little in the political process beyond voting for Republican candidates. Apparently the only African American to seek elective office before the end of the nineteenth century was Edward Parker, who in 1871 lost his bid to become one of the three members of a Richlands Township school committee. As early as 1872, however, the county commissioners began to appoint blacks as poll watchers during elections.[43]

Nonetheless, blacks keenly felt their minority status. They organized, generated their own leadership, and protested their isolation. At a convention in Jacksonville in January 1882, Onslow blacks claimed civil and political equality under the Constitution and drafted a resolution to petition the county commissioners for the recognition of their rights, particularly that to serve on juries. The following month a delegation of black citizens led by W. P. Fenderson went before the board of county commissioners. After building a case against racial discrimination on the basis of the American Revolution, the Civil Rights Act of 1875, and the Bible, Fenderson asked, "Has one race any rights given them by law to denounce another on account of color?" and answered his own question, "no; a myriad of times no."[44]

Dr. Ward, chairman of the board of commissioners, responded by temporizing. He claimed that five days before the January meeting the board of commissioners had proposed the names of twenty-five Onslow blacks for jury duty. Indeed, opined Ward, no injustice was intended by omitting blacks from jury panels; the commissioners only felt that they must be better qualified. To that end Ward told the blacks to "work and educate your children and make good citizens of yourselves." Perhaps the commissioners relented under pressure. Blacks may have appeared on jury lists by the end of 1882, but the evidence is not conclusive.[45]

The brief Republican ascendancy in the South after the Civil War, followed by a resurgence of the Democratic Party in the 1870s and 1880s, proved a prelude to the politically turbulent decade of the 1890s, which witnessed the rise of a third party, the Populists, to challenge Republicans and Democrats. The third party movement originated in the agrarian despair that pervaded the country during the three decades after the Civil War. Farmers blamed their chronically depressed condition on usurious interest rates, high transportation costs (usually associated with railroads), deflation, foreign competition, tenancy, and the crop lien system.

Farmers organized on a state, regional, and national basis to remedy their ills. Among the more popular farm organizations in the 1870s was the Patrons of Husbandry or Grange. But that essentially nonpolitical group gave way to the more political and militant Farmers' Alliances. The Southern Alliance, or the Farmers' Alliance and Industrial Union, appeared in North Carolina in 1887 and quickly attracted Onslow farmers. Becoming a vehicle for political protest, it advocated railroad regulation and ceilings on interest rates, among other reforms. Failing to secure the cooperation of the major parties, in particular the Democratic Party in the South, the radicals of the Alliance throughout the country organized a third party, the People's or Populist Party, in 1892.

Dr. Cyrus Thompson, son of former Democratic state legislator Frank Thompson Sr., led the Populists in Onslow. Born in the Rich Lands vicinity, Cyrus Thompson obtained his medical degree from Tulane University in 1878, then returned to Onslow to institute a successful practice and enter the political arena. He represented the county in the state house of commons in 1883 and in the state senate in 1885. Upon the formation of the Farmers' Alliance in North Carol[i] Thompson became one of its principal spokesmen, spendin[g] traveling across North Carolina as state lecturer.[46]

With the appearance of the Populist Party Thompson a[t] Democrats. After actively supporting the party for four [years,] elected secretary of state on the Populist-Republican fusion ticket in 1896. With the demise of the Populists, Thompson joined the Republicans, perhaps in reaction to the obloquy heaped upon him by the Democrats. After unsuccessfully seeking another term as secretary of state in 1900, Thompson retired from active politics and resumed his medical practice in Jacksonville. Periodically, however, the Republican Party sought his service as a political candidate.[47]

Cyrus Thompson was a physician and political leader in his native Onslow County. He represented the county in both houses of the General Assembly, served as North Carolina's secretary of state, and was active in the Farmers' Alliance and the Populist Party. Photograph from the files of the Division of Archives and History.

Hill E. King of Folkstone was also prominent among Onslow Populists. A Confederate veteran and active member of the Democratic Party in the post–Civil War era, King served two terms in the state house of commons (1885, 1887). However, suffering with his fellow farmers during the 1880s, King became an active member of the Alliance, working as publicity agent, lecturer, and organizer. From this affiliation with the Alliance, King gravitated to the Populists. In 1894 King undertook the publication of a newspaper, the *Onslow Blade*, as a mouthpiece of the Populists in eastern North Carolina. During the fusion era, when Republican and Populist tickets were combined, King served as clerk of the state senate in 1897 and became a trustee of the State A. and M. College in Raleigh, member of the Board of Agriculture, and chief clerk for the North Carolina Experiment Station, at which point he moved to Raleigh.[48]

Another political maverick was Francis D. Koonce, attorney, who was born in 1837 and admitted to the bar in 1858. Though opposed to secession, he supported the Confederacy. Yet he drifted from the Democrats following the conflict, appearing as a congressional candidate for the Greenback Party in 1878. His withdrawal from that race resulted in a victory for Republican Daniel L. Russell, who served in the Forty-sixth Congress. Subsequently Republican President Benjamin Harrison appointed Koonce to federal office, but Koonce's Greenback ties inclined him toward Populism in the 1890s, and the party supported his unsuccessful bid for a congressional seat in 1892. At the beginning of the twentieth century Koonce practiced law in Jacksonville, where he served as mayor in 1902.[49]

Despite the obvious appeal of Populism in Onslow, the Democrats maintained a firm grip on politics in the county. The numbers of Democrats going to the polls in the gubernatorial elections barely declined from the 1888 figure, and in the presidential elections Democratic voters rose by 33 percent from 1888 to 1896. In contests for governor and president in 1892 and 1896, Democrats won 54 and 60 percent, respectively, of the total vote, easily outpolling the Populists and Republicans.[50] While the tactic of fusion in 1894 and 1896 often proved rewarding for Republicans and Populists— Daniel L. Russell was elected governor of North Carolina in 1896— Onslow remained a Democratic stronghold.

Leading the Democrats in the 1890s were Rodolph Duffy and Frank Thompson, who represented Onslow in the state house of commons from 1895 to 1901. The decline of Populism in the late 1890s, due to rising prices and the return of prosperity to the agricultural sector of the economy, led to the reestablishment of Democratic hegemony in North Carolina. In the process Democrats resorted to white supremacy campaigns in 1898 and 1900 to lure Populists and discredit Republicans. White supremacy materialized in the form of White Government Unions in the state, including one in Jacksonville in 1898 that tried to terrify blacks in the town. The white supremacy movement resulted in a suffrage amendment to the North Carolina Constitution in 1900, approved in Onslow by a vote of 1,531 to 671, that virtually disfranchised blacks and left them bereft of political influence until the second half of the twentieth century.[51]

The years following the Civil War witnessed significant changes in the form of county government in North Carolina. Reflecting the democracy inherent in the postwar Republican reform efforts in the South, the state constitution of 1868 replaced the county court with a board of county commissioners as the principal agency of county government, though retaining the position of justice of the peace. The commission plan provided for a board of five commissioners in each county who were popularly elected for two-year terms. Other county officials, such as the sheriff, register of deeds, treasurer, surveyor, and coroner, were also subject to popular election. The commissioners assumed the administrative powers of the justices of the peace over public buildings, schools, roads and bridges, and finances; the judicial responsibilities of the former county courts were distributed among the justices of the peace, the superior court, and the clerk of the superior court.[52]

The Constitution of 1868 also created the township unit as a subdivision of county government for the more effective administration of local affairs. Onslow commissioners divided the county into five townships—Stump Sound, Jacksonville, Richlands, Swansboro, and White Oak.[53] A board of trustees composed of a clerk and two justices of the peace, all popularly elected for two-year terms, controlled financial affairs and directed local government projects in the township. However, the board of trustees was strictly accountable to the county commissioners. Other township officials included a school committee of three and a constable.

Although the county commission and township introduced a measure of local self-government previously unknown in North Carolina, the new policies immediately encountered opposition. Democrats discovered that the Republicans, whose power rested principally upon the black vote, controlled several counties in which blacks outnumbered whites. Thus a constitutional convention in 1875, in which James G. Scott represented Onslow, authorized the General Assembly to modify the county government plan.[54] The legislature in its 1876-1877 session proceeded upon the mandate of the convention by arrogating the right to appoint the county justices of the peace, who in turn selected the board of county commissioners (though in some counties the board was also subject to legislative appointment). Although the commissioners retained their powers of local governance, all substantive decisions made by the board, such as the imposition of taxes, had to be approved by a majority of the justices of the peace. Since the Democratic Party had gained control of the legislature by the mid-1870s, the Democrats, in effect, assured themselves of command of the county governments by the altered scheme in which the General Assembly named the justices of the peace.

The advent of Populism and fusionism in the 1890s worked to reverse the process. Legislation in 1895, passed by the Populist-Republican fusion General Assembly, restored the popular election of county commissioners and justices in most counties and relieved the justices of the peace of any control over county administration. Townships remained, but principally for road building and maintenance purposes. In 1905 the legislature restored the popular election of county commissioners to all counties. Essentially elective commission control over county government has existed through the twentieth century, though the commissioners might create subordinate boards or transfer responsibility for particular aspects of county government to other organizations.

Onslow's county commission organized in Jacksonville on September 22, 1868, at which time the newly elected commissioners took their oath of office. Among the five was Jasper Etheridge, whose Republican proclivities apparently were not obvious to the predominantly Democratic electorate at the time. Indeed, Etheridge chaired the first board of commissioners, which once met in Etheridge's home. However, the commission seat was Etheridge's last elected office, for he lost a bid for reelection two years later and in 1872 was defeated by James G. Scott in a state senatorial contest. In fact, Democrats controlled the county commission from the outset, and by 1870 the party elected all five members of the board.[55]

The economic and social dislocations engendered by the war imposed severe hardships on Onslow's county government. Not only was the tax base curtailed by the ravages of war and depressed agricultural conditions, but expenses rose. The county commissioners found that public buildings, roads, and bridges demanded repair or replacement; an enlarged public school system encompassing both races necessitated funding; and a greatly increased number of poor required support. It was a circumstance repeated many times over in North Carolina and throughout the South.

The county and state continued their antebellum reliance upon poll and ad valorem property taxes to raise the preponderance of public revenues, though state law set maximum limits on county poll and property levies. Additional funds were derived from impositions on a variety of subjects, including playing cards, gypsies, circuses, and theatrical companies, and from fees collected on deeds, mortgages, marriage licenses, and other public instruments. Onslow usually imposed the maximum poll and property taxes, using most of the revenues to fund education and to support the poor.

The Onslow County commissioners, however, found that the maximum tax levies permitted by state law were insufficient. Consequently they continuously sought legislation from the General Assembly to allow the imposition of special taxes to underwrite ordinary expenses, to pay for unusually expensive projects, and to fund a county debt that stubbornly refused to disappear. The General Assembly invariably acquiesced, beginning in its 1868-1869 session, when it authorized a tax to build a poorhouse and repair bridges. The following session the legislature approved another tax to pay the county's outstanding debt.[56]

When the General Assembly for a third consecutive year in 1870-1871 permitted a tax of one-half of one percent of the value of real property, the legislators apparently felt that they ought to make the tax contingent upon the approval of the Onslow electorate. After that tax was defeated by a vote of 340 to 114, the Onslow commissioners requested another authorization to reduce county indebtedness in order to make "checks on the County Treasurer . . . good as cash." The legislature responded with yet another law, which also required approval by the electorate. A positive vote, 407 to 271, was forthcoming in 1872 as Onslow residents succumbed to the inevitable.[57]

After a respite of several years the General Assembly again reacted to the debt-ridden condition of Onslow. Legislation in 1877 permitted a special tax for two years, predicated on the approval of county voters.[58] Subsequently, in 1879, the legislature authorized Onslow commissioners to issue bonds not exceeding six thousand dollars over six years. However, Dr. E. W. Ward, appointed agent by the commissioners to confer with county creditors, found that most of those to whom the county owed money objected to payment by bonds. Moreover, Ward did not believe that the bonds could be sold for cash unless they were offered at a "ruinous discount."[59] Thus in 1881 the General Assembly returned to the practice of allowing the county commissioners to levy a special tax (in 1881, 1882, and 1883, and not to exceed in total seven thousand dollars) to pay outstanding debts, with the oldest obligations being paid first.[60]

As a result of mounting public consternation, the Onslow justices of the peace in 1879 appointed a Special Investigatory Committee of Finance. The committee spent a week examining county accounts from 1868 to January 1, 1879. Although it exonerated all county officers, particularly Register A. C. Huggins and Sheriff Elijah Murrill, of malfeasance or misappropriation of county or state funds, the committee found that the board of commissioners had failed to require county officials to record their accounts properly and punctually as required by law, thus rendering impossible a calculation of the county indebtedness. Opined the committee, "While we do not believe the present or any past Board of Commissioners, or any individual member thereof, guilty of any willful wrong-doing, in connection with their various duties, yet there has been a seeming looseness, which the present and future Boards would do well to steer clear of. "[61]

Still, troublesome fiscal questions continued to plague the county. The General Assembly in its 1887 session appointed a board of audit and finance to ascertain county indebtedness and authorized poll and property taxes to underwrite bonds of one-to-four-years duration to meet the debt.[62]

Meanwhile, funding for special projects required legislative approval of additional taxes. When Onslow contemplated subscribing capital to the proposed Wilmington, Onslow, and East Carolina Railroad in 1885, the General Assembly approved a special tax for that purpose. Two years later the need for a new jail produced an enactment that allowed impositions in 1887 and 1888 to raise the necessary funds. More money was collected than needed for the jail, and in 1889 the General Assembly allowed the county commissioners to use the surplus to repair bridges. In 1897 and again in 1900, the legislators permitted commissioners to use the surplus from the railroad tax of 1885 for repairing or replacing bridges and other county purposes.[63]

Still, the county debt could not be ignored, and the century ended much as Reconstruction had begun, with the Onslow commissioners grappling with their creditors. Legislation in 1891 permitted the commissioners to impose additional taxes to underwrite bonds, maturing over a five-year period, for paying creditors. Two years after a judgment against the county in 1896 that compelled Onslow to subscribe to forty thousand dollars worth of railroad bonds, the county commissioners claimed that they were in arrears on principal and interest payments. Bondholders were "pushing for their money." Thus the commissioners sought legislation to issue an additional five thousand dollars in bonds to cover delinquencies and to levy taxes to underwrite the bonds.[64]

Compounding the fiscal problems of the county was the delinquency of longtime sheriff Elijah Murrill. The sheriff seemed invariably in arrears when accounting for the proceeds of his collections and had the misfortune early in his tenure to have been robbed (as he claimed) of three thousand dollars in county money, which he was taking to Raleigh to pay the state treasurer. Representative of Murrill's status were his arrearages in 1883, which amounted to almost 10 percent of the tax collections. In 1890 an exasperated board of county commissioners gave Murrill ten days to pay all county funds that he had collected but had not paid to the county treasurer. Yet legislation in 1893 indicated that Murrill (by that time deceased) had failed to collect all taxes due in the years 1886-1890.[65]

The General Assembly attempted to mitigate the financial distress of towns and counties by permitting them to hire to private interests prisoners committed to jail for failure to pay fines or court costs. That not only relieved the governmental authorities of the cost of incarceration but allowed them to realize income from indigent lawbreakers. The Onslow County commissioners quickly availed themselves of the statute by ordering the sheriff to hire out several men to "Some Suitable person or Corporation," with the stipulation that proper food, clothing, and medical attention be accorded the prisoners. By 1893 the procedure had become so routine that the commissioners simply directed one of their number, Dr. Cyrus Thompson, to engage those sentenced to jail by Onslow Superior Court. The county realized as much as four dollars a month per prisoner, who might be hired out for as long as two years.[66]

A substantial portion of the county revenues provided support for the indigent, whether in their homes, in the care of others, or in the county poorhouse. Often the commissioners allotted from one to five dollars a month for the maintenance of the "out of doors" poor. Under conditions that required immediate aid the commissioners would grant money for a particular purpose, such as five dollars for clothing to one Toney Simpson. In the mid-1870s the annual number of paupers ranged from thirty-two to fifty-seven. However, only a small number were maintained in the poorhouse. Occasionally they included children—the commissioners consigned Hilda Garrett and her two offspring to the poorhouse in August 1877.[67]

The county poorhouse required constant attention and proved a major item of expense in the county budget. During the war the poorhouse at Alum Spring had disintegrated so badly that the county obtained authorization from the legislature in 1869 to erect a new structure in the Catharine Lake area, which was ready by April 1871. Those who had kept the indigent in their homes in the meantime were directed to take the paupers to the new poorhouse. Subsequently the legislature permitted the sale of the Alum Spring site. The commissioners periodically improved the new poorhouse, including the construction of a shed in 1881 "for the purpose of preaching and the comfort of the Poor."[68]

Annually the county commissioners appointed a superintendent of the poor to supervise the poorhouse. Usually a contract was let to the lowest bidder—A. H. Rhodes in 1871 for one hundred dollars, who was instructed to provide the inmates with "such necessaries as he may Consider actually Necessary for their Comfort and reasonable Convenience." Women—Amanda Wells in 1879 and Sarah Heritage in 1886—served as superintendents of the poorhouse. Those in charge billed the county for expenses. The commissioners pointedly told the superintendent in 1876 to call upon a physician when necessary, claiming the county would pay the fee. The county also paid the superintendent for burial expenses of deceased paupers, though not exceeding five dollars per person.[69]

Deterioration of the poorhouse convinced the commissioners in 1879 to replace the structure with another on the same site. They envisioned a building that would be thirty by fifteen feet with a partition in the middle and a stack chimney in the center or stick-and-mud chimneys at each end. The new poorhouse was occupied by 1884, and a grand jury report that year found the building "comfortable." However, the jurors claimed that the food was insufficient in quantity and badly prepared. Moreover, bedclothing and wearing apparel were "Scanty in the extreme and barely afford[ed] covering to the person." The well, which apparently had not been cleaned out in three years, was inadequate, and the physician paid by the county to care for the poor rarely visited them.[70]

The courthouse and jail at Jacksonville, the county seat, proved less troublesome than the poorhouse. Upon appointing a bridge keeper for the drawbridge at Jacksonville, the county commissioners often directed the bridge keeper to clean and make minor repairs to the courthouse. Substantial repairs to the courthouse were let at public contract to the lowest bidder—improved underpinning and gutters in 1875 and roof repair and painting (at least two coats of "good paint") for the courthouse and jail in 1880. A grand jury report in 1884 indicated that the jail was in "Very good condition in all respects." The building was clean; food and bedding were adequate. There were "No complaints among the inmates." Nonetheless, by 1887 the physical deterioration of the jail led to its replacement.[71]

The enormity of the economic devastation of the Civil War in Onslow may be seen immediately and starkly by a comparison of census figures for agriculture in 1860 and 1870.

	1860	1870
Improved land in acres farmed	63,783	37,618
Cash value of farms	$1,337,923	$349,640
Horses	1,068	469
Mules	403	323
Cattle	8,722	1,700
Oxen	603	431
Sheep	3,936	1,849
Hogs	25,628	8,786
Value of livestock	$293,758	$142,230
Wheat, bus.	418	———
Corn, bus.	273,937	117,420
Oats, bus.	1,990	125
Rice, bus.	43,938	10,590
Tobacco, lbs.	10	———
Cotton, bales	336	881
Potatoes, Irish, bus.	6,399	2,632
Potatoes, Sweet, bus.	175,354	62,186

Improved land declined by 41 percent; the value of livestock, by more than 50 percent. The cash value of farms, consequently, dropped about 75 percent.[72]

Immediate efforts by Onslow farmers to improve their circumstances were unavailing. Several in 1872 formed the Onslow Agricultural Society, electing Franklin Thompson president and Z. M. Costin recording secretary, and appointing Elijah Murrill, Jasper Etheridge, and Dr. Charles Duffy Sr. to prepare a constitution. James G. Scott and Andrew J. Murrill were also present in what amounted to a gathering of the political as well as agricultural elite of the county. Absent, however, was E. W. Fonville, a progressive farmer of the Wolf Pit community, who later challenged those of Onslow and surrounding counties to match his rather impressive cotton crops.[73] Despite its promise, the Agricultural Society apparently was short-lived, and cotton failed to revive farm fortunes.

Manufacturing in Onslow also suffered greatly from the shock of war. The 1870 census listed sixteen manufactories, but they employed only 38 people whose production was valued at $56,042. This represented a decline from 1860, when 302 people worked in manufactories and production was valued at $455,891. Although the number of manufactories rose to twenty-three in 1880, their output amounted to $45,089. As before the Civil War the establishments reflected the importance of agricultural and extractive industries—corn mills, turpentine distilleries, cotton gins, and lumber mills. Less significant, but still closely associated with farming and forests, were smith and wheelwright establishments, cooperages, and a tannery at Peanut (Folkstone) in 1884.[74]

A long-standing manufacturing industry, shipbuilding, declined after the Civil War, at least in the instance of oceangoing vessels, because the West Indies trade had virtually disappeared, the coastal trade had declined, and Onslow's inlets, most notably Bogue, were silting up. Three schooners were built in the county in 1866, but thereafter only five oceangoing vessels—four schooners and one sloop—appeared before the end of the century. One of the schooners, constructed in 1882 by Captain A. L. Willis, was a sharpie, forty-five feet long and designed to carry freight on New River.[75]

Shipyards existed throughout the county, though Swansboro appears to have been the shipbuilding center. Swansboro contained only one shipyard in 1877, and that "on a small scale," but two decades later the town boasted two shipbuilders, probably Edward Hill and Reinhold Foster. But shipbuilding was not confined to Swansboro and the vicinity of White Oak River. Louis C. Brown of Gillett and Walter Marine and

Reinhold Joseph Foster was a shipbuilder from Kiel, Germany, who settled in Swansboro in the late 1870s. He became one of the leading shipwrights in Onslow County during the late nineteenth century. Photograph from the files of the Division of Archives and History.

Luther Harrision of Marines constructed small craft along the banks of New River.[76]

The production of cotton, a valuable prewar crop, diminished after 1880, a result of the soil depletion properties of the crop and the shifting of cotton cultivation to the Gulf Coast states. Looking for crops to replace or at least supplement cotton, Onslow farmers turned to peanuts and rice, neither of which became the cash crop so desperately needed. However, Onslow did rank third among North Carolina counties in the production of peanuts in 1890. Following a surge in rice production in the 1870s, F. S. Coburn and E. H. Conville of Duck Creek intended to erect a rice mill. Yet, the output of rice reached its zenith of 92,565 pounds in 1880 and thereafter declined.[77]

Eventually tobacco filled the void. Postwar experiments with the crop lagged, for Onslow farmers were discouraged by legislation that required them to sell tobacco only to licensed manufacturers. The county produced only 730 pounds of tobacco in 1880. By the turn of the century, however, Isaac N. Henderson of Hubert and Dr. J. L. Nicholson of Richlands brought experienced tobacco curers to the county to promote the crop in Richlands Township. As a result Onslow produced 508,500 pounds of tobacco in 1900. Tobacco subsequently became the agricultural mainstay of Onslow's economy.[78]

Although the naval stores industry, so critical to Onslow's economy before the Civil War, suffered as a result of the conflict, North Carolina remained the nation's leading producer of such products. Onslow, however, dropped from fourth in 1860 to eleventh in 1870 among the counties in the value of naval stores produced. The monetary decrease was staggering—from almost $400,000 in 1860 to $38,700 in 1870, another indication of the impact of the Civil War. The number of turpentine distilleries in Onslow rose from three in 1870 to seven by the end of the decade. At the beginning of the twentieth century the number of distilleries remained at seven.[79] But naval stores never regained its favored prewar position in Onslow, and by 1900 the industry had largely run its course in North Carolina, which acknowledged the Gulf Coast states as the industry leaders.[80]

The bountiful natural resources along the North Carolina coast plus the advent of rail transport attracted northern as well as local investment capital, resulting in the appearance of several businesses in the latter part of the nineteenth century that affected Onslow. Among them were the Enterprise Lumber Company of Goldsboro, incorporated in 1889; the North Carolina Land and Lumber Company based in New Hanover County, 1889; the Pender and Onslow Land and Improvement Company, 1889; the Jones and Onslow Tram-Way Company, 1891; and the Onslow Land and Improvement Company, 1893. Most sought to take advantage of Onslow's timber. However, the Onslow Land and Improvement Company first intended to enter the lumbering business, then to cultivate oysters, and subsequently to open a cannery for fruits and vegetables.[81]

The most immediately successful of the lumbering operations was the Onslow Lumber Company, incorporated in 1889 by New York financiers Thomas A. McIntyre, Ewen McIntyre, and Richard Lamb. Two years later the company sent its first shipment of lumber—225,000 feet—to Wilmington. After becoming the sole proprietor in 1893, Thomas A. McIntyre sold the business to Parmele Eccleston Lumber Company of New Jersey, which obtained 139 leases to land in Onslow between 1893 and 1897. Although a stimulus to the Onslow economy in the 1890s, lumbering affected the county more markedly in the twentieth century.[82]

The seafood industry played a particularly prominent role in Onslow's economy in the last years of the nineteenth century. Always a local pursuit, fishing assumed a regional, even national, importance. Nineteen fisheries were located in the vicinity of Swansboro in 1890. The General Assembly attempted to protect the movement and migration of fish in New and White Oak Rivers and to encourage Onslow citizens to propagate diamondback terrapins. Legislation also sought to promote the growth of oysters in New River by forbidding the removal of the bivalves from their natural beds between May and September of each year.[83]

Shellfish, principally the New River oysters that had been praised so highly by antebellum denizens of the area, proved more important commercially than finfish. In 1869 Wilmingtonians noted "the fine luscious New River oysters that are making their appearance in our markets." Wilmington agents also sold New River oysters as far away as Columbia, South Carolina. By 1883 New River oysters were entered in the Boston Exposition and won acclaim from R. R. Higgins and Company, the city's largest dealer in oysters. Closer to home Onslow County commissioners appropriated money in 1888 and 1889 to assist those who wanted to participate in New Bern's annual fish and oyster fair.[84]

The General Assembly continued a prewar statute to encourage the cultivation of oysters and clams along the coast, though amending the antebellum law to empower the superior courts rather than the county courts to recognize private claims to oyster beds not exceeding ten (later fifteen) acres. In 1887 the General Assembly instructed the Onslow County commissioners to select biennially three interested citizens to compose a Board of Shellfish Commissioners for the county. The board exercised exclusive jurisdiction over all oyster grounds and fisheries in the county, and surveyed and allotted natural oyster beds to private individuals. In effect the shellfish commissioners assumed the duties previously exercised by the county court and then the superior court.[85]

Several companies organized to take advantage of Onslow's seafood potential as well as the county's agricultural and lumbering resources. The General Assembly incorporated the Eastern Carolina Piscatorial Association in 1891 to encourage "the propagation and cultivation of native and other fish," including shellfish. The law located the headquarters of the company in Burgaw, the seat of Pender County, but the association utilized land and water in Onslow. By the fall of 1897 the company owned a large truck farm bordering New River and that season shipped ten thousand packages of fruits and vegetables in addition to oysters.[86]

The New River Oyster Company, also incorporated in 1891, was owned by interests in Onslow, Wilmington, and Raleigh and centered its operations at Stones Bay in Onslow. It likewise contemplated growing and canning fruits and vegetables as well as harvesting oysters. By March 1892 the company had planted 107,000 bushels of oysters and expected to begin harvesting in the winter. In June 1892 the company held its annual picnic for stockholders, taking the participants to Stones Bay by train and then mule cart and treating the guests to oysters from the company's waters.[87]

The New River oyster boom abruptly terminated at the end of the century. A hurricane in late October 1899 produced wave action along New River and the sound that covered the oyster beds in silt. While Onslow oystermen obviously suffered, outside investors in the oyster enterprises probably lost more.[88]

Overland transportation changed little in the aftermath of the Civil War and did not noticeably improve until the twentieth century. The supervision of roads, bridges, and ferries remained the same, though after 1868 it fell under the purview of the county commissioners and the township trustees. The commissioners, as had the justices formerly, approved or rejected requests to open new roads and discontinue old ones. Illustrative of the difficulties faced by county residents was the withdrawal of a petition to the commissioners to discontinue a road from Yopps Meeting House on the condition that the township trustees assign more men to work on the road, appoint an overseer, and agree not to prosecute those who previously had failed to work on the road. Almost a quarter century later, when the commissioners closed a public road, they noted objections and allowed appeal of their decision to the superior court of the county.[89]

Occasionally the General Assembly mandated the construction of a road as it had done in the colonial and antebellum eras, but the success of the legislative directives was moot. A proposal in 1883 to create a road from Hatch Fork to the Swansboro and New Bern road near A. J. Murrill's residence remained unfulfilled in 1897.[90] More important was an 1879 statute authorizing the construction of Quaker Bridge Road, which would extend from Tar Landing on New River through White

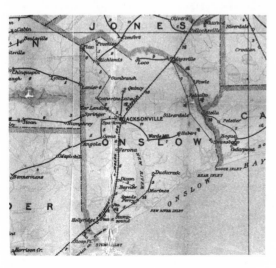

Detail of a post route map indicating post offices, mail routes, and distances as of June 1, 1896.

Oak Pocosin to Trent River. That highway would have facilitated trade with New Bern. Yet as late as 1899 the road remained unfinished despite offers by the legislature to make available state convict labor.[91]

Bridge construction and maintenance differed little from antebellum practices. Road overseers and companies cared for smaller structures, though the county would offer timber for building and repair. The county commissioners assumed control of the lengthier bridges in 1873: Big Southwest Bridge, Harris Creek Bridge, Doctors Bridge, Northwest Bridge, Big Northeast Bridge, the bridge at Montfort's Mill, and the Onslow half of the bridge at Smith's Mill. Later, in 1883, state legislation compelled county supervision of bridges over streams ten feet wide or more.[92]

The commissioners might advertise publicly for bridge construction and repair, or they might place one of their own in charge of the process. Commissioner A. J. Murrill in 1883 was appointed to contract for the repair of Southwest Bridge under the following conditions: the builder must use "good timber," submit to inspection of his work by a "good mechanic," and keep the bridge in "good condition" for two years. On occasion the commissioners established private toll bridges, such as Northwest Bridge across New River in 1893, to induce the construction and upkeep of the structures.[93]

Although the several bridges in the county required constant attention, the Jacksonville or Courthouse Bridge at the county seat seemed the most troublesome. Rebuilt after the war, the Jacksonville bridge necessitated a bridgetender to maintain the draw. The commissioners awarded bridgetender contracts on a monthly or yearly basis. Robert Pelletier accepted the tender's job in January 1875 for three months at $8.33 per month, with the stipulation that he repair the bridge and mind the courthouse, adding a door with a lock at the stairway of the latter. The contract extended to Lewis A. Avery from 1881 to 1882 for $36 included the obligation of cleaning the courthouse on all public days and keeping the windows and doors shut. On occasion, the county commissioners paid the tender for the number of times that the bridge had to be opened—twenty-one between March 16 and April 5, 1891, an indication of the traffic on New River.[94]

Another prominent bridge in Onslow's transportation system was the structure across White Oak River at Barkersville (Stella), for that crossing and concomitant roads brought Onslow residents closer to the seats of Carteret and Craven Counties. Upon the completion of the 413-foot Barkersville Bridge in 1879, some fifteen hundred people from Onslow, Carteret, Craven, and Jones Counties gathered at the site to celebrate the occasion. The bridge was rebuilt in 1893 or 1894, apparently with a draw. Throughout, Onslow and Carteret shared the cost of construction.[95]

The Jacksonville bridge, like others in the county, suffered from the elements and traffic. When the county commissioners ordered the trustees of Jacksonville Township to take charge of the bridge in 1870, they directed the trustees to put the bridge in "good repair." In 1872 the county commissioners deemed the structure unsafe, posting signs at both ends to warn people that they crossed at their own risk. Five years later the commissioners paid eight men a dollar each for "saving the County Bridge" at Jacksonville "during the Storm" on September 28, 1877. In 1891, in an effort to preserve the structure, the commissioners forbade people to congregate or fish on the bridge, to drive across at more than a walk, to tie rafts or logs to the bridge, or to hitch boats to the bridge.[96]

Ferriage in the county centered on the traditional passage across New River at Sneads Ferry. The county decided in 1875 to allow residents of Onslow to cross free of charge but required nonresidents to continue to pay the usual fees. Caroline Pearsons, a former slave, was a longtime ferry operator at New River who finally retired in 1894 after two decades of service. Upon his reappointment as ferryman in 1885, Pearsons received $215 plus fees from nonresidents upon the stipulation that the "Ferryman shall always be at his post" from sunrise to dark. Although ferry service generally appeared adequate, periodically complaints reached the county commissioners about the poor condition of the ferryboat, a circumstance the commissioners quickly attempted to remedy.[97]

The railroad exerted the greatest impact on Onslow's economy in the postwar era and, indeed, affected many aspects of life in the county. Immediately following the Civil War some Onslow residents wanted railroads to transport their produce to market. Reciprocally, merchants in New Bern and Wilmington hoped to engross Onslow's trade. Thus, in its 1869-1870 session the General Assembly chartered two roads: the Planters Railroad Company, which would link the Atlantic and North Carolina Railroad near New Bern to the navigable waters of New River in Onslow, and the Onslow Branch of the Wilmington and Weldon Railroad, whose rails would run from Teachey's to New River.[98]

Agitation soon appeared for a third route, which would extend from Jacksonville directly to Wilmington. As a result the state legislature in its 1870-1871 session incorporated the Wilmington and Onslow Railroad Company, authorizing it to build a road from the New Hanover port to the Onslow county seat. Later in the same legislative session the General Assembly provided for the merger of the Planters Railroad and the Wilmington and Onslow Railroad Company, to be known as the

Wilmington and Planters Railway Company. The merger to form the Wilmington and Planters Railway Company was confirmed by law in 1872. Later the name of the railroad was changed to the Atlantic Coast Railway Company.[99]

Meanwhile the Onslow County commissioners, responding to the ground swell of support for a railroad, agreed in September 1870 to appropriate fifty thousand dollars to help finance such a venture, contingent upon approval by the county electorate. A vote in January 1871 produced overwhelming sentiment in favor of the appropriation, specifically for the Wilmington and Onslow Railroad, which soon became the Wilmington and Planters Railway Company. Although Onslow agreed to subscribe to fifty thousand dollars worth of stock in the company, neither the Wilmington and Onslow nor any other railroad materialized. At a March 1871 meeting in Wilmington the Wilmington and Onslow Railroad Company was organized. Subscription books were opened at Wilmington, Scotts Hill, Sloop Point, Jacksonville, New River, and Richlands, but it was an abortive effort. In 1874 a resident of Onslow tried to revive interest in a railroad, at least from Sneads Ferry to Wilmington, which would speed mail deliveries and help to market truck produce, but without success.[100]

Onslow continued to attract New Bern and Wilmington mercantile interests. That concern ultimately resulted in an Onslow rail connection with both cities. Legislation in 1885 incorporated the Wilmington, Onslow, and East Carolina Railroad, which laid tracks from Wilmington to Jacksonville by 1891 and became the Wilmington, Newbern and Norfolk Railroad in 1893. In 1887 the General Assembly chartered the East Carolina Land and Railway Company, which completed a line from New Bern to Jacksonville in 1893. The Wilmington, Newbern and Norfolk Railroad absorbed the East Carolina Land and Railway Company in 1894, control of which passed to the Atlantic Coast Line Railroad in 1897. The Wilmington, Newbern and Norfolk operated a daily passenger train between Wilmington and New Bern that stopped in Jacksonville. It also sent a triweekly passenger-freight train between those terminals that called at Holly Ridge, Folkstone, Dixon, Verona, Jacksonville, Northeast, and White Oak.[101]

The railroad company and Onslow did not enjoy a harmonious relationship. The Onslow County commissioners allowed the railroad to use county land, including the Quaker Bridge Road, for a roadbed. However, the commissioners refused to issue bonds, as authorized by county voters in a special election in January 1888, to underwrite railroad construction costs. Upon suit by the railroad in the Lenoir Superior

Court, Onslow County and the railroad reached a compromise in 1896. According to the agreement the railroad surrendered any claim to previous bonds and interest thereon and agreed to pay court costs. In turn Onslow County relinquished any past claims to capital stock in the company and agreed to issue forty thousand dollars worth of bonds for the benefit of the railroad.[102]

Additional railroad schemes abounded in the late nineteenth century. Among them was the Burgaw and Onslow Railroad, incorporated in 1879 to run a line from the Pender County seat to Jacksonville. In 1888 the incorporators finally opened the subscription books and apparently attempted to organize the company. The Neuse and Swansboro Railroad Company received statutory recognition in 1893 to run a line from Riverdale in Craven County through Carteret and Jones Counties to Swansboro. During the same legislative session the Eastern Carolina Piscatorial Association was allowed to build a line for company purposes from New River to some point on the Wilmington, Onslow, and East Carolina Railroad. And the General Assembly chartered the Kinston and Jacksonville Railroad Company in 1899. Of these only the Eastern Carolina Piscatorial Association road—the Bay View Railroad—was constructed.[103]

As road and bridge capabilities improved but slowly and the railroad made a tardy appearance, water—slow but cheap—remained a crucial component of Onslow's internal transportation system. Periodically state law reinforced the authority of the county commissioners to maintain the navigability of the county's watercourses. Legislation forbade the felling of trees in watercourses and prohibited other obstructions, including fishing hedges, in the streams and rivers of Onslow.[104]

In order to improve their economic prospects, Onslow residents embraced several major internal improvement projects, among which was a canal to connect New River with the Northeast Cape Fear, thus allowing residents of lower Onslow better access to the Wilmington market. For that purpose the legislature in its 1871-1872 session incorporated the New River Canal Company. Three years later a gathering in Jacksonville chaired by Dr. E. W. Ward appointed committees throughout the county to take subscriptions to underwrite the funding of the canal.[105] The project waned after 1878, when the federal government expressed interest in building an intracoastal waterway along the eastern coast of the United States.

Citizens of Onslow and adjacent counties eventually felt compelled to seek the aid of the federal government to clear obstructions from local watercourses, for private enterprise had proven unable to do so. The government responded positively, allocating money to clear the oyster rock at the mouth of New River that had plagued navigation since the colonial era. By 1884 Congressman W. J. Green secured an appropriation of five thousand dollars to improve New River and to conduct marine surveys from New River to Beaufort. The Army Corps of Engineers, in charge of the work, began its dredging operations in October 1886 and eventually deepened the river channel.[106]

The federal government continued to evidence interest in Onslow's coast. Capt. William H. Bixby of the Army Corps of Engineers conducted a preliminary survey of White Oak River in 1889, recommending deepening the channel to admit steamboats and flatboats. The government failed to act, however, in large part because the completion of the railroad through Onslow in the 1890s offered a feasible alternative to the water carriage of such bulky items as naval stores and timber. In 1896 Congress considered deepening Bogue Inlet in order to facilitate traffic from Swansboro. The chief proponent of the project was the Swansboro Lumber Company, which would have been an immediate beneficiary. Congress abandoned the effort because the benefits were not deemed commensurate with the cost.[107]

Onslow's maritime trade centered on White Oak River and Swansboro. Naval stores, cotton, peanuts, lumber, and fish constituted the principal exports of the White Oak River area. Swansboro's importance as a naval stores center declined, but in the 1890s the town still shipped about 150 barrels of rosin and 30 barrels of turpentine weekly. Imports consisted primarily of fertilizer and general merchandise. Most exports and imports, however, passed through Beaufort and Bogue Sound rather than Bogue Inlet at Swansboro.[108]

A variety of craft, ranging from flats to sailing sloops and schooners to steamers, provided transport on Onslow's watercourses. Schooners, whose captains had to be warned by the county commissioners not to tie their boats to the bridge in Jacksonville for fear of damaging the structure, might ultimately take their cargoes of foodstuffs, cotton, and naval stores to market in Wilmington. The ocean voyage was risky for the schooners, particularly after the closing of New Inlet leading to the Cape Fear in 1879. Some failed to reach even that point, however, for one went aground off Wrightsville Beach in New Hanover County in 1882.[109]

Steamers added a new perspective to waterborne craft, as people came to depend upon them for their relative reliability. The New Bern, Beaufort, and Onslow Inland Coasting Company, organized in 1883, briefly ran a steamer between New River and Morehead City—probably the *Tarboro*, which had been built in Washington, North Carolina. For a connection to the Cape Fear, the Wilmington and New River Steam Navigation Company incorporated in 1877 to carry freight and passengers through the coastal sounds from Fort Fisher to New River. Apparently unsuccessful, it was supplanted by the Wrightsville and Onslow Navigation Company in 1889, which was given the same monopoly right.[110]

After the *Tarboro*, only a few steamers appeared in Onslow before the turn of the century, all of which served mainly lumber or oyster interests in the county. In 1887 Hilery Terry, a northern businessman who had come to North Carolina the previous year, built the *Minnie B.* at Stella to haul lumber from the sawmill that he had erected at the village. In the 1890s the *George D. Purdie* of the New River Oyster Company provided freight and passenger service on the New River. The Swansboro Lumber Company finished another steamer, the *Nina*, in 1897.[111]

Matching the political reconfiguration and economic disruption occasioned by the Civil War was the profound impact of the conflict on societal relationships. In the wake of emancipation former slaves with little property or education were left to fend for themselves, except for the immediate assistance of the Freedmen's Bureau, an agency of the War Department, and such northern philanthropic organizations as the American Missionary Society. For its part Congress envisioned a radical readjustment of racial relations by the integration of blacks into the civil and political framework of the United States.

The disruption caused by the war produced distress among whites and blacks alike. The South's traditional agrarian economy was in shambles. Farms suffered from neglect. Mounting indebtedness forced the sale of large and small properties, impoverishing men of wealth as well as those of ordinary means. The abolition of slavery transformed labor as well as race relations. No longer able to rely upon forced labor, white landlords developed various forms of tenancy. Blacks and whites increasingly found themselves caught in a web of tenancy and debt through the crop lien system that reduced many to a state of semi-servitude. In Onslow tenancy stood at 35 percent of the farms in 1880, dropped to 27 percent in 1890, and then rose.[112]

The twin impact of emancipation and poverty exerted a powerful effect on Onslow blacks and consequently the county population. Blacks availed themselves of their newfound freedom and mobility to seek better economic opportunities elsewhere. Thus the federal census showed that Onslow's population dropped from 8,856 in 1860 to 7,569 in 1870, a decline of 14.5 percent due almost entirely to the out-migration of blacks. As a result the percentage of blacks in Onslow's population dropped from 41.3 in 1860 to 31.7 in 1870. Although the number of county residents rose steadily during the ensuing three decades, reaching 11,940 in 1900, the percentage of blacks decreased slightly to 30.2 at the turn of the century.[113]

Onslow's population remained overwhelmingly rural. The railroad, which passed through the county linking Jacksonville to New Bern and Wilmington, spawned several villages. Clusters of people, ranging in number from 25 at Stump Sound to 75 at Catharine Lake, produced post office communities, and the Eastern Carolina Piscatorial Association established Bay View on New River, which had a population of 50 in 1896. Joining Jacksonville and Swansboro as an incorporated community in 1880 was Richlands, not to be confused with Rich Lands on New River. A mayor, three commissioners, and a marshal constituted the governing officials of Richlands, which had a population of 160 in 1900.[114]

Legislation in 1877 and 1895 renewed the incorporation of Swansboro. A mayor and four commissioners, elected annually, appointed a town secretary, treasurer, marshal, and other necessary officials. The legislation invested the commissioners with the usual authority to enact ordinances, levy taxes, organize a fire company, erect a market, establish a cemetery, and control the spread of infectious diseases. Violators of town ordinances, if unable to pay their fines, might at the discretion of the mayor be put to work on the public streets for as long as two days.[115]

Until the last decade of the nineteenth century Swansboro remained a quiet place. Although known particularly for its recreational opportunities, overnight visitors must have been few, for there was only one boarding-house in town in 1896. However, the advent of commercial lumbering found three sawmills in the town by that date, from which vessels from New York, Philadelphia, and Baltimore annually took some 150,000 board feet of lumber. Swansboro's inlet accommodated ships of ten-foot draft. As a result of the lumber boom the town's population jumped from 141 in 1870, to 233 in 1890, and 265 in 1900.[116]

The railroad and lumber mills also led to a burgeoning population in Jacksonville by the end of the century. Its sixty residents in 1870 must have been frightened by a fire the next year that destroyed the home and outbuildings of A. C. Huggins, superior court clerk, but the town began to grow. Legislation in 1883 enlarged its corporate limits, and laws in 1891 and 1897 provided for a government headed by a mayor and four commissioners. By the end of the century, Jacksonville contained three corn mills, a cotton gin, and a carriage maker's shop. Its population rose from 170 in 1890 to 309 in 1900. Nine boardinghouses in the town indicated the expectation of numerous visitors.[117]

Although Onslow's population was overwhelmingly native to the county and North Carolina, investment opportunities in lumber and railroads as well as recreational advantages attracted northern capitalists. New Yorker Thomas A. McIntyre, associated with the Onslow Lumber Company and the Wilmington, New Bern and Norfolk Railroad, purchased twenty-six hundred acres around Holly Ridge in 1889 as a hunting preserve. In 1892 he built a twenty-seven-room mansion, Onslow Hall, on his twenty-six-hundred-acre Town Point plantation and established a model farm, Glenoe (Glencoe, Glen Oaks), on the property. Onslow Hall, renamed Coddington after its sale by McIntyre, remained a showplace well into the twentieth century.[118]

Additional northern investors appeared in the 1890s. A Mr. Lamb, doubtlessly Richard Lamb, who was one of McIntyre's partners in the Onslow Lumber Company, erected a "fine house" in the Frenchs Creek area in 1893. By 1896 E. M. Koonce and Company had built the New River Inn near the mouth of New River, one of the first tourist accommodations in Onslow. Ownership of the inn subsequently passed to New York investors. A storm in March 1899 greatly damaged the structure; a hurricane the following October demolished the inn and twelve of its adjoining cottages.[119]

Northern investors brought a welcome infusion of capital to Onslow, but depressed agricultural conditions, both nationally and locally, bore heavily on the county. When the county sheriff sought to collect tax arrearages from two elderly widows eking out an existence in a one-room log cabin, he was greeted at gunpoint and informed that the women were penniless. Landless and unemployed men sought and received licenses from the Onslow commissioners to peddle goods in the county. But in 1899 the commissioners permitted David Burton to peddle "free of any license" due to his "Physical Infirmities."[120] Another gauge of poverty was insolvency, or the inability to pay taxes. The number of insolvents stood at 165 in 1868, rose to 191 in 1880, and declined to 150 in 1898, but still constituted 8 percent of the taxpayers in Onslow at the end of the century.[121]

Despite depressed economic conditions, the school system revived after the war. At a private school near the home of Edward W. Fonville at Wolf Pit, the teacher, Miss O. J. Ireland, taught an eight-month term. When graduation exercises were held in July 1866, the *Wilmington Journal* announced that the ceremony was "the first of its kind" since the interruption caused by the war. Four years later, in 1870, Onslow contained two academies. The number of private academies in Onslow rose to six in 1884 but declined thereafter to one in 1896, located near Catharine Lake.[122]

Formal education for blacks began in 1868, when the American Missionary Association opened a school in Swansboro. The term lasted from March to June, and many of the pupils were adults who attended morning and evening classes. When the AMA closed its operations, the teacher of the school, Mary D. Williams, reported that there were only a few students, but they were "smart & making good progress." Williams endeared herself to the blacks of the Swansboro area, who unsuccessfully beseeched the AMA to return her to Swansboro. However, the AMA may have operated three schools for blacks along New River in 1869.[123]

Reconstruction witnessed the reinvigoration of public education, a circumstance attributable mainly to the Republican Party and the 1868 state constitution. The constitution required the county commissioners to organize a public school system for both races, though according to state legislation in 1869 segregated facilities existed throughout the state. The Onslow commissioners organized the county system in 1869, dividing the county into twenty-three school districts within the five townships. In a singular instance the commissioners ordered the school committee in Richlands Township No. 5 to pay Jonas Williams in order that he might teach his children at home.[124]

Several factors worked against a successful public school program. Poverty, a sparse population, the need for labor to assist in farming and fishing, and unqualified teachers were consequential. Public attitude was also important. According to a correspondent from Swansboro to the Beaufort *Weekly Record* in 1887:

Our school here is progressing, but not progressing as well as it might be. The people are too poor, or they don't take the interest they should in schools. Out of about 50 children subject to schools here, about 15 go to school. Even the good schools don't have the children they ought. It seems most of our people are too conceited and too self willed; they all want to be boss, and if they can't boss, they won't do anything; rule or ruin is what some of them want.[125]

At the outset educational support for blacks suffered in comparison with that for whites but later achieved virtual parity. The county always maintained fewer school districts for blacks, which reflected the imbalance of the population and meant that greater distances had to be traversed to black schools. Moreover, in 1885 only ten of nineteen black school districts contained schoolhouses, three of which were log and only one of which had a fireplace. By 1897-1898 districts for whites numbered forty-nine and those for blacks twenty, reflecting almost exactly the racial composition of the county's population—70 percent white and black. The school year approximated twelve weeks for whites ai weeks for blacks.[126]

Public education struggled to meet the needs of the people the quality of instruction the county inaugurated teachers' institutes tor whites and blacks in 1890 and continued the practice for several years. By the end of the decade white teachers had organized the White Teachers Library Association, which was given space in the courthouse by the county commissioners to maintain a library. Yet literacy improved little. By 1900, 80 percent of the white adult males in Onslow were literate, a slight increase over the 73 percent literacy rate in 1870. In Swansboro Township the literacy figures were 80 percent for white males, 84 for white females, 55 for black males, and 60 percent for black females.[127]

Literacy may have increased in Onslow, but residents lacked a newspaper until the last decade of the nineteenth century and perforce relied upon sheets from New Bern and Wilmington. Partisan politics in the 1890s produced the first newspaper, when Hill E. King of Folkstone (Peanut) in 1893 founded the *Onslow Blade*, a mouthpiece for the Populist Party. The Democrats countered in 1894 with the *Times* in Jacksonville, edited by Arthur Whiteley, which was followed by the *New River Herald* in 1899. Whiteley not only denounced the Populists but also entrenched Democratic politicians who controlled county government. On one occasion Frank Thompson, county attorney and Democratic political candidate for the house of commons, personally confronted Whiteley to seek satisfaction for the editor's criticism. Armed with an umbrella, Thompson challenged Whiteley, who with his printer's rule inflicted a shoulder wound on his opponent.[128]

Contention was not confined to political disagreements. Although Sheriff Elijah Murrill claimed in 1870 that "there is not a more law-abiding and law-loving community in North Carolina" than Onslow County, the lawless had not entirely disappeared. Grand jury presentments in 1879 revealed two cases of assault and battery, three of theft, two of vagrancy, and one each of willfully firing turpentine woods, obtaining money under false pretenses, and fornication. In 1895 a grand jury indicted H. A. Harman for distributing intoxicating liquor during an election and the subsequent tabulation of votes. During that same year Justice of the Peace Hill E. King issued a warrant for the arrest of Andrew Peterson on a charge of slander for using "defamitory [*sic*] language against all of the unmarried ladies of Stump Sound Township."[129]

A mitigating and comforting force in the lives of Onslow inhabitants was the church. Although the number of churches fluctuated greatly, among whites, Baptists—mainly Primitive Baptists—predominated, distantly followed by Methodists. Stones Bay Primitive Baptist Church was organized in 1867, Enon (Cow Head Church) Chapel Missionary Baptist Church in 1872, and Atlantic Missionary Baptist Church in 1897 at Marines. During the mid-1890s Onslow contained several congregations: one Baptist, one Missionary Baptist, three Primitive Baptist, and one Methodist.[130]

Following the Civil War black society often relied upon religion and the church for individual and collective sustenance. As in the case of whites, most were Baptists and Methodists. Joining the Sandy Run Baptist Church, which was organized in Jacksonville possibly as early as 1854, were Blooming Hill AME in Richlands (1865), Saint Thomas AME in Swansboro (1869), Saint Paul AME Zion in Silverdale (1870), Saint Julia AME Zion in Jacksonville (1873), Little Zion AME Zion in Sneads Ferry (1870), Marshall Chapel Baptist in Piney Green (1879), and three additional churches in the 1880s, an indication of the burst of organizational religious activity and the importance of churches in the post-Civil War era.[131]

One of the more troubling social issues with which the churches had to deal in the late nineteenth and early twentieth centuries was temperance or prohibition. The county commissioners licensed liquor dealers in Onslow (including some of the commissioners), but many residents were clearly sympathetic to the temperance movement that gained momentum after the Civil War. Legislation in 1872 forbade the sale of liquor in Swansboro and its environs, though the act was repealed two and a half years later. Legislative enactments banned the sale of alcoholic beverages in the vicinity of certain schools and churches in the county as well as within the limits of the town of Richlands after its incorporation. Nonetheless, Onslow voters helped reject a prohibition amendment to the state constitution in 1881 by a vote of 1,500 to 145.[132]

If not troubled by intemperance the rural populace of Onslow contended with ill health, often occasioned by an imperfect knowledge of hygiene. Although approximately ten physicians continually inhabited the county from the end of the Civil War to the beginning of the twentieth century, not all utilized their training fully. Dr. Edward W. Ward became a gentleman farmer; Dr. Cyrus Thompson fell to the lure of politics in the 1880s and 1890s. Numerous Onslow citizens in 1869 beseeched Dr. E. Porter, formerly of Onslow but then a resident of New Hanover, to return to Onslow to practice medicine, at least from mid-

July to mid–October, the "most sickly season" of the year. The physician politely declined.[133]

In 1877, however, Dr. James L. Nicholson moved to Richlands and served Onslow and sections of Duplin and Jones Counties for the next four decades. A longtime member of the State Board of Health, Nicholson was best known for his successful campaign in the first years of the twentieth century to treat and eradicate hookworm. According to Dr. Edward J. Wood, Nicholson "blazed a trail through Onslow and adjoining counties. From lethargy and retarded development . . . have sprung . . . new life and renewed hope." Nicholson offered a promising future to people "far advanced . . . in a degeneracy which owed its origins largely to this soil-infesting parasite."[134]

Easing the burdens of agricultural toil and poverty were simple pleasures long appreciated by residents of Onslow. The coast provided a ready opportunity for fishing, sailing, swimming, oyster roasts, and "Banks parties." In touting Swansboro one individual invited those who wished "a quiet rest from the turmoils of a busy life, . . . [to] visit the place and enjoy its invigorating sea breezes." However, Swansboro citizens bestirred themselves to celebrate with relish the Fourth of July. People of the village of Marines liked square dancing and on the weekends went by boat to New River Inlet for a day's respite.[135]

Onslow County's coast offered a variety of recreational opportunities. In this early twentieth-century photograph, participants in a "Banks party" are returning to Swansboro after a trip to Bear Beach. Photograph from the files of the Division of Archives and History.

Hunting remained a popular pastime. Nathan Gornto in 1882 reported killing two alligators in one day, only to be topped by G. W. Ward, who killed five the following day. Bears constituted such a threat to livestock that state legislation in 1893 permitted the county commissioners to offer a bounty for killing the animals. A description of a deer hunt in Onslow in 1873 reported that every township in the county, plus some in neighboring New Hanover, contributed participants. Each hunter brought his pack leader. During the three-and-a-half-day hunt the sportsmen bagged seventeen deer and believed that several more had been taken before their hounds by outsiders.[136]

County residents gathered for picnics. A fine outing was provided by Mr. and Mrs. H. A. Whiting for their daughter at the famed Glenoe Farm, owned by businessman Thomas A. McIntyre. Numerous guests were taken by train to Jacksonville and then by steamer down New River to the farm. The party spent the day sailing, dancing, and playing tenpins and billiards. On a larger if more plebeian scale were the annual picnics at Alum Spring, site of the county poorhouse, for the benefit of inmates. Long after the removal of the poorhouse, the "Big August" picnic flourished as a countywide social gathering.[137]

Onslow residents also left the county to pursue recreational pleasures. One man wrote feelingly about a sailing party to Morehead City, which included "some right pretty girls" on a night when "the moonlight was in its glory." In the opposite direction, after the construction of the railroad, people enjoyed "excursions," particularly to Wilmington, Ocean View, and Carolina Beach. As many as three hundred people a day made one-day trips on the rails.[138]

At the close of the nineteenth century the serenity of rural, agrarian life still characterized Onslow. The abolition of slavery produced a readjustment of race relations which eventuated in segregation and the virtual elimination of blacks from the political process. The "New South" doctrine of progressivism and industrialization barely touched Onslow, though the railroad and steamboats portended significant changes. Agriculture languished, and the lumber industry had just begun to affect the county significantly.

Chapter Five
Twentieth-Century Onslow

Onslow entered the twentieth century as a rural, agrarian county, but four decades later World War II brought immediate and irreversible change with the establishment of the military installations Camp Davis and Camp Lejeune. The population of Onslow immediately reflected the impact of the military. Rising slowly from 11,940 in 1900 to 17,939 in 1940, the number of county residents jumped to 42,157 in 1950. The expansion of the military presence vaulted population to 149,838 in 1990, making Onslow the ninth most populous county in North Carolina. While the black population increased in absolute numbers over the years, it declined relatively from 27.1 percent of the total in 1940 to 13.3 percent in 1970, before rising to 19.9 percent in 1990.[1]

Not only did population increase dramatically in the aftermath of World War II, but the demography of the county changed as well. The military bases brought large numbers of single men and families with young children to Onslow. In 1990 males outnumbered females three to two in Onslow, whereas women constituted a majority of the populace throughout the state. While 74 percent of Onslow's residents were younger than thirty-five, only 53 percent of North Carolina's inhabitants fell below that age. In addition, the military produced a comparatively transient population—only 50 percent of the people age five and older in 1990 had lived in North Carolina in 1985 as opposed to 87 percent statewide.[2]

Most of Onslow's residents lived in a rural setting until World War II. Not until 1950 did the county contain a town of sufficient size, Jacksonville and its environs, for the United States Census Bureau to consider Onslow to have an urban population. With the growth of

Jacksonville, Onslow's urbanites rose from 18.2 percent of the population in 1950 to 57.5 percent in 1970 and 64.6 percent in 1980. Much of that urbanization reflected the impact of the military personnel in the vicinity of Jacksonville.[3]

Jacksonville opened the twentieth century with the principal distinction of being the county seat of Onslow. Its population of 309 in 1900 rose to only 873 by 1940 but burgeoned to 3,960 at midcentury after the construction of Camp Lejeune at the beginning of World War II. The town limits continued to expand, a council-city manager form of municipal government replaced the mayor-commission, and the municipality became a city in the 1950s. A population of 13,491 in 1960 reflected the growth of Jacksonville, which continued to enlarge in area and in numbers until the population reached 30,013 in 1990.[4]

Other than Jacksonville, Onslow's incorporated municipalities remained small. Legislation in 1905 reaffirmed the incorporation of Richlands, replacing the mayor-commission government with one headed by a mayor and board of aldermen. For many years Richlands was the cultural center of Onslow, boasting the first graded school, the first public high school, and the first library in the county. During the first two decades of the twentieth century its population jumped from 160 to 548. Growth thereafter slowed, for Richlands counted 996 residents in 1990.[5]

Swansboro enjoyed increasing prosperity in the early years of the twentieth century as a result of a rapidly expanding lumber industry. The

Front Street in Swansboro, 1929. Note the post office to the left. Photograph from the files of the Division of Archives and History.

town's population rose from 265 in 1900 to 420 in 1920. New houses appeared, built from the wood of the Swansboro Land and Lumber Company, as well as new commercial buildings on Front Street. The boom slowed during the depression thirties, but subsequently the retirement opportunities in the Swansboro vicinity and the completion of a high-rise bridge over Bogue Sound, connecting Emerald Isle to Highway 24 near Swansboro, brought increased interest in the town, resulting in a population of 1,165 in 1990.[6]

Of the remaining incorporated areas Holly Ridge was the oldest. A small crossroads community of 28 in 1940, the village briefly became known as "Boom Town" as a result of the appearance of Camp Davis, an antiaircraft training facility operated by the War Department from 1941 to 1944. Holly Ridge residents incorporated in 1941, but flush times ended following the dissolution of Camp Davis and the conclusion of missile testing on Topsail Island. Population dwindled from 1,082 in 1950 to 415 in 1970, but rebounded to 728 in 1990. Chadwick Acres, incorporated in 1961, had a population of 15 in 1980 but never became an active incorporated community. North Topsail Beach, Onslow's latest municipality, incorporated in 1990 with 792 residents.[7]

Politically, Onslow, like North Carolina and other former Confederate states, exhibited an affinity for the Democratic Party throughout the first half of the twentieth century. Democratic candidates carried all but one presidential election between 1904 and 1964 and all of the gubernatorial and United States senatorial contests. Nevertheless, a strong undercurrent of Republican sentiment persisted. Despite the virtual disfranchisement of blacks at the beginning of the century, Republicans mustered 35 to 45 percent of Onslow's vote in the presidential elections of 1904 and 1908, evidence perhaps of the personal popularity of the Rough Rider, Theodore Roosevelt, and his handpicked successor, William Howard Taft, respectively. Desiring, in the phraseology of Warren G. Harding, a return to "normalcy" after World War I, Onslow gave the Republican candidate 36 percent of the vote in 1920. In 1928 the county favored Herbert Hoover, the Republican of rural background and prohibitionist sentiment, over the New York City Democrat Al Smith.[8]

In the 1960s the backlash against integration and Democratic social programs led to political realignment. George Wallace, representing the American Party in the presidential election of 1968, won a plurality of the vote in Onslow; the Democratic candidate placed third, after Republican Richard M. Nixon, who won the presidency that year. Moreover, the Republican gubernatorial nominee, James C. Gardner, carried Onslow in 1968, though he lost statewide. Subsequently Republican presidential candidates enjoyed the support of Onslow in elections from 1972 to 1992, with the exception of 1976 when the county backed Democrat Jimmy Carter of Georgia. Successful Republican gubernatorial candidate James G. Martin triumphed in Onslow in 1984 and 1988, as did Gardner in 1992, though again Gardner lost statewide. And Republican United States senatorial candidates found favor with the Onslow electorate in 1980, 1984, 1990, and 1992.[9]

In elections for the state legislature, Democrats in Onslow proved successful throughout the century until the 1980s. A few dominant figures emerged, including Senators Edward W. Summersill (1933-1935, 1955), William D. Mills (1971-1976, 1979-1982), and Alexander D. Guy (1983-1991). Serving in the lower house for extended terms were Elijah Koonce (1905-1913), Horace V. Grant (1915-1917, 1923-1925), Carl V. Venters (1949-1959, 1963, 1971), Hugh Ragsdale (1963-1969), Mills (1965-1967, 1989-1991), Wilda H. Hurst, the first female state legislator from Onslow (1975-1978), Bruce Ethridge (1978-1987), and Guy (1979-1983). Republicans broke the stranglehold of the Democrats in the mid-1980s, when Gerald B. Hurst won election to the lower house in 1985 and was followed by Robert Grady in 1987, 1989, and 1991. The party also captured the senate seat with Tommy Pollard's victory in 1991.[10]

In the wake of the *Brown* desegregation decision by the Supreme Court and subsequent federal civil rights legislation, blacks in Onslow moved to reenter the political arena in the 1950s. Their entree was inauspicious. In 1955, apparently for the first time since Reconstruction, an African American sought political office in Onslow, when Lewis A. McIver lost his bid to win a seat on the Jacksonville City Council. In the 1960s, federal civil service worker Ronnie J. Bell, the only black in the county to file for political office in that decade, failed in his effort to win a state senate seat.[11]

Blacks redoubled their efforts to win political office in the following two decades and ultimately realized success. In 1976 J. W. Broadhurst, the last principal of Georgetown High School, became the first Onslow black elected to a major political office when he won a seat on the county board of education. Subsequently Paul Hardison (1986) and Mary Jones (1990) were elected to the board of education, and Hardison in 1990 successfully sought a district judgeship. Fannie Coleman and Jerome Willingham in 1991 obtained positions on the Jacksonville City Council, and Ernest Wright in 1992 won a seat on the Onslow County Commission. African Americans had finally joined the political mainstream in Onslow.[12]

The board of commissioners continued to control county government in the twentieth century. By law the electorate chose three commissioners in a countywide ballot. Legislation in 1924 recognized five voting districts in Onslow—White Oak Township, Stump Sound Township, Richlands Township, Jacksonville Township, Swansboro Township—and offered the option of each township choosing one member of the board of commissioners rather than continue countywide elections. The duties of the county commissioners bore great similarity to the demands of earlier years. Overseeing the transportation system (roads, bridges, and ferry), caring for the poor (outdoors and in the county home), issuing licenses (for peddlers and liquor dealers), supervising public buildings, and directing county fiscal affairs consumed most of their time.[13]

The commissioners constantly wrestled with financial exigencies. Not only did they have to face an onerous debt left from the court-mandated issuance of forty thousand dollars worth of railroad bonds in 1896, but the commissioners had to meet normal operating expenses, such costly projects as replacing the courthouse, and unforeseen crises, including a smallpox epidemic. When the county fell behind in payment of principal and interest on the railroad bonds in 1909 and creditors were "pushing for their money," the commissioners successfully sought legislative approval to issue five thousand dollars worth of bonds to cover the demands. At the same time the county managed to save money in the future by refinancing the original forty thousand dollars at a lower interest rate. Interestingly, John W. Burton, who became one of the county commissioners, purchased the five thousand dollar bond issue; the Bank of Onslow, of which Burton was president, refinanced the forty thousand dollars.[14]

Since tax collections covered only basic expenses, the commissioners looked to the General Assembly to authorize special taxes or bonds to underwrite extraordinary demands on the county. Thus legislation permitted additional impositions in 1903, 1904, and 1905 to liquidate the debt incurred during a smallpox epidemic and offered the commissioners the opportunity to float bonds to pay for a new courthouse and county home and to improve roads. Despite heightened taxation and provisions for sinking funds to retire bonds, indebtedness continued to rise, and in 1927 the General Assembly authorized a two hundred thousand dollar bond issue to fund the county's current debt.[15]

Fiscal difficulties stemmed in part from the poverty of the county and a low tax base. Most citizens were farmers struggling to cover their own expenses. Other than the railroad and lumber companies, corporate enterprises were small and unable to bear substantial taxes. Moreover, sheriffs often fell years behind in their tax collections.[16] To dissuade those people who were dilatory in their tax payments, the commissioners beginning in 1918 obtained by law the option of assessing a penalty on

109

unpaid taxes.[17] And to meet any questions about their own integrity, the commissioners appointed a finance committee to oversee fiscal affairs. Subsequently legislation mandated a board of finance and audit, created the office of county auditor, and required the commissioners to publish monthly a list of expenditures.[18]

The construction of a new courthouse early in the twentieth century added to the county's financial burdens. In March 1904 the commissioners justified a new building by declaring that the increase in population and business during the past decade demanded a larger facility. Moreover, grand juries and judges had long recommended the replacement of the current structure. Construction, begun by September 1904, was concluded in 1905, when the building was insured for seven thousand dollars. Acting on legislation in 1905 that authorized a special, ten-year tax to fund construction, Onslow commissioners floated bonds in 1906 and used the proceeds of the tax to retire the debt. Improvements were made to the courthouse about 1940, and a new district court building was constructed in 1978.[19]

The county also erected a new jail. The maintenance of the jail and prisoners remained an ongoing concern of the county. In addition to

Onslow County has had numerous courthouses through its history. This structure was the county courthouse from 1884 until 1904, when county commissioners decided that the building was too small to serve Onslow's growing population. Photograph from the files of the Division of Archives and History.

hiring a jailer and providing food, furnishings, and medical care for the inmates, the commissioners constantly repaired the building. The installation of a new sewer and the drilling of a well in 1903 entailed extra expenses. The following year a grand jury found sanitary conditions in the jail appalling and recommended fumigating the structure. By 1915 the need for a new jail was so acute that Judge R. B. Peebles ordered the county grand jury to indict the county commissioners if they did not provide a new structure. Goaded into action, the commissioners contracted with Southern Building Company of Goldsboro to construct a jail and borrowed ten thousand dollars by another bond issue to underwrite the expense. The county replaced the jail in 1972 and enlarged the structure in 1986.[20]

Another major outlay consisted of support for the county poor in the form of stipends, medical and burial expenses, and maintenance of the county home. By 1904 a grand jury found the county home in "a very bad Condition." It recommended selling the site and building a new facility in the vicinity of Jacksonville, the county seat. Although the commissioners closed the county home in 1904, a replacement did not materialize immediately. Only in 1908 did the General Assembly authorize the sale of the existing property and the issuance of five thousand dollars worth of bonds to fund the purchase of a new site and the construction of a building. The commissioners failed to act, however, until the legislature in 1923 allowed the county to borrow twenty-five thousand dollars by means of floating bonds. The following year the commissioners voted to spend that sum for a new home, hiring Kinston architect L. L. Mallard and Raleigh builder U. A. Underwood for that purpose.[21]

County government throughout the century remained under the control of the commissioners, who in 1969 hired a county manager for professional expertise and advice. Indebtedness per capita was relatively high compared to the rest of the state in 1930. It worsened with the depression but was alleviated somewhat by the appearance of the military installations in the 1940s, when the federal government spent considerable moneys to ease the impact of the population increase on Onslow's public facilities. By the latter part of the century indebtedness had been reduced to manageable proportions. At that time 50 percent of the county's expenditures supported health and human services and education. The county derived almost two-thirds of its revenues from ad valorem property taxes, state grants, and sales taxes.[22]

Until the advent of the military installations, Onslow's economy remained firmly based on the bounty of nature, emphasizing agriculture, fishing, lumbering, and related enterprises. Although farmers in the

111

United States prospered during the first two decades of the twentieth century, in Onslow farm land peaked at 277,219 acres in 1890, declining to 193,173 acres in 1920. Land under cultivation also fell, from 77,220 acres to 54,196 acres, but the number of farms rose, thus reducing the average size of the individual farm to 89 acres in 1920. Still, as a result of mechanization and other improvements, the value of farm property rose more than fivefold between 1900 and 1920.[23]

Onslow's principal crops, corn, cotton, and tobacco, reached peak production levels in 1920. Farmers devoted more acreage to corn than to any crop, but most was used for feeding workstock, fattening hogs, and to some extent making bread. And still the county raised insufficient corn to meet its needs. Tobacco, the bright leaf variety used for the manufacture of cigarettes and light smoking tobacco, replaced cotton as the principal cash crop. Whereas only 508,500 pounds of tobacco from 570 acres had been harvested in 1899, 2,323,701 pounds of tobacco from 3,164 acres were realized twenty years later. The emphasis on tobacco may have accounted for the reduction in farm size and acreage under cultivation, for tobacco was a labor intensive crop, and few farmers could afford to cultivate large holdings. In addition to the major money crops, farmers marketed large quantities of sweet potatoes, peanuts, hay, peas, apples, and peaches.[24]

Farmers throughout the country organized as they had in the nineteenth century. Succeeding the Grange and the Farmers' Alliance was the Farmers' Union. The North Carolina Farmers' Union appeared in 1905. By 1912 the Union had over 33,000 members, including 492 organized into twenty-five locals in Onslow. Through educational endeavors and cooperatives the Union hoped to improve the lot of the farmer. However, the Farmers' Union declined almost as quickly as it had arisen, virtually disappearing by the late 1920s.[25]

An economic boom in the United States followed World War I, with the exception of agriculture. Farm prices collapsed after the recovery of the European economies and the removal of the artificial stimulation of the war. Moreover, American farmers to a great extent became the victims of their own success by producing more than their domestic markets could consume. Continued advances in seeds and fertilizers combined with the introduction of new machinery, particularly gasoline-powered vehicles, created surpluses that contributed to lower prices. When the Great Crash occurred in 1929, farmers hardly knew the difference, for theirs had been a depressed state for most of the decade.

Before the New Deal of the 1930s the federal government extended little relief to farmers, particularly small farmers, with the exception of the establishment of the county agency under the auspices of the land grant colleges in the various states. The county agent offered instruction in the latest methods of land preparation, fertilization, and crop production. J. C. Parker, appointed in 1909, apparently was Onslow's first county agent. The agents were accompanied by home demonstration personnel as a result of the passage of the federal Smith-Lever Act in 1914. Onslow County commissioners generously funded home demonstration work in 1917-1918, paying Ava Wyatt a salary of twenty-five dollars a month for ten months for her work. Late in the twentieth century the Onslow County Cooperative Extension Service, a branch of North Carolina State University, continued the work begun before World War I, disseminating information to farmers and hosting 4-H clubs. The home economics branch offered workshops on such subjects as clothing, home furnishings, and nutrition as well as sponsored homemakers' clubs.[26]

Onslow agriculture reflected the trying years of the twenties and the depression thirties. Although the number of farms held steady—2,188 in 1940 as opposed to 2,179 in 1920—average size dropped to seventy-one acres. Mortgages hung over a quarter of the properties in 1930; tenancy of the farms jumped to almost 50 percent.[27] Helping to mitigate farm problems were New Deal programs, including the Agricultural Adjustment Administration, Farm Credit Administration, and Rural Electrification Administration.

Near the end of the century farming in Onslow reflected the ongoing trend of agricultural consolidation throughout the United States. The number of farms declined steadily and substantially, to 871 in 1974 and 436 in 1987. Farm acreage declined as well, but not correspondingly. Thus the size of the average farm rose from 98 acres in 1974 to 158 acres in 1987, and the value of the average farm from $52,192 to $183,442. Indeed, farming for some was a lucrative enterprise, for in 1987 fifteen Onslow operations recorded sales exceeding five hundred thousand dollars, and another seventy topped one hundred thousand dollars. More farms were operated by owners or part owners, and tenancy dropped to 14 percent by 1987.[28]

During the last quarter of the twentieth century livestock proved more remunerative than cash crops for Onslow farmers, contributing 57 percent of total farm sales. Poultry, followed by hogs, proved most valuable among livestock. Tobacco was the principal cash crop in Onslow, though the future of tobacco looked increasingly dubious given the concerns raised over its deleterious effects on health. The sale of grains, mainly corn and soybeans, provided most of the remainder of cash crop income. Although not planted in 1987, cotton began to stage a comeback soon thereafter, as farmers earned $1.5 million from four thousand acres in 1991.[29]

113

Although the state legislature increasingly attempted to protect and promote the fishing industry along the North Carolina coast, few in Onslow relied upon fishing for their sole support. Competition from many sources decreased individual catches. Onslow residents shared their waters with sport and commercial fishermen from other counties. Cape Fear menhaden fishing boats, though standing offshore, may have interfered with fish running into Onslow waters. Additionally, Carteret County fishermen from the vicinity of Beaufort and Morehead City came to Onslow in sharpies to set out nets at New River Inlet. As a result most Onslow fishermen were farmers who supplemented their agricultural income by fishing.[30]

Oystering continued on a limited scale in Onslow in the twentieth century. Although storms in 1899 had effectively ended the operation for the large companies that had moved into the county in the 1890s, individuals still pursued the bivalves. However, such activity was confined to New River, Sneads Ferry, and waters southward. Most oysters were consumed locally, though some were sold in Wilmington. The intrusion of sand and salt water, in part the result of government dredging, further damaged oyster beds, leading to the popularity of mussels and clams. Although little effort was made to promote mussels and clams, at least one resident owned a clam garden in 1911, and others marketed clams commercially.[31]

Onslow fishermen showed little enthusiasm for state intervention and regulation of fishing, but the General Assembly persisted in pursuing its nineteenth century efforts to promote shellfishing. The legislature in 1901 created the office of oyster commissioner to enforce laws relating to the bivalves. Specific statutes affecting Onslow prohibited oystering along New River and in Stump Sound during certain seasons of the year. Meanwhile the Board of Shellfish Commissioners in Onslow continued to monitor oyster grounds in the county. Funds obtained from the sale of franchises for cultivating oysters and from taxes levied on oyster grounds remained separate from the general county fund, and any surplus went into the public school fund. In 1909 the legislature also attempted to regulate clamming in Brown's Sound and Queens Creek.[32]

The General Assembly also tried to protect finfish. Creating the office of fish commissioner in 1907, the legislators directed the occupant to map the coastal area, collect fees and taxes on fisheries, study the migratory habits of fish, and through deputies and inspectors enforce fishing laws. To ensure the free run of fish through inlets, sounds, and streams, and to prevent indiscriminate fishing that might damage the industry in Onslow, legislation prohibited or regulated the use of seines and nets in all of Onslow's coastal waters and in New River.[33]

An extensive coastline and a long history of fishing combined to render seafood an integral facet of Onslow's economy throughout the twentieth century. Onslow ranked ninth among the coastal counties in the value of fish caught between 1936 and 1940, though it lagged far behind such counties as Dare, Carteret, and Brunswick. Production averaged annually 1,367,000 pounds valued at $45,856. An average of 325 men sought a living from the water, placing Onslow seventh among the counties, though many may have been employed only part time in the business.[34]

Later in the century neighboring Carteret might claim to be the seafood capital of North Carolina, but Onslow's total of finfish and shellfish in 1978 placed the county tenth in poundage and seventh in value among the state's coastal counties. By 1991 total poundage of 4,062,397 (2,328,725 of finfish and 1,733,672 of shellfish) was two and one-half times greater than that of 1978. Total value of the seafood in 1991 was over four and one-half times that of 1978. Sea bass and mullet were the most remunerative finfish; shrimp and clams were the most valuable shellfish.[35]

The first two decades of the twentieth century witnessed the denouement of the naval stores industry in Onslow because the longleaf pine forests, upon which the activity rested, had mostly been depleted. Remnants of the industry lingered, for improved roads and the railroad made it possible to conduct operations farther from the usual locales. Backboxing or boxing the reverse side of older trees and boxing younger trees grown to maturity offered possibilities for some small operators. And, in 1912, the founding of the Lackanawa Naval Stores Company in Jacksonville evidenced the possibility of extracting naval stores chemically from old pinewood as opposed to continued reliance on gum naval stores. However, the era of naval stores for Onslow and North Carolina had passed by World War I.[36]

Lumbering cushioned the decline of naval stores, however. With the exception of Thomas A. McIntyre's Onslow Lumber Company, lumbering operations in Onslow remained small-scale until the twentieth century, when the industry boomed across the state. By the outbreak of World War I the Swansboro Land and Lumber Company, started by J. F. Prittyman in 1893, and the New River Land Company dominated lumbering in Onslow. Several other companies appeared before 1920: Jacksonville Lumber Company (1909); J. C. Foster Lumber Company (1913); Onslow Lumber Company (1913); and Hitch Logging Company (1919). In addition, the Blades Lumber Company of New Bern built a spur railroad into Onslow to take advantage of 514 leased tracts of land between 1899 and 1929, and the Goldsboro Lumber Company constructed the Dover and

The Swansboro Land and Lumber Company, founded in 1893 by J. F. Prittyman, played a key role in the lumber boom of the early twentieth century. Pictured above are the company's store and office, ca. 1900. Photograph from the files of the Division of Archives and History.

South Bound Railroad to connect Richlands to its mills in Dover in Craven County.[37]

Although the larger companies had cut most of Onslow's virgin timber by the mid-1920s, smaller operations appeared, using mobile mills and taking advantage of the logging roads cut by their predecessors. Lumber remained an important facet of manufacturing in Onslow. In the latter part of the twentieth century firms dealing in lumber and wood products comprised approximately one-third of the manufactories in Onslow, though most were relatively small operations.[38]

Onslow and Jones Counties served as the site of an experimental forestry project, Hofmann Forest, named for Dr. J. V. Hofmann, who in 1932 became director of the Division of Forestry at North Carolina State College (now University). Hofmann initiated an effort to purchase a large tract of land to serve as a living laboratory for forestry students and a model of progressive forestry techniques. In addition to demonstrating the success of the scientific approach to forestry, Hofmann and his successors converted the Hofmann Forest into an excellent game preserve.[39]

Onslow coastal shipping at the beginning of the twentieth century centered on the exportation of lumber from the county's forests. From mills in Swansboro lumber was lightered to vessels waiting inside Bogue Inlet. After that inlet shoaled so badly that ships of sufficient size were unable to navigate the opening, Swansboro lumber was taken through Bogue Sound to Beaufort where it was loaded on oceangoing vessels.[40]

Timber and sawed lumber constituted the bulk of the commerce on the White Oak River in the early twentieth century. In 1906 they accounted for 19,000 tons of the total 21,532 tons carried on the river. The remaining trade consisted principally of seafood, agricultural products, and general merchandise. The shallow depth of the river restricted commerce to the area between Stella and the mouth. The federal government in 1915 considered creating a navigable waterway from the mouth of the White Oak River to the town of Maysville, located on the railroad connecting New Bern and Wilmington. However, trade on the river had declined approximately 50 percent during the previous ten years, and the volume of water traffic could not justify the expense needed to dredge and maintain a river channel.[41]

Maritime commerce along the Swansboro coast did warrant the creation of the Bogue Inlet Lifeboat Station by the federal government. Authorized by Congress in 1902 and opened in 1905, the Bogue Station undertook sixteen rescue missions. Alex R. Moore, formerly keeper of the Core Bank Lifeboat Station, was the officer in charge of the Bogue Station before it became part of the United States Coast Guard in 1915.[42]

After World War I Onslow's limited maritime trade centered on the Intracoastal Waterway, a protected water transit system that traversed the eastern coast of the United States. Proponents of the waterway argued that it would stimulate local commerce along the route by opening areas to waterborne trade that previously had little or no access to transportation outlets or found railroads prohibitively expensive. Particularly, the coastal area between New River and Cape Fear River, then virtually untapped, might contribute to waterway commerce by some half million dollars annually.[43]

The Waterway materialized in segments. That connecting Beaufort and Wilmington proceeded from the Rivers and Harbors Act of 1927 and opened in 1932. The legislation called for a twelve-foot-deep channel at low water with a bottom width of ninety feet and included a channel three feet deep and forty feet wide from the mouth of New River to Jacksonville. Not only did the waterway aid shipping, but it probably lowered competitive railroad rates, a boon to coastal residents facing the depression years of the 1930s. In 1938, six years after the completion of the Beaufort to Wilmington section of the Intracoastal Waterway, Onslow traffic consisted of approximately 8,500 motor vessels, 200 barges, and 300 tugs.[44]

Manufacturing in Onslow remained closely dependent upon the water and timber resources of the county and generally continued on a small-scale, often individual, basis. According to census figures in 1919, Onslow contained twenty-one manufactories employing 264 workers and producing $595,000 worth of goods. Twenty years later the numbers had declined to nine establishments, employing 148 and producing $277,000.[45]

Boatbuilding was among the principal manufacturing industries. The construction of small vessels continued apace at the beginning of the twentieth century. Nine—two sloops, three schooners, a barge, two gasoline-powered boats, and a steam tug—emerged from Swansboro between 1899 and 1904. Builders were also active in the vicinity of Sneads Ferry and Marines along New River. Apparently unique to the New River was the long-bow skiff, a small boat rigged like a shipjack with a bow that was cut from a solid log and fitted to the hull. In 1910 there were ten small shipyards in North Carolina, one of which was located in Onslow.[46]

Gasoline-powered craft, built in Onslow as early as 1906, began to replace steam vessels. The last steam vessels constructed in Onslow were the *Lallah* and the *Fawn*, screw propeller boats used to haul lumber barges. Toward the end of the nineteenth century the state and Onslow witnessed a transition in ship construction from trading or commercial vessels to

Monte Hill (left) and Isaiah Willis, shown standing on a newly completed boat, were leading shipbuilders in Onslow County during the first half of the twentieth century. Photograph from the files of the Division of Archives and History.

fishing boats. The gasoline engine hastened the conversion, for outboard motors and then automobile engines were adapted to the fishing boats. Most were built by fishermen and individual artisans.

Although many individuals constructed small boats along the waterways of Onslow after 1920, the Willis and Hill families remained the most prominent among county shipbuilders to the middle of the twentieth century. The partnership of Isaiah Willis and Monte Hill produced perhaps as many as one hundred vessels over the years, ranging in length from twelve to fifty feet. After 1950 professional building, particularly in woodcraft, declined significantly; this was attributable largely to the competition offered by fiber glass and the commercial manufacture of fishing craft.

The population boom of the last half of the twentieth century spurred manufacturing in Onslow, though the county never achieved a manufacturing base of great importance. Government figures showed a rise in manufactories from thirteen in 1954 to forty in 1977 and forty-eight in 1987. Value added by manufacturing moved from a half million dollars in 1954 to $31.8 million in 1977 and $116.2 million in 1987. The leading industry in the last year was lumber and wood products, followed by apparel and textile products, printing and publishing, and food products. The largest private employers in 1992 were Thorne Apple Valley of California and Del-Mar Garments.[47]

An inadequate transportation system impeded the development of manufacturing. The waterways of Onslow served as important conduits of business and trade in the early twentieth century as they had in the colonial era. As formerly, the county commissioners and the General Assembly by legislation attempted to maintain the navigability of the watercourses of Onslow. New River proved a valuable artery of traffic. Shipping on that river averaged 37,062 tons annually from 1910 through 1914. The freight consisted of bricks, fertilizer, lime, salt, gasoline, hardware, furniture, and dry goods. As late as 1940 many in the New River area received their groceries by water.[48]

Until the state and federal governments began to assume responsibility for road construction and maintenance after World War I, the county commissioners continued to oversee Onslow's roads, bridges, and ferry. An expanding population demanded ever more roads, and the commissioners continually entertained petitions to that end. To aid the improvement of local highways the General Assembly in 1911 permitted the county to issue one hundred thousand dollars worth of bonds to construct "a system of sand, clay, or macadamized roads." Because the county was burdened with debt at the time, the Onslow commissioners exhibited an understandable reluctance to take advantage of the legislative offer. Governor Locke Craig, at the beginning of his administration in 1913, pressed for improved roads in North Carolina, and the Onslow commissioners "heartily" endorsed Craig's proclamation, "calling upon all Citizens to help in the upbuilding of Good roads" in Onslow County.[49]

The governor and commissioners hoped to persuade Onslow residents to adopt a proposal by the General Assembly in 1913 to decentralize the administration of county roads. Legislation authorized each of the county townships to elect a Board of Road Trustees, which in turn would control all affairs relating to roads (but not bridges). Such duties included appointing a superintendent of roads, hiring a surveyor, purchasing machinery, and issuing bonds to be retired by special taxes on residents of the respective townships. Apparently only Jacksonville and Richlands Townships took advantage of the opportunity to create a road board and float bonds, but subsequently the General Assembly directed the county commissioners to appoint road superintendents in the other townships. Later, legislation established a road commission specifically for Stump Sound Township. By 1922, however, responsibility for the roads had reverted to the county commissioners, who found the highways and bridges in such poor condition that they contemplated borrowing $15,000-$25,000 for a repair and construction program.[50]

The General Assembly in 1924 determined that the respective township supervisors would constitute the Onslow County Road Commission. The legislation empowered the Road Commission to elect a county road commissioner and to issue bonds for road purposes upon the approval of the county electorate.[51] Doubtlessly the state legislature reacted to the obvious need for better transportation facilities throughout the state and in promoting better roads wanted to deal directly with a central county authority rather than subdivisions of the counties.

North Carolina quickly pursued Governor Craig's concern for improved roads when the legislature in 1915 created the State Highway Commission. The following year Congress in the Federal Aid Road Act appropriated money on a matching basis to the states for road building. And during the administration of Governor Cameron Morrison (1921-1925) North Carolina acquired the reputation of the "Good Roads State." Legislation in 1921 enlarged the powers of the State Highway Commission; directed a road construction program to connect all county seats, state institutions, and major towns; and authorized a successful multimillion dollar bond issue to raise money for highway building.

When the state legislature began to contemplate funding roads, it made sixty-seven hundred dollars available to Onslow on a matching basis for preliminary surveys. The funds were derived from the Federal Aid Road Act of 1916. Eventually county and state settled upon a route for

Highway 24, though most Onslow commissioners at first so strongly opposed the proposed route that they instructed the county attorney to obtain an injunction against the state. Later, however, the Onslow commissioners withdrew their objection and passed a resolution that left all future locations of state-funded roads to the discretion of the State Highway Commission. By 1934 North Carolina Highway 24 had been extended from Beaufort through Swansboro to Jacksonville. Construction of Highway 24 from the Onslow county seat to Burgaw in Pender County was completed only in 1949.[52]

The other major highway crossing Onslow was U.S. 17, the Ocean Highway, which paralleled the eastern coast. Providing an immediate link between Wilmington and New Bern, U.S. 17 in Onslow passed through Holly Ridge, Folkstone, Dixon, Verona, Jacksonville, and Belgrade. Finished in 1925 and constantly improved, U.S. 17 proved an inestimable boon to farmers for marketing their crops and to Onslow residents generally who wanted better access to the state and nation beyond.[53]

Bridges in the county demanded constant attention and care. The commissioners frequently appropriated funds for the purchase of wood and the payment of workmen to repair bridges, but they did not always act swiftly enough. The county in 1903 paid F. W. Hargett one hundred dollars for the loss of a horse that fell through South West Bridge. The General Assembly tried to protect bridges by forbidding anyone to ride on horseback or to drive vehicles faster than a walk across any bridge exceeding thirty feet in length. Moreover, the legislature made individuals or companies operating sawmills responsible for damage to Onslow's bridges when transporting logs across the structures. All the while Onslow commissioners cooperated with Carteret County commissioners in the maintenance and repair of the drawbridge at Stella.[54]

However, the drawbridge over New River at Jacksonville, which carried so much traffic, proved the most vulnerable to damage and the most expensive to maintain. By 1906 the county commissioners decided first to rebuild, then to repair, the structure. In the interim they procured a flat and ferryman to supplant the bridge. More than a year elapsed before the bridge once more was operational. The bridge was replaced in 1943, with extensive repairs undertaken in 1957.[55]

Sneads Ferry remained the only ferry crossing in the county. The commissioners contracted with C. C. Brown to maintain the ferry for two hundred dollars annually. Additional expenses included the purchase of a cable for the ferry in 1903; the purchase of rope, nails, and paint for the ferry flat in 1906; and the construction of a ferry house for the ferryman in 1907. The ferry flat, first rowed across New River and then pulled by hand along a cable that stretched across the river, eventually was propelled by a motor launch attached to the side of the boat. In 1939, however, a steel drawbridge, built in part with Works Progress Administration funds, replaced the ferry, and in 1993 a high-rise bridge supplanted the draw, further facilitating traffic across the river.[56]

Railroads supplemented road transport. Before World War I, the state legislature incorporated numerous railroads, many of which would have affected Onslow but failed to materialize. Legislation in 1913 permitted certain townships in Onslow to issue bonds to raise funds to build the Central Carolina Railroad and the Goldsboro, Seven Springs and Swansboro Railroad. However, the townships did not act until 1917, when additional legislation permitted the county commissioners to initiate township funding for railroads subject to township electorate approval. In elections in 1917 Jacksonville, Richlands, and Swansboro Townships voted to subscribe to Central Carolina Railroad stock. White Oak Township agreed in 1918, after first rejecting a subscription proposal.[57] As had been the case in the 1890s, short lines designed to facilitate lumbering operations were popular, including the White Oak River and Onslow Tramway Company and the line of the Goldsboro Lumber Company, both authorized in 1901.[58]

Ultimately, however, few of those proposals benefited Onslow. Early in the twentieth century the Atlantic Coast Line connection between Wilmington and New Bern crossed central Onslow. The Dover and South Bound Railroad from Richlands to Dover began as a timber road but later carried passengers, freight, and mail in the northwestern section of the county. Another lumber railroad also traversed northern Onslow. The advent of trucks and buses, together with an improved and expanded road system, proved too competitive for the railroads. In 1984 the last railroad (except for that serving Camp Lejeune) disappeared when the Seaboard Air Line, formerly the Atlantic Coast Line, obtained permission from the Interstate Commerce Commission to discontinue its route from Wilmington to New Bern.[59]

Onslow embraced a more modern mode of transportation in 1971, when the Albert J. Ellis Airport opened between Richlands and Jacksonville. From a 5,200-foot runway and a 4,000-square-foot terminal facility at the outset, the airport expanded to a 7,100-foot runway and 32,000 square feet of passenger facility twenty years later. The FAA funded 90 percent of projects involving air operations (runway) and 80 percent of those involving terminal operations. With certain exceptions the state of North Carolina and Onslow divided equally the remainder of costs. As a result of the expansion and improvements to air traffic, county passenger traffic at Albert

J. Ellis Airport averaged 196,092 enplanements and deplanements per year from 1989 through 1992.[60]

During the first four decades of the twentieth century the slow and simple pace of life in Onslow continued, governed as it was by the routines of farming and fishing. Illiteracy was high; per capita income low—$206 in 1940 compared to $199 in Pender, $260 in Carteret, and $494 in New Hanover. At the onset of World War II only 13.3 percent of the homes had electricity, 9 percent had running water, and 7.3 had inside plumbing. According to one study at the time, "facilities are . . . primitive, but sufficient if wants are few and ambition is low."[61]

Prohibition, a reform whose momentum had been gathering intensity since Reconstruction, threatened the tranquillity of Onslow during the early years of the century. Onslow residents successfully sought state legislation to prohibit the manufacture or sale of spirituous liquors within two miles of various churches and schools in the county. As a result of an election in Jacksonville in 1903 that found "a good majority" favoring prohibition, the county commissioners declined to issue licenses to sell spirituous or malt liquors in the town. Nonetheless, in a statewide referendum on prohibition in 1910, Onslow voters, by a majority of 1,273 to 490, showed that they were not prepared to join the rest of the state, and eventually the nation, in the prohibition experiment.[62]

During Prohibition in the 1920s law enforcement officers in Onslow found numerous stills, indicating that Onslow, like the rest of the country, had not totally endorsed the reform. Four years after the repeal of the Prohibition amendment in 1933, North Carolina established a State Board of Alcohol Control to license and supervise the sale of certain alcoholic beverages. Subsequent legislation allowed part of the profits from the Alcoholic Control Board in Onslow to be used for the support of the Onslow County Hospital and to be distributed to the incorporated towns of the county.[63]

Fueling the demand for Prohibition were the Missionary Baptists and Methodists who predominated among Onslow's church adherents. Baptists easily were the most numerous of Onslow's declared communicants, followed in order by Methodists, AME Zion, and Presbyterians. The appearance of Camp Lejeune brought greater diversity to the religious scene in Onslow, in particular the establishment of a large community of Roman Catholics among a hitherto Protestant county. Still, in 1987, among the eighty-one churches and synagogues in Onslow, the Baptists, Methodists, and AME Zion maintained their numerical superiority.[64]

Although Prohibition proved a fleeting social phenomenon, Onslow life-styles began to succumb to more permanent changes in the early twentieth century. The consumer durable goods revolution, electricity, improvements in communication, and the introduction of the gasoline engine began to make their impress upon the county. The automobile revolutionized business as well as social relations. Hardly less important were the gasoline-powered boats that altered the course of the seafood industry and tractors that transformed farming. And school trucks, then buses, led to the consolidation of school districts.

Some amenities of modern life, including electricity and telephone service, came slowly to Onslow. Before 1925 small, locally operated electric companies provided illumination for a few businesses, homes, and street corners in Jacksonville and Richlands. In 1914 the county commissioners agreed with the Jacksonville Electric Company to install electric lights in the courthouse. Two years later the commissioners contracted with the company to put lights on the New River bridge in Jacksonville.[65]

Growth and consolidation of electric facilities ensued. The Neuse River Electric Company acquired the Jacksonville facility in 1925 and in turn was purchased by Tide Water Power Company of Wilmington. Tide Water, after expanding its operations to meet the demands of Camp Davis and Camp Lejeune, merged with Carolina Power and Light Company in 1952. Meanwhile, in 1939 the Jones-Onslow Electric Membership Corporation, a product of New Deal reform, organized to bring low cost electric power to rural areas of those counties. Carolina Power and Light and the Jones-Onslow Electric Membership Corporation continued to provide electricity for Onslow residents in the latter part of the twentieth century.[66]

Onslow obtained telephone service as early as 1909, when the county commissioners allowed the Onslow Telephone Company to use county roads for erecting poles and stringing wires. Four years later the General Assembly passed legislation specifically to protect telephone wires in Onslow from vandalism. The local company was purchased by the Southern Appalachian Company, which in turn was bought by Carolina Telephone and Telegraph Company. Carolina converted the telephones in Richlands, Swansboro, and Jacksonville to dial in 1936-1937, and eventually the company extended service throughout the county.[67]

Public education at the beginning of the twentieth century found a racially segregated system on a sound but hardly flourishing basis. Of the school age children in the years 1900-1902, only 77 percent of the whites and 68 percent of the blacks were enrolled. The length of the school terms averaged 14.6 weeks for whites and 11.6 weeks for blacks. Resource allocations slightly discriminated against blacks. Although white children constituted 70 percent of the total, they occupied 71 percent of the schoolhouses and received 78 percent of educational expenditures. At the same time whites in Onslow paid 90 percent of the school funds raised in the county.[68]

The energetic Walter M. Thompson, elected superintendent of public schools in Onslow in 1903 but not employed full time until 1907, tried to improve public education. When Thompson concluded his twenty-three-year tenure, consolidation of the numerous schools had begun as a result of the purchase of thirteen school trucks (which preceded buses) in 1925 and the decision to build central high schools in each township. Richlands in 1906, followed by Jacksonville, had established the first high schools in the county. High schools subsequently appeared in Dixon, White Oak, and Swansboro, followed much later by Southwest High School in Jacksonville Township.[69]

The introduction of graded schools had a beneficial impact on public education. After state legislation authorized local districts to petition county commissioners to impose a special school tax to create graded schools, the town of Richlands in 1904 became the first district in Onslow to implement a graded school. The following year local districts in Swansboro, Jacksonville, and Stump Sound Townships sought and obtained approval from the county commissioners to erect graded schools.

Graded schools came to Onslow County in 1904. Pictured above are students from the Swansboro Graded School, ca. 1912-1913. Photograph from the files of the Division of Archives and History.

The requests mounted over the years until the number reached ten by July 1911, and petitions continued to besiege the commissioners.[70]

Despite the best efforts of Superintendent Thompson and the introduction of graded schools, the status of public education in Onslow was disappointing. The county ranked fifty-second among the one hundred in the state in rural expenditures per child enrolled in 1926-1927, eighty-fourth in length of term of rural white schools in 1924-1925, ninety-fourth in white high school graduates in 1927, and seventy-fourth in rural white school systems in 1926-1927. An illiteracy rate of 20.6 and 22 percent of males and females, respectively, declined too slowly.[71]

The thirties and forties brought significant changes to public education in Onslow. During the depression years a lack of local funds forced the state to underwrite an increasing proportion of the financial burden of county education. During the following decade Camp Lejeune brought additional students to the county, but the base opened its own school in 1943 for civilian and military personnel living on federal property, alleviating pressure on county resources. Still, the shortage of gasoline to power the school buses, the lack of teachers, and the general scarcity of the wartime years brought hardship to the classrooms.[72]

Georgetown High School in Jacksonville, the only high school for blacks in Onslow in the era of segregation, was a major focus of black education. Founded by the Trent River Oakey Grove Missionary Baptist Association, Georgetown opened in 1908 as the Trent River Oakey Grove Collegiate and Industrial Training School under the principalship of William Washington Parker. It was a private, nonsectarian boarding school dependent upon student tuition and private support from such sources as county teachers, PTA groups, and New York physician William Sharpe, who owned Hammock Beach.[73]

By 1932 the school had been renamed Georgetown. Although control of the school had been transferred to the county in 1919, little public support was accorded Georgetown until the 1930s. During that decade a new building replaced the original structure, establishing the basis of a modern elementary and high school complex. The 1950s witnessed the construction of a new cafeteria and gymnasium, the organization of a band, and the beginning of male and female athletic programs. Georgetown closed in 1966 as a result of desegregation.[74]

The fifties and sixties brought new challenges. Onslow's population rose by 145 percent between 1950 and 1970, resulting in comparable increases in the number of schoolchildren. Following the 1954 *Brown* decision by the Supreme Court and the federal Civil Rights Act of 1964, the school system began the process of desegregation. The task was accomplished in the mid- to late sixties with minimum friction under the leadership of Superintendent of Education J. Paul Tyndall.[75]

By 1980 Onslow boasted a far better record in the field of educational accomplishment than it had displayed in the 1920s. The county exceeded the state average in virtually all significant categories: percentage of high school graduates among the adult populace, percentage of residents having four or more years of college education, and average median years of school completed. Still Onslow ranked ninety-first among the state's counties in per-pupil expenditures in 1982. The state supplied 69 percent of the funding; local and federal contributions amounted to 19 and 12 percent, respectively.[76]

Coastal Carolina Community College in Jacksonville provided the opportunity for advanced education in Onslow. Chartered as Onslow County Industrial Education Center in 1963 and opening the following year as a satellite of Lenoir County Technical Institute, the IEC became independent in 1965. It was renamed Onslow Technical Institute in 1967 and then Coastal Carolina Community College in 1970, the latter change reflecting its offering of college-transfer courses. Subsequently Coastal Carolina Community College offered a college-transfer curriculum, technical degree programs, and vocational studies.[77]

As the public became more literate, newspapers flourished in Onslow, mainly in Jacksonville, despite the limited population of the county seat. The sheets of the politically disputatious 1890s were followed by the *New River Herald, Messenger, Enterprise* (under various titles), the *New River News,* and the *Onslow County Record.* The latter was published in Wallace, ca. 1928 to 1941, then purchased by Wilmington publisher R. B. Page, retitled the *Jacksonville Record,* briefly edited by Sam Ragan, and greatly improved and enlarged. In addition to Jacksonville, Belgrade briefly boasted a newspaper, the *Courier,* in 1901, published by Fred C. Henderson, school principal and postmaster.[78]

Challenging the *Jacksonville Record* was the *Onslow County News and Views.* Subsequently the *News and Views* purchased the *Record,* and after several years of semiweekly publication, the newspaper became the *Daily News* in 1953 upon the decision to publish six days a week. Additional news sheets served Onslow residents: the weekly *Advertiser-News* provided coverage of the Richlands (and Beulaville) area, and the weekly *Tideland News* went to press in Swansboro. The *Globe* at Camp Lejeune and the *Rotovue* at New River Marine Corps Air Station served the military communities.[79]

Onslow did not neglect its cultural heritage and historic past. In the late twentieth century the county boasted the Council for the Arts of Onslow County, the Onslow Art Society, the Onslow Arts and Crafts Association, and the Onslow County Museum in Richlands. The Onslow Historical Society, established in 1954, was greatly invigorated by the work of the indefatigable local historian Tucker Littleton, and after his death the society continued assiduously to promote the long and distinguished history of Onslow.[80]

At the beginning of the twentieth century concern for health, sanitation, and hygiene among the rural and small town populace of North Carolina, including Onslow County, had advanced little from colonial times. Rural communities proved resistant to reform, as found by the Rockefeller Sanitary Commission when it tried to combat hookworm in North Carolina. Organized in 1909, the commission seized upon North Carolina as a sort of testing ground for its hookworm crusade. The appearance of the Rockefeller Commission coincided with a reinvigorated state health bureaucracy in North Carolina, all representative in part of the Progressive Era reforms that swept the United States before World War I.[81]

The Rockefeller Commission realized some success in North Carolina, mainly by working with local physicians and public officials. The county commissioners in 1911 funded medical demonstrations in Richlands and other communities in cooperation with the Rockefeller Commission to explain the nature and treatment of hookworm. Although the incidence of hookworm infection was reduced, a number of factors retarded significant progress in treating hookworm and other diseases: indifference; suspicion of outside influences, including state bureaucrats; and even opposition by local physicians. Thus the state did not attempt compulsory vaccination for smallpox until after World War I.[82]

As a result the superintendent of public health in Onslow and the Sanitary Board, composed of county physicians, contended with smallpox as well as other epidemic diseases, such as diphtheria and scarlet fever. Although inoculation for smallpox, then vaccination, had been available for more than a century, few possessed the knowledge, means, or desire to take advantage of such protection. Thus smallpox flared occasionally in North Carolina. An outbreak appeared in Onslow in November 1902, dissipated, reappeared in 1904, and concluded early in 1905.

When the first smallpox epidemic occurred in late 1902, county physicians moved quickly to avert a catastrophe. Led by Dr. E. L. Cox, superintendent of public health, they quarantined a number of residents in a "pesthouse." In addition, the Onslow commissioners purchased vaccine to be administered by county physicians. The smallpox epidemic abated in 1903, but later in the year diphtheria threatened Onslow. Cases of diphtheria appeared intermittently throughout 1904, when smallpox reemerged. The second smallpox epidemic lasted from early November to late January 1905, according to Dr. Cox. During the course of the second smallpox epidemic several cases of scarlet fever also appeared.[83]

Although smallpox and other contagions finally disappeared in 1905, their effects lingered in the form of county debt incurred to pay the many expenses attending the epidemics, including Dr. Cox's bill for $800. The county commissioners declined to pay, deeming Cox's charges excessive, and later settled with the physician for $450. Realizing that ordinary county taxes were insufficient to meet the additional financial burden imposed by the epidemic, the General Assembly authorized the Onslow commissioners to levy special taxes in 1903, 1904, and 1905 to liquidate the smallpox debt, measures which the commissioners gratefully utilized.[84]

With the onset of World War II and the consequent influx of people to the area, an Onslow-Pender Health District was instituted under the direction of Dr. H. W. Stevens. The physician resided in Jacksonville but established branch offices and clinics in Atkinson, Burgaw, Richlands, Holly Ridge, and Camp Lejeune. Dr. Stevens helped to convince the federal government to erect Onslow County Hospital, which opened in 1943 and was subsequently acquired by the county. The construction of a new hospital in 1974 provided Onslow with a 150-bed facility and acute-care service.[85]

In addition to Onslow Memorial Hospital, public and private agencies in Onslow offered a wide range of health services. The county health department provided assistance in areas ranging from family planning and prenatal care to communicable diseases, environmental health concerns, and care for the mentally and physically handicapped. Urgent care clinics, a birthing center, and outpatient, elective surgery clinics offered additional options. The Onslow County Area Mental Health Developmental Disabilities and Substance Abuse Program and Brynn Marr, a private facility in Jacksonville, treated psychiatric and chemical dependency disabilities.[86]

The recreational opportunities that had enticed northerners to Onslow in the late nineteenth century piqued the interest of nonresidents in the twentieth. Private fishing and hunting clubs began to appear, particularly along New River. Most often they were patronized by wealthy gentlemen from beyond the county. One of the earliest was the Onslow Rod and Gun Club, to which noted brain surgeon William Sharpe belonged. Dr. Sharpe, seeking a suitable personal retreat for fishing and hunting, subsequently purchased the "Hammocks," forty-six hundred acres of woods and fields almost surrounded by water, including a four-mile stretch of beach on the Atlantic Ocean. Other private organizations included the New River Hunting Club, the Guilford Fishing Club, and the Charlotte Gun and Reel Club.[87]

Various public entertainments appealed to Onslow citizens. The county commissioners in 1905 allowed M. L. Burton to use the courthouse for a concert to benefit the Oxford Orphan Asylum, making Burton responsible for cleaning the building and for repairing any damages to the structure. In the same year J. T. Canady gave "magic lantern" and moving picture exhibitions throughout the county. Also popular were shooting matches, which too frequently endangered the public safety and evoked legislation to prevent such contests within four hundred yards of public buildings and highways. On the eve of World War II three Richlands men attempted to establish a horse racetrack and pari-mutuel betting facility.[88]

Although hunting continued apace in Onslow in the twentieth century, the General Assembly undertook a more determined effort to protect and preserve various animals and birds. Legislation in 1909 designated the county commissioners as the game protection commission of Onslow. Among the duties of the game commission were the appointment of a game warden and the prescription of the form of hunting licenses issued by the clerk of the superior court, but only to nonresidents of Onslow. In 1925 the General Assembly reconstituted the game commission to consist of the game warden and his assistants, all appointed by the county commissioners, and entrusted the commission with the authority to enforce the game laws, including a ban on shooting deer in New River and its tributaries and on using airplanes and automobiles for hunting.[89]

Hunting and fishing retained their recreational significance late in the century. The North Carolina Wildlife Resources Commission licensed and regulated hunting for bear, deer, fox, rabbit, squirrel, dove, and migratory game birds. Saltwater and freshwater fishing were readily available along the coast and inland streams. In fact, Onslow's extensive beach and riverfront property beckoned to tourists and retirees alike, who might take advantage of sailing, golf, cycling, and countless other leisure activities available in the county.[90]

Although the establishment of Camp Lejeune and the accompanying air station doubtlessly had the greatest impact on Onslow in the twentieth century, the county first had to contend with World War I and the Great Depression. For three years after the onset of World War I in Europe the United States maintained officially a neutral position but then declared war on Germany and other Central Powers in 1917. The war ended a year and a half later in November 1918, but not before the country had thoroughly mobilized for the conflict and Onslow had placed 503 men in the military services—433 in the army, 68 in the navy, and 2 in the marines—of whom five were killed.[91]

The Great Depression, which began in 1929 in the aftermath of the stock market crash, left its mark on Onslow, but the county, mainly dependent on agriculture, probably did not experience the hardships endured by the more urban, industrialized areas of the nation. Franklin D. Roosevelt's New Deal helped to ameliorate the distress of the nation and county. Roosevelt's first goal was to revive confidence in the banking system. Of the two banks in Onslow, the one in Jacksonville closed briefly for federal inspection and then reopened. However, the bank in Richlands, which had already closed, was deemed unfit to continue business. Still, the liquidation of its assets paid depositors in full.[92]

Onslow benefited from the emergency relief efforts of the New Deal as county residents struggled to meet the demands of the economic crisis. Through the North Carolina Emergency Relief Administration, Onslow received funds for improving drainage in towns; repairing roads, streets, and public buildings; planting oyster beds; and supporting educational projects. Camp Hofmann, a Civilian Conservation Corps facility, employed young men in reforestation and flood and erosion control. County farmers anticipated improved incomes as a result of various federal programs to raise farm prices.[93]

The New Deal response to the depression proved instrumental in the institution of the first public library in Onslow County. Sponsored by the Women's Club of Richlands, which used WPA money, the library opened in Richlands in 1936. Needing additional funding, the library in 1940 received an appropriation from the Onslow County commissioners, after which it became the Public Library of Onslow County. With the appearance of Camp Lejeune in Jacksonville and the tremendous population growth in the area, county officials decided to move the library to the county seat. Initially the Richlands library shared books with what was considered by many to be an extension of the Richlands library in Jacksonville. But in 1949 the Jacksonville library was designated the headquarters of the library system. Subsequently a branch remained in Richlands, and other branches were established in Swansboro and Sneads Ferry.[94]

Despite the impact of World War I and the Great Depression, World War II marked a turning point in the history of modern Onslow. Not only did Onslow send 1,814 into military service in World War II, but the United States government erected Camp Davis and Camp Lejeune in the county

Women's Airforce Service Pilots (WASPs) towed targets for gunnery practice at Camp Davis. WASPs were civilian pilots employed by the military during World War II to free male pilots for combat duty. This photograph of members of a target-towing squadron was taken at Camp Davis in November 1943. Photograph from the files of the Division of Archives and History.

during the war years. Camp Davis, operated by the War Department in the vicinity of Holly Ridge, made a forceful impact upon the southern part of the county. Camp Lejeune, which became operational in 1941 and subsequently evolved into the largest, most sophisticated Marine Corps training base in the world, survived the war to exert an enormous influence on Jacksonville and central Onslow. The war, in effect, forced Onslow into the American mainstream, modernizing the county in many ways.

Camp Davis existed briefly. Named for Major General Richmond P. Davis of Statesville, North Carolina, the army installation erected at Holly Ridge opened in 1941 and closed in 1944, though later the Department of the Navy utilized its facilities for a missile testing program. In late 1940 the War Department decided to lease land north of Wilmington for an antiaircraft training center. Ultimately it obtained 46,483 acres, including Topsail Island, for an installation that trained six white and two black regiments of coastal artillery. The post conducted antiaircraft training in Fort Fisher, some fifty miles south, and at Topsail Island, approximately four miles east. From 1941 to 1942 the base also housed the Barrage Balloon Training Center, the first of its kind in the army.[95]

Camp Davis was the site of the army's first Barrage Balloon Training Center. This photograph, dated September 4, 1941, shows soldiers filling a balloon with helium. U.S. Army Photo in the files of the Division of Archives and History.

Following World War II Camp Davis and Topsail Island served as a successful testing site for the ramjet missile program. After the army transferred Camp Davis to the Marine Corps, which used the base as a training and separation center, the Navy Department assumed possession. In 1946 the Navy began to build a control tower, launching platform, and eight observation towers on Topsail Island for missile testing and used Camp Davis at Holly Ridge to house personnel. After the completion of construction in early 1947, the Applied Physics Laboratory of Silver Spring, Maryland, supervised the development and testing of the missiles during the next eighteen months. Despite success, which facilitated the development of jet aircraft engines on the ramjet principle, the navy abandoned the Topsail facility in 1948 and moved its operations to sites in California, New Mexico, and Florida. At that time Camp Davis and the land and buildings on Topsail Island were deeded back to landowners, and equipment was given to local town and county agencies.[96]

Amid the war in Europe the United States Marine Corps decided that it had outgrown its facilities at Quantico, Virginia, and Parris Island, South Carolina, and sought a new training area. At least partially responsible for the decision to locate the new camp along New River and the Atlantic coast was Onslow native George Gillette. An electrical engineer who graduated from North Carolina State College (later University), Gillette served in World War I and won the Silver Star for heroism in France. Just prior to World War II, Gillette, a colonel, mapped the coast of the Carolinas. The geography, topography, oceanfront, climate, and isolation of Onslow rendered the county's coast an ideal location for a Marine Corps base.[97] Absorbing more than one-fifth of the landed area of Onslow, altering the demographic complexion of the county, and fueling the local economy, Camp Lejeune in many ways changed life in Onslow.

Once Congress approved and funded the New River project, Camp Lejeune arose quickly and massively. Construction began in 1941 at what was called the Tent Camp or Tent City, a temporary residence for the marines first sent to New River. First Division marines arrived at Tent City in September to accompany a few already present as fireguards. Meanwhile, work started on the north side of New River between Hadnot Point and Frenchs Creek for the permanent installation. Following the attack on Pearl Harbor on December 7, 1941, efforts were redoubled. By the end of 1942, Camp Lejeune officially replaced the Marine Barracks at New River. Despite the haste of construction and the

Thousands of African American marines trained at Camp Lejeune during World War II. In this photograph, ca. 1942, black marines are undergoing bayonet training. Photograph from the Library of Congress Collection in the files of the Division of Archives and History.

vast area encompassed by the base, Camp Lejeune was carefully designed from the outset. At the same time it was self-sufficient, providing its own electric power, hospital, railroad, schools, library, and newspaper.[98]

Camp Lejeune served as a training site for more than the traditional leathernecks during World War II. The Women's Reserve Battalion, organized in February 1943, began to train women at Camp Lejeune later in the year. They provided support in virtually all areas of military endeavor but actual fighting, thus releasing men for combat duty. Blacks enlisted in the marines in 1942 for the first time in the history of the Corps. More than eighteen thousand trained at Camp Lejeune, though under segregated conditions demanded by the times. And over 450 canines prepared for combat action at the base in the Marine Corps' only War Dog Training School. Franklin D. Roosevelt, the first president to visit Onslow since George Washington, was greatly impressed by Camp Lejeune on his tour of the base in 1944.[99]

Although success marked the establishment of Camp Lejeune, the base brought havoc and misery to Onslow residents who were forced to yield their property to the government. Approximately 720 families, or twenty-four hundred people, were dispossessed, left homeless and in some cases destitute. An average of two years elapsed between the time they were evicted and the receipt of compensation for their property. Most did not receive adequate compensation to obtain comparable property. Resettlement took from two to five years. Among the deprived were some one hundred black families, who subsequently purchased land along Highway 24 from William Kellum. On that land arose Kellumtown, a community of huts and other crude shelters where inhabitants eked out a living as best they could.[100]

Following the war the military presence in Onslow not only left bitter memories for some but contributed to ongoing friction with the local populace. Swansboro residents complained to their district congressman that heavy bombing on the base threatened their homes, where walls were cracking and plaster was falling, as well as placed "a terrible strain on the nerves." Onslow citizens also complained about the Marine Corps' decision to close lucrative fishing waters for extended periods of time for rifle and artillery practice, though actual practices were short and sporadic. Additional complaints involved the stoppage of creeks by the military and the dumping of waste materials into New River.[101]

Accompanying Camp Lejeune was New River Marine Corps Air Station. Commissioned Peterfield Point in 1944, the installation closed at the end of World War II but was reactivated as an air facility in 1951 during the Korean War. The deployment of helicopters to the area in 1954 spurred the growth of the base, which was designated a Marine Corps air station in 1968. Encompassing some twenty-six hundred acres, the air station principally provided support for Marine Aircraft groups of the Second Marine Aircraft Wing, headquartered at Cherry Point, and for the Second Marine Division at Camp Lejeune.[102]

The emergence of a permanent military establishment not only altered significantly the demographic structure of Onslow but also the complexion of the county's labor force. By 1979, 54 percent of Onslow's population consisted of military personnel, dependents, and retirees. In addition, in 1981 the county contained 4,034 federal civilian employees and boasted a $15.5 million federal civilian payroll, which placed Onslow third and seventh, respectively, in those categories among North Carolina counties.[103]

The military and its civilian auxiliary thus became the dynamic of the economy. After an initial construction boom in the 1940s, service and retail industries superseded agriculture. By 1954 retail trade in Onslow was valued at $35 million; crops were valued at $10 million. From 1950 to 1982 retail sales rose 29-fold in the county as opposed to 17-fold throughout the state. The Gulf War in Kuwait and Iraq in 1991 evidenced the importance of the military. The conflict drew many military personnel overseas and caused many of their family members to leave Onslow temporarily, thus producing an economic crisis in the county. Unemployment soared, retail sales plunged, and bankruptcy filings increased.[104]

Although the federal government's presence in the form of the military improved economic conditions in Onslow, the county's economy began to regress in the last quarter of the twentieth century. After approximating the state average through the early 1970s, Onslow's per capita income declined. Figures in 1991 revealed a per capita income of $10,537 for the county (and $11,495 for Camp Lejeune) but $16,848 for North Carolina. The percentage of persons living below the poverty level dropped from 21.7 in 1969 to 16.9 in 1979, but Onslow still exceeded the state average. In 1990 the percentage fell to 12.1, which brought Onslow below the state average. Still, mean household income remained substantially below the state norm in 1990.[105]

As Onslow looked to the twenty-first century, the county reflected the tremendous impact of the military installations. At the same time Onslow retained its ties to a more traditional world of sea and soil that had first brought settlers to the region and subsequently sustained life for some two centuries. A rural agrarianism flavored life beyond Jacksonville, Camp Lejeune, and Marine Corps Air Station, New River. Yet settlement, expansion, and even the appearance of the marine bases in Onslow emanated from the maritime setting of the county.

Water originally provided access to Onslow, and thereafter influenced all facets of life. Streams and rivers flowing to the sounds and ultimately the ocean constituted avenues of social interaction and economic development. Naval stores, wood products, and farm produce found their way to markets via water, at least before the advent of the railroad and a modern highway system. The coastal and river setting also rendered Onslow an appropriate site for Camp Lejeune. And later beaches, sounds, and rivers laid the basis for a thriving tourist and retirement industry. Ultimately Onslow arose in a maritime setting and retained a close association with, if not dependence upon, water resources.

NOTES

CHAPTER ONE
NATIVE AMERICANS AND EUROPEAN SETTLEMENT

1. Theda Perdue, *Native Carolinians: The Indians of North Carolina* (Raleigh: Division of Archives and History, North Carolina Department of Cultural Resources, 1985), 4-7; David Sutton Phelps, "Archaeology of the North Carolina Coast and Coastal Plain: Problems and Hypotheses," in *The Prehistory of North Carolina: An Archaeological Symposium*, ed. Mark A. Mathis and Jeffrey J. Crow (Raleigh: Division of Archives and History, North Carolina Department of Cultural Resources, 1983), 18-26; Thomas C. Loftfield, "Excavations at 31 on v 33, A Late Woodland Seasonal Village" (typescript, Marine Science Fund, University of North Carolina at Wilmington, n.d.), 4-5; Thomas C. Loftfield, "Testing and Excavation at 31 on 196 Permuda Island" (typescript, Department of Anthropology, University of North Carolina at Wilmington, 1985), 10-11.

2. Perdue, *Native Carolinians*, 8-9; Loftfield, "Excavations at 31 on v 33," 5, 7-8, 90-94.

3. Thomas C. Loftfield, principal investigator, and Tucker R. Littleton, comp., *An Archaeological and Historical Reconnaissance of U.S. Marine Corps Base, Camp Lejeune, Part 2, The Historic Record* (n.p., 1981); Loftfield, "Testing and Excavation at 31 on 196," 12-15; Loftfield, "Excavations at 31 on v 33," 1-11, 90-94; Loftfield, "Testing and Excavation at 31 on 82" (typescript, Department of Anthropology, University of North Carolina at Wilmington, 1985), 1-12; Phelps, "Archaeology of the North Carolina Coast and Coastal Plain," 1-2, 37; Lawrence Lee, *The Lower Cape Fear in Colonial Days* (Chapel Hill: University of North Carolina Press, 1965), 74-83.

4. Lawrence C. Wroth, *The Voyages of Giovanni da Verazzano, 1524-1528* (New Haven: Yale University Press, 1970), 133-141.

5. Loftfield and Littleton, *Reconnaissance*, 20, 22-25.

6. David Leroy Corbitt, *The Formation of the North Carolina Counties, 1663-1943* (Raleigh: State Department of Archives and History, 1950), 18, 57, 74, 159; Loftfield and Littleton, *Reconnaissance*, 41-42.

7. Loftfield and Littleton, *Reconnaissance*, 30-33.

8. Minutes of the Carteret Court of Pleas and Quarter Sessions, State Archives, Division of Archives and History, Raleigh, December 1723, March 1724/25, March 1725/26, June 1726. Hereafter all references to county court minutes of pleas and quarter sessions will be cited as County Minutes with the appropriate county noted and will be found in the State Archives, Division of Archives and History, Raleigh.

CHAPTER TWO
COLONIAL ONSLOW

1. William L. Saunders, ed., *The Colonial Records of North Carolina*, 10 vols. (Raleigh: State of North Carolina, 1886-1890), 3:256-257; Joseph Parsons Brown, *The Commonwealth of Onslow: A History* (New Bern, N.C.: Owen G. Dunn, 1960), 3-4.

2. Saunders, *Colonial Records*, 3:440-457, 561-562, 575-576; Onslow Court Minutes, January 1733/34, April 1734, July 1734, October 1734, January 1734/35.

3. Walter Clark, ed., *The State Records of North Carolina*, 16 vols. (11-26) (Winston and Goldsboro, N.C.: State of North Carolina, 1895-1907), 23:119-120; Saunders, *Colonial Records*, 3:634-635, 640-641, 643; 4:121, 137, 155; Corbitt, *Formation of the North Carolina Counties*, 164-166.

4. Saunders, *Colonial Records*, 4:633; Clark, *State Records*, 22:262; Loftfield and Tucker, *Reconnaissance*, 75-76.

5. Saunders, *Colonial Records*, 5:163; 8:669, 677, 701-702; Clark, *State Records*, 19:838; 22:336-344; Brown, *Commonwealth of Onslow*, 387-391; *Philadelphia Pennsylvania Gazette*, July 11, 1771.

6. John L. Cheney Jr., ed., *North Carolina Government, 1585-1979: A Narrative and Statistical History* (Raleigh: Department of the Secretary of State, 1981), 35-41, 43-49; Saunders, *Colonial Records*, 6:319, 324, 800-802, 893-894; Lawrence Lee, *The Lower Cape Fear in Colonial Days* (Chapel Hill: University of North Carolina Press, 1965), 94, 102, 126; Brown, *Commonwealth of Onslow*, 348.

7. Onslow Court Minutes, 1735-1765 passim; Cheney, *North Carolina Government*, 1217; Samuel A. Ashe, *Biographical History of North Carolina*, vol. 5 (Greensboro, N.C.: C. L. Van Noppen, 1906), 379-382; Clark, *State Records*, 23:349-350, 400; Jack P. Greene, *The Quest for Power: The Lower Houses of Assembly in the Southern Royal Colonies, 1689-1776* (Chapel Hill: University of North Carolina Press, 1963), 463-464, 466, 489-492.

8. Saunders, *Colonial Records*, quotations in order, 5:948; 6:297; 5:948; Greene, *Quest for Power*, 6; Jack P. Greene, "The North Carolina Lower House and the Power to Appoint Public Treasurers, 1711-1775," *North Carolina Historical Review* 40 (winter 1963): 45-51; Cheney, *North Carolina Government*, 1217.

9. Cheney, *North Carolina Government*, 1223; Saunders, *Colonial Records*, 8:578, 595, 597, 689, 692-693, 701-702; 9:298, 1237; Brown, *Commonwealth of Onslow*, 30-33.

10. Cheney, *North Carolina Government*, 1223; Alan D. Watson, "The Appointment of Sheriffs in Colonial North Carolina: A Reexamination," *North Carolina Historical Review* 53 (autumn 1976): 385-398; Loftfield and Littleton, *Reconnaissance*, 97.

11. Onslow Court Minutes, April 1735, April 1742, April 1745, April 1751, April 1755, August 1760, May 1761, August 1762, March 1763, October 1763, December 1766, January 1769, January 1772, April 1774; Saunders, *Colonial Records*, 4:346, 1239; 6:1013.

12. Watson, "The Appointment of Sheriffs," esp. 390-391; Onslow Court Minutes, October 1763.

13. Craven Court Minutes, June 1741; Hyde Court Minutes, September 1745, September 1750; Tyrrell Court Minutes, December 1753, March 1763; Onslow Court Minutes, April 1749, April 1751, January 1751/52, July 1754, July 1756, July 1757, July 1759, August 1761, August 1762, August 1763, June 1765.

14. James Davis, *The Office and Authority of a Justice of the Peace* (Newburn, N.C.: James Davis, 1774), 115-123; Clark, *State Records*, 23:15-16, 162-163; Onslow Court Minutes, July 1742, October 1742, January 1751/52, April 1753, June 1765.

15. Clark, *State Records*, 23:149; Onslow Court Minutes, July 1746, July 1747, July 1753, April 1774.

16. Clark, *State Records*, 23:120; Onslow Court Minutes, July 1732, April 1733, July 1733, July 1734, July 1735, October 1735.

17. Onslow Court Minutes, October 1735, January 1735/36, July 1736, October 1736, January 1736/37, April 1737.

18. Clark, *State Records*, 23:170-171; Onslow Court Minutes, April 1744.

19. Onslow Court Minutes, July 1744, October 1746, April 1747, July 1747, July 1748, April 1749, July 1751, July 1752.

20. Clark, *State Records*, 23:387-388; 25:329-330; Onslow Court Minutes, April 1753; quotation from the *Boston Evening Post*, October 23, 30, 1752, reprinted in David M. Ludlum, *Early American Hurricanes, 1471-1870* (Boston: American Meteorological Society, 1963), 47.

21. Onslow Court Minutes, January 1756, July 1757, August 1760, August 1761, September 1763, September 1764.

22. Onslow Court Minutes, October 1736, July 1744, October 1745, April 1746, July 1753, July 1756, September 1763, December 1763, September 1764, March 1767, October 1770, October 1772, October 1775.

23. Alan D. Watson, "County Fiscal Policy in Colonial North Carolina," *North Carolina Historical Review* 55 (summer 1978): 289-294; Clark, *State Records*, 23:289-291, 346; Account of Thomas Johnston, Sheriff, 1774-1775, County Accounts, Onslow County, Miscellaneous Records, 1732-1950, State Archives; Onslow Court Minutes, July 1752.

24. Clark, *State Records*, 23:346; Onslow Court Minutes, July 1752.

25. Clark, *State Records*, 23:178-180; Onslow Court Minutes, October 1742, April 1749, January 1758, July 1758, August 1760, February 1761.

26. Clark, *State Records*, 25:232-233; Onslow Court Minutes, July 1743, January 1746/47, July 1748, April 1749.

27. Clark, *State Records*, 23:617-618, 862, 914-915; Certificate of William ———, January 14, 1774; Certificate of William Jones, November 5, 1775; Account of Thomas Johnston, Sheriff, 1774-1775, County Accounts, Onslow County, Miscellaneous Records.

28. Clark, *State Records*, 23:171, 785-786; 25:311-312, 330, 348, 389, 478-482; Alan D. Watson, "The Ferry in Colonial North Carolina: A Vital Link in Transportation," *North Carolina Historical Review* 51 (summer 1974): 255-256; Onslow Court Minutes, April 1744, July 1755, July 1757, June 1763, January 1775.

29. Marvin L. Michael Kay, "The Payment of Provincial and Local Taxes in North Carolina, 1748-1771," *William and Mary Quarterly*, 3d ser., 26 (April 1969): 218-240; Watson, "County Fiscal Policy," 303-304.

30. Inventory of James Gray, January 10, 1758; Appraisal of Estate of James Ambrose, May 17, 1762, Onslow County, Estates Records, 1735-1914, State Archives; Samuel Johnston Jr. to Samuel Johnston Sr., October 5, 1755, Hayes Collection, Southern Historical Collection, University of North Carolina Library, Chapel Hill; Proclamation of Governor (William Tryon), February 12, 1767, *The Correspondence of William Tryon and Other Selected Papers*, ed. William S. Powell, vol. 2 (Raleigh: Division of Archives and History, Department of Cultural Resources, 1981), 422-423; Charles Christopher Crittenden, *The Commerce of North Carolina, 1763-1789* (New Haven: Yale University Press, 1936), 59-60.

31. Loftfield and Littleton, *Reconnaissance*, 68; Marcus B. Simpson Jr. and Allie W. Simpson, "The Pursuit of Leviathan: A History of Whaling on the North Carolina Coast," *North Carolina Historical Review* 65 (January 1988): 12-20.

32. Lee, *Lower Cape Fear*, 150-151; Loftfield and Littleton, *Reconnaissance*, 63-65.

33. Onslow Court Minutes, 1740-1775 passim.

34. Clark, *State Records*, 23:380-381, 790-801; 25:313-319, 378-387; Paul M. McCain, *The County Court in North Carolina before 1750* (Durham, N.C.: Duke University Press, 1954), 116, hereafter cited as McCain, *County Court before 1750*; Onslow Court Minutes, October 1741, April 1742, October 1743, October 1744, October 1745, July 1748, July 1752, January 1756, January 1757, April 1757, July 1759, December 1764, March 1766, March 1767, December 1767, October 1768, January 1769, April 1769, January 1770, January 1771, January 1772, January 1773, January 1775, April 1775.

35. Onslow Court Minutes, January 1733/34, October 1734, January 1734/35; Clark, *State Records*, 23:46-48; Alan D. Watson, "Regulation and Administration of Roads and Bridges in Colonial Eastern North Carolina," *North Carolina Historical Review* 45 (autumn 1968): 399-402.

36. Clark, *State Records*, 23:118-119; Onslow Court Minutes, July 1735, January 1736/37; Watson, "Regulation and Administration of Roads and Bridges," 402-403, 412-413; McCain, *County Court before 1750*, 124-125, 131-132.

37. Onslow Court Minutes, October 1741, April 1744, July 1744, quotation from April 1744; Clark, *State Records*, 23:220-229, esp. 220-221.

38. Clark, *State Records*, 23:489-490; Onslow Court Minutes, February 1762, September 1764; undated petition and complaint, ca. 1770, Road Papers, Onslow County, Miscellaneous Records.

39. Onslow Court Minutes, 1758-1775 passim; Lee, *Lower Cape Fear*, 171-172; Hugh B. Johnston, ed., "The Journal of Ebenezer Hazard in North Carolina, 1777 and 1778," *North Carolina Historical Review* 36 (July 1959): 377-378; Johann David Schoepf, *Travels in the Confederation (1783-1784)*, trans. and ed. Alfred J. Morrison (Philadelphia: William J. Campbell, 1911), 2:145. Legislation in 1764 mandated the marking of the roads, and Onslow attempted to comply. Clark, *State Records*, 23:610-611; Onslow Court Minutes, September 1764.

40. Carteret Court Minutes, June 1726, June, 1728; Onslow Court Minutes, January 1733/34, June 1765, April 1768; "William Logan's Journal of a Journey to Georgia, 1745," *Pennsylvania Magazine of History and Biography* 36 (1912): 12.

41. Onslow Court Minutes, October 1736; Will of Robert Courtney, 1751, *North Carolina Wills and Inventories*, ed. J. Bryan Grimes (Raleigh: Edwards & Broughton, 1912), 138; Clark, *State Records*, 23:510-511; Treasurers' and Comptrollers' Papers, Ports, Port Brunswick Shipping Register, 1765-1775, State Archives.

42. Clark, *State Records*, 23:163, 542-544; Crittenden, *Commerce of North Carolina*, 6; Saunders, *Colonial Records*, 6:702-703, quotation on 703.

43. Clark, *State Records*, 23:510-511; Loftfield and Littleton, *Reconnaissance*, 68.

44. Loftfield and Littleton, *Reconnaissance*, 70-71.

45. Loftfield and Littleton, *Reconnaissance*, 35, 88-89.

46. John LaPierre to the Bishop of London, April 23, 1734, Anglican Church Records (microfilm, State Archives); Saunders, *Colonial Records*, 3:439, 450.

47. Onslow Court Minutes, July 1744, October 1774; Saunders, *Colonial Records*, 5:320; 7:145-146; Account of Thomas Johnston, Sheriff, 1774-1775, County Accounts, Onslow County, Miscellaneous Records; H. Roy Merrens, *Colonial North Carolina in the Eighteenth Century: A Study in Historical Geography* (Chapel Hill: University of North Carolina Press, 1964), 54-55.

48. Alan D. Watson, "Household Size and Composition in Pre-Revolutionary North Carolina," *Mississippi Quarterly* 31 (fall 1978): 564-565; Saunders, *Colonial Records*, 5:320; Onslow County, Tax List, 1771, Legislative Papers, State Archives.

49. Trial of Simon and Mingo, July 19, 1765; Trial of Titus, August 25, 1777; Trial of Isaac, June 26, 1779, Slave Papers, Onslow County, Miscellaneous Records.

50. Clark, *State Records*, 23:389; Onslow Court Minutes, July 1758, November 1761, June 1766, April 1768, April 1772, April 1774.

51. Onslow Court Minutes, January 1735/36, April 1754; McCain, *County Court before 1750*, 89.

52. Onslow County, Tax List, 1769, Secretary of State Papers, 837, State Archives; Onslow County, Tax List, 1771; Onslow Court Minutes, April 1742, June 1753; Account of Andrew Fuller, 1763-1764, Slave Papers, Onslow County, Miscellaneous Records.

53. Clark, *State Records*, 23:225, 435-437; Onslow Court Minutes, October 1746, February 1761.

54. Onslow County, Tax List, 1769; Onslow County, Tax List, 1771; Samuel Johnston Sr. to Samuel Johnston Jr., November 6, 1754, Hayes Collection; Onslow Court Minutes, December 1765; Robert Orme to Dr. William Gibson, June 24, 1777, Onslow County, Miscellaneous Records.

55. Watson, "Household Size and Composition," 569; Onslow Court Minutes, January 1745/46, October 1748, April 1749, July 1751, June 1763, September 1766, April 1772, April 1774, January 1775, April 1775.

56. John LaPierre to the Bishop of London, April 23, 1734, Anglican Church Records; Daniel Blake Smith, *Inside the Great House: Planter Family Life in Eighteenth-Century Chesapeake Society* (Ithaca, N.Y.: Cornell University Press, 1980), 42-52, 286.

57. Clark, *State Records*, 23:70-71; Onslow Court Minutes, April 1734.

58. Onslow Court Minutes, March 1764, March 1766, March 1767.

59. Inventory of Richard Ward, April 1, 1755; Inventory of William Wells, July 4, 1744, Onslow County, Estates Records.

60. Appraisal of the estate of James Ambrose, May 17, 1762; Inventory of Joseph Ward, August 26, 1761; Inventory of James Glenn, March 14, 1764; Inventory of James Gray, January 10, 1758, Onslow County, Estates Records.

61. Inventory of James Glenn, March 14, 1764; Inventory of Richard Ward, April 1, 1775, Onslow County, Estates Records.

62. George Burrington to the Bishop of London, May 10, 1732; John LaPierre to the Bishop of London, April 23, 1734, Anglican Church Records; Saunders, *Colonial Records*, 6:562; 8:540; Clark, *State Records*, 23:119-120; Onslow Court Minutes, July 1735, October 1743, September 1765.

63. Onslow County Minutes, January 1734/35, August 1761; Saunders, *Colonial Records*, 6:562; Loftfield and Littleton, *Reconnaissance*, 92-93.

64. Loftfield and Littleton, *Reconnaissance*, 94-98; Brown, *Commonwealth of Onslow*, 233-235.

65. Onslow Court Minutes, April 1735, January 1735/36, April 1736, October 1736.

66. Onslow Court Minutes, July 1751, October 1759, March 1767; Johnston, "Journal of Ebenezer Hazard," 377-378.

67. Onslow Court Minutes, 1740-1775 passim; Clark, *State Records*, 23:171, 728.

CHAPTER THREE
FROM REVOLUTION TO CIVIL WAR

1. Cheney, *North Carolina Government*, 153-159.

2. Brown, *Commonwealth of Onslow*, 32; Leora H. McEachern and Isabel M. Williams, eds., *Wilmington-New Hanover Safety Committee Minutes, 1774-1776* (Wilmington, N.C.: Wilmington-New Hanover County American Revolution Bi-Centennial Association, 1974), 45; Alan D. Watson, Dennis R. Lawson, and Donald R. Lennon, *Harnett, Hooper & Howe* (Wilmington, N.C.: Louis T. Moore Memorial Commission, 1979), 12.

3. McEachern and Williams, *Wilmington-New Hanover Safety Committee Minutes*, 33; Brown, *Commonwealth of Onslow*, 29; Oath of Allegiance to the United States by Civil and Military Officers, July 1777 Court, Oath to Support the Constitution, Onslow County, Miscellaneous Records.

4. Petitions of Obed Scott, September 22, 1818; James Rowe, February 6, 1821; Fabin Gilgo, May 7, 1821; Aron Davis, November 7, 1821, Revolutionary War Service (Records), Onslow County, Miscellaneous Records.

5. Loftfield and Littleton, *Reconnaissance*, 105-106; Clark, *State Records*, 17:709, 787, 789.

6. Loftfield and Littleton, *Reconnaissance*, 106.

7. Presentments of the Onslow County Grand Jury, n.d., Onslow County, Miscellaneous Records.

8. Clark, *State Records*, 15:569; 22:537, 541, 544.

9. Gregory De Van Massey, "The British Expedition to Wilmington, January-November, 1781," *North Carolina Historical Review* 66 (October 1989): 387-411; Brown, *Commonwealth of Onslow*, 27-28.

10. Clark, *State Records*, 15:632; Loftfield and Littleton, *Reconnaissance*, 107.

11. Cheney, *North Carolina Government*, 162-163, 177, 211, 1223-1224.

12. Cheney, *North Carolina Government*, 767; William C. Pool, "An Economic Interpretation of the Ratification of the Federal Constitution in North Carolina, Part II: The Hillsboro Convention—Economic Interests of the Antifederalists," *North Carolina Historical Review* 27 (July 1950): 305; Clark, *State Records*, 22:30.

13. Cheney, *North Carolina Government*, 769; William C. Pool, "An Economic Interpretation of the Ratification of the Federal Constitution in North Carolina, Part III: The Fayetteville Convention, 1789," *North Carolina Historical Review* 27 (October 1950): 439 n. 9; Clark, *State Records*, 22:48; Sarah McCulloh Lemmon, "Onslow County During the War of 1812" (paper presented to the Seminar on Onslow County History, Swansboro, N.C., 1982), 9.

14. *Private Laws of North Carolina, 1819*, cc. 124, 73; *New Bern Carolina Sentinel*, April 21, 1821; Report of the Commissioners, January 26, 1822, Records relating to the building of a new courthouse, Onslow County, Miscellaneous Records.

15. *Private Laws of North Carolina, 1850-1851*, c. 264.

16. Lemmon, "Onslow County During the War of 1812," 5; Report of Danl. Ambrose et al., May 1824; Census Records. Products of Industry and Social Statistics, 1850. County Accounts and Reports, Onslow County, Miscellaneous Records.

17. *Private Laws of North Carolina, 1819*, c. 47; *Laws of North Carolina, 1836*, c. 79; Account of Lewis T. Oliver, former Shff., 1819-1821; Report of Danl. Ambrose et al., May 1824; Report of the Committee of Finance, September 1, 1863, County Accounts and Reports, Onslow County, Miscellaneous Records.

18. A Statement of the Revenue of North Carolina (for 1827), *Laws of North Carolina, 1828-1829*, unpaginated; A Statement of the Revenue of North Carolina (for 1837),

Public and Private Laws of North Carolina, 1838-1839, unpaginated; *Raleigh North Carolina Standard,* October 17, 1855.

19. Joseph M. French to Mary French, March 8, 1835; Robert Montford to Joseph M. French, May 13, 1860, Joseph M. French Papers, J.Y. Joyner Library, East Carolina University, Greenville.

20. Guion Griffis Johnson, "Antebellum Onslow County: A Social History" (paper presented to the Seminar on Onslow County History, Swansboro, N.C., 1982), 2, 17.

21. Clark, *State Records,* 24:534-535; Petition, March 29, 1778, Road Records, Onslow County, Miscellaneous Records.

22. Clark, *State Records,* 24:534-535; Account of Lewis Hicks, Sheriff, for 1787, County Accounts and Reports, Onslow County, Miscellaneous Records.

23. Alice E. Mathews, "The Social History of Onslow County" (paper presented to the Seminar on Onslow County History, Swansboro, N.C., 1982), 2; Alonzo Thomas Dill Jr., "Eighteenth Century New Bern: A History of the Town and Craven County, 1700-1800. Part VIII," *North Carolina Historical Review* 23 (October 1946): 515; J. E. B. DeBow, comp., *The Seventh Census of the United States. 1850* (Washington, D.C.: Robert Armstrong, 1853), 308.

24. *Newbern Weekly Progress,* January 31, February 21, 1860.

25. *Laws of North Carolina, 1806,* c. 57; *Laws of North Carolina, 1810,* c. 58; *Laws of North Carolina, 1816,* c. 132; *Private Laws of North Carolina, 1848-1849,* c. 233.

26. Clark, *State Records,* 18:355, 33-34; *Private Laws of North Carolina, 1842-1843,* c. 35; *Private Laws of North Carolina, 1848-1849,* c. 225.

27. James Battle Avirett, *The Old Plantation: How We Lived in the Great House and Cabin Before the War* (New York: F. Tennyson Neely Co., 1901), 157; Johnson, "Antebellum Onslow County," 5-6.

28. Avirett, *Old Plantation,* 36-37.

29. Avirett, *Old Plantation,* 25, 157; Donnie D. Bellamy, "Slavery in Microcosm: Onslow County, North Carolina," *Journal of Negro History* 62 (October 1977): 342; "Historic and Architectural Resources of Onslow County, North Carolina," National Register of Historic Places Multiple Property Documentary Form, Section F, 1-10, kindly supplied by Claudia Brown, National Register Coordinator, Division of Archives and History, Raleigh.

30. Avirett, *Old Plantation,* 70-71; Johnson, "Antebellum Onslow County," 5, 18.

31. Petition of Fabin Gilgo, May 7, 1821, Revolutionary War Service (Records), Onslow County, Miscellaneous Records.

32. Clark, *State Records,* 24:738-739; *Laws of North Carolina, 1797,* c. 52; *Private Laws of North Carolina, 1834-1835,* c. 161; Census Records, 1850, County Accounts and Reports, Onslow County, Miscellaneous Records.

33. M. L. F. Redd to ———, November 15, 1859, Marcus Lafayette Redd Papers, Private Collections, State Archives.

34. *Heads of Families at the First Census of the United States Taken in the Year 1790* (Baltimore: Genealogical Publishing Company, 1966), 194-197; Johnson, "Antebellum Onslow County," 22-23; Contract between the County of Onslow and Nancy Ambrose, February 9, 1831, Ferry Records, Onslow County, Miscellaneous Records.

35. John Hope Franklin, *The Free Negro in North Carolina, 1790-1860* (Chapel Hill: University of North Carolina Press, 1943), 232; Donnie D. Bellamy, "Onslow

County's Black History" (paper presented to the Seminar on Onslow County History, Swansboro, N.C., 1982), 7.

36. Bellamy, "Slavery in Microcosm," 345-347; Grand Jury Presentment, July 9, 1816; Petition of Kilby and William Ferrand, October 6, 1809, Freedom of Slaves (Papers), Onslow County, Miscellaneous Records.

37. Bellamy, "Onslow County's Black History," 3, 5.

38. Bellamy, "Onslow County's Black History," 5.

39. Franklin, *Free Negro in North Carolina*, 214-216.

40. *Newbern Weekly Progress*, January 19, May 29, 1860.

41. Bellamy, "Onslow County's Black History," 8; Franklin, *Free Negro in North Carolina*, 231, 233, 237.

42. Franklin, *Free Negro in North Carolina*, 160, 235-237; Bellamy, "Onslow County's Black History," 11. Not all free blacks held slaves for benevolent purposes, however. See Loren Schweninger, "John Carruthers Stanly and the Anomaly of Black Slaveholding," *North Carolina Historical Review* 67 (April 1990): 159-192.

43. Avirett, *Old Plantation*, 118.

44. Avirett, *Old Plantation*, 124-126.

45. Avirett, *Old Plantation*, 118.

46. Bellamy, "Onslow County's Black History," 16; John W. Blassingame, *The Slave Community: Plantation Life in the Antebellum South* (New York: Oxford University Press, 1972), 159; Avirett, *Old Plantation*, 47-48.

47. See various trials of slaves dated July 19, 1765, June 26, 1779, April 15, 1786, April ?, 1787, November 27, 1798, August 2, 1800, April 30, 1802, June ?, 1807, Criminal Actions Concerning Slaves, Onslow County, Miscellaneous Records.

48. *New Bern North Carolina Gazette*, December 17, 1796; *Wilmington Gazette*, January 27, 1807; *Private Laws of North Carolina, 1834-1835*, c. 89; *Public Laws of North Carolina, 1850-1851*, c. 47.

49. Guion Griffis Johnson, *Ante-Bellum North Carolina: A Social History* (Chapel Hill: University of North Carolina Press, 1937), 514-515.

50. Johnson, "Antebellum Onslow County," 12; Memorandum of the examination of the Negroes charged with insurrection, 1831, September ?, 1831, Onslow County, Miscellaneous Records. See also *Laws of North Carolina, 1830-1831*, c. 153.

51. Petition of Harvey Cox, December Term, 1833, Onslow County Court, Grist Mills and Saw Mills, Onslow County, Miscellaneous Records; Avirett, *Old Plantation*, 166-167.

52. Avirett, *Old Plantation*, 120; *Wilmington Journal*, June 18, 1846; Cheney, *North Carolina Government*, 1223-1224; Loftfield and Littleton, *Reconnaissance*, 114, 132.

53. *New Bern State Gazette of North Carolina*, January 18, 1787.

54. *Newbern Weekly Progress*, January 10, 1860; DeBow, *Seventh Census*, 316.

55. Onslow Court Minutes, November 1839; Report by David W. Sanders, ca. September 1858, Education Records, Onslow County, Miscellaneous Records.

56. Report by David W. Sanders, ca. September 1858; Report by the School Committee of District 4, December 1859; Report of School Committee in District 5, January 23, 1855, School Reports and Lists of School Children, 1850-1859, Education Records, Onslow County, Miscellaneous Records.

57. Clark, *State Records*, 24:534-535.

58. *Laws of North Carolina, 1791*, c. 42; *Laws of North Carolina, 1809*, c. 23; *Laws of North Carolina, 1810*, c. 67; *Private Laws of North Carolina, 1824*, c. 123.

59. *Wilmington Journal*, April 28, December 29, 1848; Johnson, "Antebellum Onslow County," 27.

60. *Wilmington Journal*, April 28, 1848; March 28, December 5, 1851; February 27, August 20, 1852; February 29, 1856.

61. *Wilmington Journal*, December 29, 1848; March 25, 1851; September 10, 1852; *Newbern Weekly Progress*, April 17, 1860; *New Bern Weekly Union*, March 22, 1860.

62. Charles Duffy to S. J. Sedgwick, July 15, 1859, Charles Duffy Papers, Special Collections Department, Duke University Library, Durham; *Wilmington Journal*, December 29, 1849.

63. Avirett, *Old Plantation*, 97-98, 158-161.

64. Avirett, *Old Plantation*, 102.

65. *New Bern North Carolina Gazette*, March 25, 1797; Onslow Court Minutes, September 1856; Petition of Daniel Bates et al. to the Onslow County Court, March 1778, Road Records, Onslow County, Miscellaneous Records; Avirett, *Old Plantation*, 33.

66. Avirett, *Old Plantation*, 184-189; *Newbern Weekly Progress*, January 24, 1860.

67. Avirett, *Old Plantation*, 99-104.

68. Avirett, *Old Plantation*, 106-109.

69. Avirett, *Old Plantation*, 23, 136-138; Johnston, "Journal of Ebenezer Hazard," 378.

70. Avirett, *Old Plantation*, 33, 35, 88, 120-121, 193.

71. *Newbern Weekly Progress*, May 15, July 17, 1860.

72. Avirett, *Old Plantation*, 172-194; Johnson, *Ante-Bellum North Carolina*, 550-553.

73. Statement of Retailers, Store & Tavern and Pedlars Tax for the Year 1847, ending the first day of October 1848, County Accounts and Reports 1840-1849, Onslow County, Miscellaneous Records; Avirett, *Old Plantation*, 113; *Newbern Weekly Progress*, May 15, 1860.

74. *New Bern Carolina Sentinel*, August 17, 1831; Johnson, "Antebellum Onslow County," 30-31.

75. Loftfield and Littleton, *Reconnaissance*, 97-98, 130; Johnson, "Antebellum Onslow County," 29.

76. Grady L. Carroll, ed., *Francis Asbury in North Carolina* (Nashville, Tenn.: Parthenon Press, n.d.), 69-70, 184, 212.

77. Carroll, *Francis Asbury*, 195-196; Johnson, "Antebellum Onslow County," 10; Avirett, *Old Plantation*, 147; Brown, *Commonwealth of Onslow*, 247.

78. Statement of Retailers, Store & Tavern and Pedlars Tax for the Year 1847, ending the first day of October 1848, County Accounts and Reports, 1840-1849, Onslow County, Miscellaneous Records; Avirett, *Old Plantation*, 118-119.

79. *Laws of North Carolina, 1802*, c. 88; *Laws of North Carolina, 1832-1833*, c. 81; *Wilmington Gazette*, October 7, 1806; *Newbern Weekly Progress*, January 24, 1860; *Wilmington Journal*, June 20, 1860.

80. *Private Laws of North Carolina, 1825*, c. 110; *Wilmington Journal*, August 2, 1850.

81. Johnson, *Ante-Bellum North Carolina*, 170; *Wilmington Journal*, August 2, 9, 1850.

82. *Wilmington Journal*, December 26, 1855.

83. Avirett, *Old Plantation*, 118-119.

84. DeBow, *Seventh Census*, 319-324; Joseph C. G. Kennedy, comp., *Agriculture of the United States in 1860* . . . (Washington, D.C.: Government Printing Office, 1864), 108-111; Avirett, *Old Plantation*, 31.

85. Clark, *State Records*, 24:749-750; *Laws of North Carolina, 1791*, c. 27; Avirett, *Old Plantation*, 32; *Newbern Weekly Progress*, August 7, 1860.

86. Avirett, *Old Plantation*, 30-31, 56-57, 83.

87. Loftfield and Littleton, *Reconnaissance*, 123; *Raleigh Register*, February 14, 1811; *Wilmington Journal*, November 16, 1849; August 16, 1860; Bellamy, "Slavery in Microcosm," 347.

88. *Wilmington Journal*, May 8, September 10, 1852; August 23, December 8, 1860; *Newbern Weekly Progress*, January 24, 1860.

89. *Raleigh Minerva*, September 15, October 6, December 1, 1815; *Raleigh Register*, February 14, 1811; *Manufactures of the United States in 1860* . . . (Washington, D.C.: Government Printing Office, 1865), 430.

90. *Newbern Weekly Progress*, January 24, 1860; Brown, *Commonwealth of Onslow*, 11-12; Products of Industry in Onslow, Census of 1850, for the year ending June 1, 1850. Businesses producing articles to the value of $500 per year, County Accounts and Reports, Onslow County, Miscellaneous Records.

91. Avirett, *Old Plantation*, 63-71; Products of Industry in Onslow, Census of 1850, for the year ending June 1, 1850. Businesses producing articles to the value of $500 per year, County Accounts and Reports, Onslow County, Miscellaneous Records.

92. William N. Still Jr., "Shipbuilding in Onslow County" (paper presented to the Seminar on Onslow County History, Swansboro, N.C., 1982), unpaginated. For shipbuilding at Bogue see *New Bern Martin's North Carolina Gazette*, August 1, 1787.

93. Still, "Shipbuilding in Onslow"; *Wilmington Gazette*, January 13, 1816.

94. Still, "Shipbuilding in Onslow"; James Sprunt, *Chronicles of the Cape Fear River, 1660-1916*, 2d ed. (Raleigh: Edwards & Broughton Printing Company, 1916), 139.

95. Johnston, "Journal of Ebenezer Hazard," 276-279; Louis B. Wright and Marion Tinling, eds., *Quebec to Carolina in 1785-1786: Being the Travel Diary and Observations of Robert Hunter, Jr., a Young Merchant of London* (San Marino, Calif.: The Huntington Library, 1943), 279; Donald Jackson and Dorothy Twohig, eds., *The Diaries of George Washington*, vol. 6 (Charlottesville, Va.: University of Virginia Press, 1979), 118.

96. Complaint by Christian Free, April 26, 1779, Bridge Records, Onslow County, Miscellaneous Records; Lemmon, "Onslow County During the War of 1812," 2.

97. Petition of Franklin Thompson and Charles Gregory to Onslow County Court, December 1847, Road Records, Onslow County, Miscellaneous Records.

98. *Laws of North Carolina, 1830-1831*, c. 118.

99. Robert B. Starling, "The Plank Road Movement in North Carolina," parts 1 and 2, *North Carolina Historical Review* 16 (January/April 1939): 2-3, 173; *Public Laws of North Carolina, 1850-1851*, c. 138; *Private Laws of North Carolina, 1854-1855*, c. 197; *Wilmington Daily Journal*, August 24, 1852.

100. *Public Laws of North Carolina, 1852*, c. 110; *Private Laws of North Carolina, 1854-1855*, c. 195.

101. *Laws of North Carolina, 1791*, c. 40; *Laws of North Carolina, 1811*, c. 23; *Laws of North Carolina, 1816*, c. 22.

102. *Laws of North Carolina, 1800*, c. 32; *Laws of North Carolina, 1804*, c. 44; *Laws of North Carolina, 1810*, c. 58; *Private Laws of North Carolina, 1858-1859*, c. 149.

103. *Wilmington Journal*, April 5, 1850; February 28, December 5, 1851; *New Bern Atlantic*, February 21, 1854; *Private Laws of North Carolina, 1854-1855*, c. 174.

104. *Wilmington Journal*, November 16, 1855; July 31, 1857; Resolutions in Regard to a Dredge Boat on New River, *Private Laws of North Carolina, 1858-1859*, unpaginated.

105. *Laws of North Carolina, 1800*, c. 31; *Public Laws of North Carolina, 1852*, c. 14; *Public Laws of North Carolina, 1846-1847*, c. 19; *New Bern Atlantic*, February 21, 1854.

106. Clifford Reginald Hinshaw Jr., "North Carolina Canals Before 1860," *North Carolina Historical Review* 25 (January 1948): 6; *People's Press. And Wilmington Advertiser*, November 13, 1833.

107. *Public Laws of North Carolina, 1854-1855*, c. 32.

108. Clark, *State Records*, 24:850-851; William H. Hoyt, ed., *The Papers of Archibald D. Murphey* (Raleigh: E. M. Uzzell & Co., 1914), 2:156; Entrances, July 1, 1789–March 10, 1790, Port Swansborough, 1788-1790, Treasurers' and Comptrollers' Papers, State Archives.

109. Agreement between Edward Ward and Bazel Hawkins, July 7, 1807; Shipping account of Z. B. Barnum of Swansborough, October 25, 1854, Shipping Records, Onslow County, Miscellaneous Records; *Wilmington Journal*, May 21, 1858; March 22, 1860; Onslow Court Minutes, June 1855.

110. *New Bern North Carolina Gazette*, October 31, 1795; Deposition of John Collier, March 11, 1799; newspaper clipping, dated March 18, 1833, Shipping Records, Onslow County, Miscellaneous Records. See also *Raleigh Register*, September 15, 1815.

111. *New Bern New Era*, November 16, 1858; *Newbern Weekly Progress*, February 21, 1860; *Wilmington Journal*, May 21, 1858; March 22, 1860.

112. "Historic and Architectural Resources of Onslow County," Section E, 11; Statement of Retailers, Store, & Tavern and Pedlars Tax for the Year 1847, ending the first day of October 1848, County Accounts and Reports, Onslow County, Miscellaneous Papers; Onslow Court Minutes, June 1855; *Wilmington Journal*, March 5, 1852.

113. *North-Carolina Chronicle, or, Fayetteville Gazette*, December 20, 1790; February 7, 1791.

114. Loftfield and Littleton, *Reconnaissance*, 119.

115. Lemmon, "Onslow County During the War of 1812," 7-8; William S. Powell, ed., *Dictionary of North Carolina Biography*, vol. 2 (Chapel Hill: University of North Carolina Press, 1986), 112-113.

116. Loftfield and Littleton, *Reconnaissance*, 119-121; Cheney, *North Carolina Government*, 1223-1224.

117. Loftfield and Littleton, *Reconnaissance*, 119; Cheney, *North Carolina Government*, 1223-1224.

118. Lemmon, "Onslow County During the War of 1812," 9.

119. Lemmon, "Onslow County During the War of 1812," 10-11.

120. Lemmon, "Onslow County During the War of 1812," 15.

121. Lemmon, "Onslow County During the War of 1812," 13; Loftfield and Littleton, *Reconnaissance*, 122.

122. Albert Ray Newsome, *The Presidential Election of 1824 in North Carolina*, The James Sprunt Studies in History and Political Science, vol. 23, no. 1 (Chapel Hill: University of North Carolina Press, 1939), 156.

123. Cheney, *North Carolina Government*, 1329.

124. *New Bern Carolina Sentinel*, January 19, 1828.

125. Cheney, *North Carolina Government*, 1329; Marc W. Kruman, *Parties and Politics in North Carolina, 1836-1865* (Baton Rouge: Louisiana State University Press, 1983), 25-26.

126. *Wilmington People's Press*, April 3, 1833; *People's Press. And Wilmington Advertiser*, November 13, 1833; *Raleigh North Carolina Standard*, August 27, 1835; William S. Hoffmann, *Andrew Jackson and North Carolina Politics*, The James Sprunt Studies in History and Political Science, vol. 40 (Chapel Hill: University of North Carolina Press, 1958), 67.

127. Thomas Jeffrey, however, does not see such a clear-cut dichotomy. See Thomas E. Jeffrey, *State Parties and National Politics: North Carolina, 1815-1861* (Athens, Ga.: University of Georgia Press, 1989), 117-142.

128. Harold J. Counihan, "The North Carolina Constitutional Convention of 1835: A Study in Jacksonian Democracy," *North Carolina Historical Review* 46 (autumn 1969): 338, 340; *Raleigh North Carolina Standard*, April 24, 1835.

129. *Raleigh North Carolina Standard*, June 12, 1835; Cheney, *North Carolina Government*, 817; Counihan, "North Carolina Constitutional Convention," 340 n. 13, 341 n. 14.

130. *Proceedings and Debates of the Convention of North Carolina, Called to Amend the Constitution of the State, Which Assembled at Raleigh, June 4, 1835,* . . . (Raleigh: Joseph Gales and Son, 1836), 80, 162, 200-201, 212, 331-332, 340.

131. *Raleigh North Carolina Standard*, November 26, 1835.

132. *Raleigh North Carolina Standard*, April 28, 1836; Cheney, *North Carolina Government*, 1329, 1331.

133. *Raleigh North Carolina Standard*, August 23, 1837; August 26, 1857; Cheney, *North Carolina Government*, 1397, 1399, 1401.

134. Cheney, *North Carolina Government*, 1223-1224.

135. *Wilmington Journal*, July 17, 1846; An Abstract of the votes taken in Onslow County . . . on the 3rd of August 1854, Election Records, Onslow County, Miscellaneous Records.

136. *Raleigh North Carolina Standard*, July 1, May 20, 1840; December 27, 1844; January 10, 1845.

137. *Raleigh North Carolina Standard*, March 19, 1856; Election Records, Onslow County, Miscellaneous Records.

138. Joseph Carlyle Sitterson, *The Secession Movement in North Carolina*, The James Sprunt Studies in History and Political Science, vol. 23, no. 2 (Chapel Hill: University of North Carolina Press, 1939), 152-154; *Newbern Weekly Progress*, January 10, 1860.

139. *Newbern Weekly Progress*, January 10, 1860; May 15, 1860; *Raleigh North Carolina Standard*, April 11, 1860.

140. *Raleigh North Carolina Standard*, April 11, 1860; Cheney, *North Carolina Government*, 1401.

141. Sitterson, *Secession Movement in North Carolina*, 175; *Wilmington Journal*, November 15, 1860.

142. *Newbern Weekly Progress*, December 18, 1860.

143. A List of votes taken in Onslow County on the 28th day of Febr. 1861, Election Records, March 1, 1861, Onslow County, Miscellaneous Records.

144. Sitterson, *Secession Movement in North Carolina*, 240-249; *Raleigh North Carolina Standard*, May 22, 29, 1861.

CHAPTER FOUR
CIVIL WAR, RECONSTRUCTION,
AND THE LATE NINETEENTH CENTURY

1. *Wilmington Journal*, June 20, 1861; Louis H. Manarin, "Onslow County During the Civil War" (paper presented to the Seminar on Onslow County, Swansboro, N.C., 1982), 6; Louis H. Manarin and Weymouth T. Jordan Jr., comps., *North Carolina Troops, 1861-1865: A Roster*, 13 vols. to date (Raleigh: Division of Archives and History, Department of Cultural Resources, 1966—), 3:481-487, 532-543, 554-565.

2. Manarin, "Onslow County During the Civil War," 6.

3. Manarin, "Onslow County During the Civil War," 7-8; Walter Clark, ed., *Histories of the Several Regiments and Battalions from North Carolina in the Great War, 1861-'65*, 5 vols. (Raleigh: State of North Carolina, 1901), 2:269-271; Brown, *Commonwealth of Onslow*, 71-73; Manarin and Jordan, *North Carolina Troops*, 7:246.

4. Manarin, "Onslow County During the Civil War," 8-9; Clark, *Histories*, 2:272-290.

5. Manarin, "Onslow County During the Civil War," 10-11.

6. Manarin and Jordan, *North Carolina Troops*, 2:178-180, 190-198, 236-245; Clark, *Histories*, 2:770-771.

7. Manarin, "Onslow County During the Civil War," 13; Clark, *Histories*, 3:503-514; Brown, *Commonwealth of Onslow*, 76-77.

8. Election returns . . . July 28, 1864, Election Records, Onslow County, Miscellaneous Records.

9. *Wilmington Journal*, October 17, 1861; September 15, 1864; February 2, 1865.

10. *Wilmington Journal*, October 31, 1861; Loftfield and Littleton, *Reconnaissance*, 134-135; Manarin, "Onslow County During the Civil War," 11-12.

11. Manarin, "Onslow County During the Civil War," 12.

12. Loftfield and Littleton, *Reconnaissance*, 135-136; *Wilmington Journal*, June 4, 1863.

13. *Wilmington Journal*, April 17, 24, 1862.

14. *Wilmington Journal*, September 4, 1862; *The War of the Rebellion: A Compilation of the Official Records of the Union and Confederate Armies*, ser. 1, 9:350-351; Manarin, "Onslow County During the Civil War," 17-18.

15. Loftfield and Littleton, *Reconnaissance*, 135; Manarin, "Onslow County During the Civil War," 18; *Wilmington Journal*, June 18, 1863.

16. *Official Records of the Union and Confederate Navies in the War of the Rebellion*, ser. 1, 8:230-232; *Wilmington Journal*, December 4, 18, 1862; Loftfield and Littleton, *Reconnaissance*, 136.

17. E. B. Barnum to Sister, May 1, 1864, Tucker Littleton Papers, Private Collections, State Archives; *Official Records (Army)*, ser. 1, 18:127-130, 166-177; 23:316; 29, pt. 1:992-994; 33:316; 40, pt. 1:819-820; Manarin, "Onslow County During the Civil War," 22-23.

18. Manarin, "Onslow County During the Civil War," 22.

19. Loftfield and Littleton, *Reconnaissance*, 137; *Wilmington Journal*, December 26, 1863.

20. *Official Records (Navy)*, ser. 1, 9:562-566.

21. Onslow Court Minutes, June, September 1861; Manarin, "Onslow County During the Civil War," 10.

22. Elizabeth J. Williams to John Wesley Williams, March 12, 1862, John Wesley Williams Papers, Special Collections Department, Duke University Library, Durham; Onslow Court Minutes, March 1863; *Wilmington Journal*, December 3, 1863.

23. Onslow Court Minutes, March, May, June, December 1863.

24. Onslow Court Minutes, March, December 1864; *Wilmington Journal*, December 15, 1864.

25. Onslow Court Minutes, September 1862, December 1862, September 1864; Loftfield and Littleton, *Reconnaissance*, 135-136.

26. *Wilmington Journal*, March 17, December 15, 1864.

27. *Wilmington Journal*, July 30, August 20, 1863.

28. Report of the Committee, School District No. 18, December 5, 1863; Report of Jasper Etheridge, Chairman of the Board of Superintendents of Common Schools, April 17, 1864, Education Records, Onslow County, Miscellaneous Records; *Wilmington Journal*, November 20, 1862.

29. Loftfield and Littleton, *Reconnaissance*, 138; Bellamy, "Onslow County's Black History," 19.

30. Cheney, *North Carolina Government*, 327-331, 387.

31. Manarin, "Onslow County During the Civil War," 11; Loftfield and Littleton, *Reconnaissance*, 135.

32. *Wilmington Journal*, November 21, 1861; July 30, October 8, 1863; August 11, 1864.

33. Onslow Court Minutes, December 1861-March 1864 passim.

34. Book 29, p. 345, Onslow County Deeds, State Archives.

35. An Abstract of Votes . . . on the 18th day of October AD 1866, Election Records, Onslow County, Miscellaneous Records; R. D. W. Connor, ed., *A Manual of North Carolina* (Raleigh: E. M. Uzzell & Co., 1913), 1017.

36. Connor, *Manual of North Carolina*, 1017; *Wilmington Journal*, May 8, August 7, 1868; September 16, 1870; Cheney, *North Carolina Government*, 1225.

37. *Wilmington Journal*, March 27, September 25, 1868; June 17, 1870; July 31, 1874; April 19, May 19, August 18, September 1, 8, October 13, 1876; Convention Delegates, April 6, 1874, County Accounts and Reports, Onslow County, Miscellaneous Records.

38. Cheney, *North Carolina Government*, 1223-1224; Brown, *Commonwealth of Onslow*, 363-364; Minutes, County Commissioners of Onslow County, May 1869, State Archives, hereafter cited as County Commission Minutes; Resolution of the Onslow Bar concerning the death of James G. Scott, 1884, Onslow County, Miscellaneous Records.

39. *Wilmington Journal*, July 14, 1882; Cheney, *North Carolina Government*, 698-699; *Congressional Record*, 47th Cong., 1st sess., March 1881-March 1882, Index, 381; 2nd sess., December 1882-February 1883, 261-262, 284-287.

40. *Wilmington Journal*, January 31, 1868; August 9, 1872; December 24, 1875.

41. Jeffrey J. Crow and Robert F. Durden, *Maverick Republican in the Old North State: A Political Biography of Daniel L. Russell* (Baton Rouge: Louisiana State University Press, 1977), 1, 12, 30-32; *Wilmington Journal*, August 14, 28, 1874.

42. *Wilmington Journal*, May 8, 1868; April 8, 1870; September 27, 1872.

43. County Commission Minutes, August 1871, July 1872, July 1874; Bellamy, "Onslow County's Black History," 34.

44. *The Wilmington Post*, January 15, February 19, 1882.

45. *The Wilmington Post*, February 19, 1882. See also County Commission Minutes, September 1882.

46. Brown, *Commonwealth of Onslow*, 122-123.

47. Brown, *Commonwealth of Onslow*, 122-123.

48. Brown, *Commonwealth of Onslow*, 127-128; Connor, *Manual of North Carolina*, 479.

49. Brown, *Commonwealth of Onslow*, 89-91; Cheney, *North Carolina Government*, 698.

50. Cheney, *North Carolina Government*, 1335-1405, 1407.

51. Brown, *Commonwealth of Onslow*, 129-132; Cheney, *North Carolina Government*, 1224; *Wilmington Weekly Star*, September 30, 1898; Connor, *Manual of North Carolina*, 1017.

52. For this and the following two paragraphs see Paul Wager, *County Government and Administration in North Carolina* (Chapel Hill: University of North Carolina Press, 1928), 6-23; Joseph S. Ferrell, ed., *County Government in North Carolina*, 2d ed. (Chapel Hill: Institute of Government, 1979), 3-5.

53. County Commission Minutes, January 1869.

54. County Commission Minutes, August 1875.

55. County Commission Minutes, September 1868, February 1869, August 1870, September 1870, August 1872; *Wilmington Journal*, July 22, 1870; June 14, 1872.

56. *Public Laws of North Carolina, 1868-1869*, c. 234; *Public Laws of North Carolina, 1869-1870*, c. 216.

57. *Public Laws of North Carolina, 1870-1871*, c. 230; *Public Laws of North Carolina, 1871-1872*, c. 125; County Commission Minutes, August 1871, January 1872, February 1872, August 1872.

58. *Public Laws of North Carolina, 1876-1877*, c. 131; County Commission Minutes, July, August 1877.

59. *Public Laws of North Carolina, 1879*, c. 134; County Commission Minutes, October, December 1879.

60. *Public Laws of North Carolina, 1881*, c. 33; County Commission Minutes, September 1881, February 1883.

61. Report of the Finance Committee of Onslow County, November 10, 1879, County Accounts and Reports, Onslow County, Miscellaneous Records.

62. *Public Laws of North Carolina, 1886-1887*, c. 43.

63. *Public Laws of North Carolina, 1885*, c. 233; *Public Laws of North Carolina, 1887*, c. 143; *Public Laws of North Carolina, 1889*, c. 241; *Public Laws of North Carolina, 1897*, c. 192; *Public Laws of North Carolina, 1900*, c. 16.

64. *Public Laws of North Carolina, 1891*, c. 202; County Commission Minutes, November 1898.

65. *Public Laws of North Carolina, 1871-1872*, c. 59; *Public Laws of North Carolina, 1893*, c. 382; County Commission Minutes, February 1884, November 1890.

66. *Public Laws of North Carolina, 1876-1877*, c. 196; County Commission Minutes, December 1877, May 1881, April 1886, November 1890, April 1893.

67. County Commission Minutes, December 1869, March 1875, April 1876, April 1877, August 1877.

68. *Public Laws of North Carolina, 1868-1869*, c. 234; *Public Laws of North Carolina, 1872-1873*, c. 146; County Commission Minutes, December 1870, April 1871, June 1881.

69. County Commission Minutes, April 1871, April 1879, April 1886, January 1876, March 1880.

70. County Commission Minutes, April 1879, April 1884; Report of the Grand Jury, Superior Court, Onslow County, Spring Term, 1884, Grand Jury Papers, Onslow County, Miscellaneous Records.

71. County Commission Minutes, April 1880, January 1884, June 1875, December 1880, November 1887; Report of the Grand Jury, Superior Court, Onslow County, Spring Term 1884, Grand Jury Papers, Onslow County, Miscellaneous Records.

72. Joseph P. Kennedy, comp., *Agriculture of the United States in 1860* . . . (Washington, D.C.: Government Printing Office, 1864), 108-109; Francis A. Walker, comp., *A Compendium of the Ninth Census* . . . (Washington, D.C.: Government Printing Office, 1872), 766-767.

73. *Wilmington Journal*, December 4, 1872; December 12, 1873.

74. *Manufactures of the United States in 1860* . . . (Washington, D.C.: Government Printing Office, 1865), 430; Walker, *Ninth Census*, 835; *Compendium of the Tenth Census*, pt. 1 (New York: Arno Press, 1976), 1003; Levi Branson, ed., *Branson's North Carolina Business Directory, 1884* (Raleigh: Levi Branson, 1884), 501-502; Levi Branson, ed., *Branson's North Carolina Business Directory, 1896* (Raleigh: Levi Branson, 1896), 465-466.

75. Still, "Shipbuilding in Onslow."

76. Still, "Shipbuilding in Onslow."

77. "Historic and Architectural Resources of Onslow County, North Carolina," Section E, 22; *Wilmington Weekly Star*, September 4, 1885; *Compendium of the Tenth Census*, 803.

78. *Wilmington Journal*, December 24, 1875; *Compendium of the Tenth Census*, 803; "Historic and Architectural Resources of Onslow County," Section E, 22; Jerry L. Cross, "Onslow County, 1865-1920: Transition, Change, and Continuity" (paper presented to the Seminar on Onslow County History, Swansboro, N.C., 1982), 9-10; Brown, *Commonwealth of Onslow*, 211-212.

79. Percival Perry, "The Naval Stores Industry in Onslow County, North Carolina, 1735-1920" (paper presented to the Seminar on Onslow County History, Swansboro, N.C., 1982), 34-35, 37; Levi Branson, ed., *The North Carolina Business Directory, 1877 and 1878* (Raleigh: Levi Branson, 1878), 228; Branson, *North Carolina Business Directory, 1896*, 465.

80. Perry, "Naval Stores Industry in Onslow County," 37.

81. *Public Laws of North Carolina, 1889*, c. 250; *Private Laws of North Carolina, 1889*, cc. 212, 109; *Private Laws of North Carolina, 1891*, c. 276; *Private Laws of North Carolina, 1893*, c. 349; *Wilmington Weekly Star*, July 28, 1893.

82. *Wilmington Weekly Star*, August 7, 1891; July 3, [August 28], 1893; "Historic and Architectural Resources of Onslow County," Section E, 16; Loftfield and Littleton, *Reconnaissance*, 156; Incorporation of Onslow Lumber Company, March 19, 1889, Articles of Incorporation, Onslow County, Miscellaneous Records.

83. Cross, "Onslow County," 14; *Public Laws of North Carolina, 1874-1875*, c. 193; *Public Laws of North Carolina, 1881*, c. 46; *Public Laws of North Carolina, 1883*, c. 359; *Public Laws of North Carolina, 1891*, cc. 200, 497.

84. *Wilmington Morning Star*, September 23, November 21, 1869; January 18, 1870; *Wilmington Weekly Star*, September 28, November 2, 1883; County Commission Minutes, March 1888, June 1889.

85. *Public Laws of North Carolina, 1871-1872*, c. 214; *Public Laws of North Carolina, 1881*, c. 46; *Public Laws of North Carolina, 1887*, c. 90; *Public Laws of North Carolina, 1889*, c. 298; *Public Laws of North Carolina, 1891*, c. 419; County Commission Minutes, June 1891, April 1892. See Petition of R. L. Williams to the Superior Court of Onslow County, November 15, 1886, for an oyster bed; Petition of E. B. Fonville to the Superior Court of Onslow County, n.d., Oyster Records, Onslow County, Miscellaneous Records.

86. *Private Laws of North Carolina, 1891*, c. 190; *Wilmington Weekly Star*, September 17, 1897.

87. *Private Laws of North Carolina, 1891*, c. 190; *Wilmington Weekly Star*, March 3, September 18, 1891; March 11, June 3, 1892.

88. *Kinston Daily Free Press*, November 18, 1899; Cross, "Onslow County," 15.

89. County Commission Minutes, August 1873, May 1897.

90. *Public Laws of North Carolina, 1883*, c. 268; *Public Laws of North Carolina, 1897*, c. 495.

91. *Public Laws of North Carolina, 1879*, c. 260; *Public Laws of North Carolina, 1881*, c. 40; *Public Laws of North Carolina, 1897*, c. 538; *Public Laws of North Carolina, 1899*, c. 445; *Newbernian*, August 16, September 6, 1879. The state envisioned the use of convict labor to complete several additional roads in the county. See *Public Laws of North Carolina, 1881*, c. 358; *Public Laws of North Carolina, 1887*, cc. 74, 260; *Public Laws of North Carolina, 1899*, c. 702.

92. County Commission Minutes, December 1873; *Public Laws of North Carolina, 1883*, c. 243.

93. County Commission Minutes, August 1874, January 1878, April 1895.

94. County Commission Minutes, May 1875, April 1880, April 1891.

95. *Newbernian*, May 10, 1879; County Commission Minutes, November 1893, August 1899.

96. County Commission Minutes, June 1870, February 1872, October 1877, September 1891.

97. County Commission Minutes, December 1874, December 1875, August 1878, January 1885, December 1897; Cross, "Onslow County," 12.

98. *Wilmington Journal*, December 17, 1869; *Public Laws of North Carolina, 1869-1870*, cc. 60, 207.

99. *Wilmington Journal*, July 1, 8, 15, 22, October 7, 14, November 4, 1870; *Public Laws of North Carolina, 1870-1871*, cc. 47, 257; *Public Laws of North Carolina, 1871-1872*, c. 13; *Public Laws of North Carolina, 1883*, c. 64.

100. County Commission Minutes, September 1870, November 1870, January 1871; *Wilmington Journal*, January 20, March 10, 31, April 21, 28, 1871; October 2, 1874.

101. *Public Laws of North Carolina, 1885*, c. 233; *Public Laws of North Carolina, 1887*, cc. 89, 299, 404; *New Bern Chronicle*, July 16, 1897; Richard E. Prince, *Atlantic Coast Line Railroad: Steam Locomotives, Ships, and History* (Green River, Wyo.: Richard E. Prince, 1966), 15.

102. County Commission Minutes, November 1890, May 1895, March 1896.

103. *Public Laws of North Carolina, 1897*, c. 71; *Private Laws of North Carolina, 1893*, cc. 155, 159; *Private Laws of North Carolina, 1899*, c. 190; *Wilmington Weekly Star*, July 17, 1888; July 19, 1889; April 5, 1895; Loftfield and Littleton, *Reconnaissance*, 156.

104. *Public Laws of North Carolina, 1880*, c. 33; *Public Laws of North Carolina, 1899*, c. 206; *Public Laws of North Carolina, 1899*, c. 550.

105. *Public Laws of North Carolina, 1871-1872*, c. 151; *Wilmington Journal*, September 17, 1875. Later legislation extended the scope of the proposed company. See *Public Laws of North Carolina, 1873-1874*, c. 55.

106. *Newbernian*, January 4, 1879; Loftfield and Littleton, *Reconnaissance*, 154; Ronald B. Hartzer, *To Great and Useful Purpose: A History of the Wilmington District U.S. Army Corps of Engineers* (n.p., n.d.), 45.

107. Wilson Angley, "An Historical Overview of Bogue Inlet," Research Branch Report, October 16, 1984, in Historical Research Reports, ser. 2, ed. and comp. Wilson Angley, Research Branch, North Carolina Division of Archives and History, Department of Cultural Resources, 1990, microfilm, 9-10.

108. Angley, "An Historical Overview of Bogue Inlet," 10-11.

109. County Commission Minutes, March 1875; *Wilmington Weekly Star*, December 22, 1882.

110. Loftfield and Littleton, *Reconnaissance*, 154; *Private Laws of North Carolina, 1876-1877*, c. 87; *Private Laws of North Carolina, 1889*, c. 36.

111. Still, "Shipbuilding in Onslow"; Loftfield and Littleton, *Reconnaissance*, 154; *Wilmington Weekly Star*, September 17, 1897.

112. "Historic and Architectural Resources of Onslow County," Section E, 22-23; *Fourteenth Census of the United States Taken in the Year 1920*, vol. 6, pt. 2, *Agriculture* (Washington, D.C.: Government Printing Office, 1922), 238.

113. Joseph P. Kennedy, ed., *Population of the United States in 1860* . . . (Washington, D.C.: Government Printing Office, 1864), 348-358; Cheney, *North Carolina Government*, 1225.

114. Cross, "Onslow County," 22; Loftfield and Littleton, *Reconnaissance*, 156; Branson, *Business Directory of North Carolina, 1896*, 464; *Private Laws of North Carolina, 1880*, c. 8; *Population of the United States . . . as Returned at the Twelfth Census: 1900* (Washington, D.C.: Government Printing Office, 1901), 292. In the colonial era a settlement called Rich Lands of New River had originated in the vicinity of an Anglican chapel. About three miles north of Rich Lands, a log chapel was built in 1813, around which arose another community, first called Oak Grove and then Upper Richlands. When the post office was moved from the older community to the newer, Rich Lands began to dwindle. Upper Richlands was incorporated in 1880 as the town of Richlands. The author is indebted to Jerry Cross, Division of Archives and History, Raleigh, N.C., for this information. Letter dated May 16, 1994, from Jerry Cross to author.

115. *Private Laws of North Carolina, 1876-1877*, c. 92; *Private Laws of North Carolina, 1895*, c. 207.

116. *Wilmington Weekly Star*, July 19, 1889; Branson, *Business Directory of North Carolina, 1896*, 464; "Historic and Architectural Resources of Onslow County," Section E, 16; *Population of the United States . . . as Returned at the Twelfth Census*, 292.

117. *Wilmington Journal*, September 15, 1871; *Private Laws of North Carolina, 1883*, c. 115; *Private Laws of North Carolina, 1891*, c. 280; *Private Laws of North Carolina, 1897*,

c. 141; Walker, *Ninth Census*, 284; *Population of the United States . . . as Returned at the Twelfth Census*, 292; Branson, *Business Directory of North Carolina, 1896*, 465-466.

118. Loftfield and Littleton, *Reconnaissance*, 156.

119. *New Bern Journal*, February 2, 1893; *Kinston Daily Free Press*, March 13, November 18, 1899; Loftfield and Littleton, *Reconnaissance*, 156-157.

120. Loftfield and Littleton, *Reconnaissance*, 143; County Commission Minutes, August 1899.

121. County Commission Minutes, December 1869, May 1881, May 1899.

122. *Wilmington Journal*, August 2, 1866; Cross, "Onslow County," 5; Branson, *North Carolina Business Directory, 1884*, 503; Branson, *North Carolina Business Directory, 1896*, 466.

123. Bellamy, "Onslow County's Black History," 24-26; Brown, *Commonwealth of Onslow*. 151.

124. County Commission Minutes, March 1869, August 1877.

125. *Beaufort Weekly Record*, May 12, 1887.

126. Bellamy, "Onslow County's Black History," 27-28; Brown, *Commonwealth of Onslow*, 151-152; *Biennial Report of the Superintendent of Public Instruction of North Carolina for the Scholastic Years 1896-'97 and 1897-'98* (Raleigh: Guy V. Barnes, 1898), 292.

127. Mathews, "Social History," 19-20; Brown, *Commonwealth of Onslow*, 151.

128. Brown, *Commonwealth of Onslow*, 133-136.

129. *Wilmington Journal*, April 8, 1870; Grand Jury Presentments, Superior Court, Spring Term, 1879, Grand Jury Records, Onslow County, Miscellaneous Records; Grand Jury Presentments, Superior Court, Spring Term, 1895, Elections, Onslow County, Miscellaneous Records; Statement of H. E. King, August 17, 1895, Justices Court, Onslow County, Redd Papers.

130. Loftfield and Littleton, *Reconnaissance*, 150; Branson, *North Carolina Business Directory, 1896*, 465.

131. Bellamy, "Onslow County's Black History," 21-24.

132. County Commission Minutes, April 1874, June 1881; *Public Laws of North Carolina, 1871-1872*, c. 166; *Public Laws of North Carolina, 1874-1875*, c. 239; *Private Laws of North Carolina, 1874-1875*, c. 4; *Private Laws of North Carolina, 1880*, c. 8; *Public Laws of North Carolina, 1893*, c. 254; Connor, *Manual of North Carolina*, 1020.

133. *Branson's North Carolina Business Directory for 1867-8 . . .* (Raleigh: Branson & Jones, n.d.), 86; Branson, *North Carolina Business Directory, 1877-1878*, 228-229; Branson, *North Carolina Business Directory, 1896*, 466; *Wilmington Journal*, December 3, 1869.

134. Brown, *Commonwealth of Onslow*, 141-143.

135. Loftfield and Littleton, *Reconnaissance*, 152, 155; *Newbernian*, July 12, 1879; *Wilmington Weekly Star*, July 19, 1889.

136. *New Bern Daily Journal*, April 12, 1882; *Public Laws of North Carolina, 1893*, c. 492; *Wilmington Journal*, December 12, 1873.

137. *Wilmington Weekly Star*, June 29, 1894; "Alum Spring," National Register of Historic Places Registration Nomination Form, kindly supplied by Claudia Brown, National Register Coordinator, Division of Archives and History, Raleigh.

138. ——— to Lizzie, August 1, 1881, Charles Duffy Papers, Special Collections Department, Duke University Library, Durham; *Wilmington Weekly Star*, September 4, 1891; June 17, 1892.

CHAPTER FIVE
TWENTIETH-CENTURY ONSLOW

1. Cheney, *North Carolina Government*, 1225; *Wilmington Morning Star*, August 8, 1992; *North Carolina State Government Statistical Abstract*, 5th ed., 1984 (Raleigh: State Data Center, n.d.), 12-13.

2. *Wilmington Morning Star*, August 8, 1992; *The Answer Book*, August 30, 1992, published by *Jacksonville (N.C.) Daily News*, 36.

3. Cheney, *North Carolina Government*, 1225; *Census Population, 1980, North Carolina*, vol. 1, pt. 35 (Washington, D.C.: U.S. Department of Commerce, 1982), 100.

4. *Population of the United States . . . as Returned at the Twelfth Census*, 292; *Session Laws of North Carolina, 1955*, c. 130; *The Heritage of Onslow County* (Winston-Salem, N.C.: Hunter Publishing Company, n.d.), 9-10; *Census of Population and Housing, 1990, North Carolina* (Washington, D.C.: U.S. Department of Commerce, 1991), 19.

5. *Private Laws of North Carolina, 1905*, c. 417; Brown, *Commonwealth of Onslow*, 157-158, 225, 353; *Population of the United States . . . as Returned at the Twelfth Census*, 292; *Fifteenth Census of the United States, 1930*, vol. 1, *Population* (Washington, D.C.: Government Printing Office, 1931), 793, hereafter cited as *Fifteenth Census, 1930*; *Census of Population and Housing, 1990*, 19.

6. "Historic and Architectural Resources of Onslow County," Section E, 10; *Population of the United States . . . as Returned at the Twelfth Census*, 292; *Fifteenth Census, 1930*, 793; *Census of Population and Housing, 1990*, 19.

7. Bill Sharpe, "The Clam that Began to Build an Airstrip," *The State*, March 26, 1955, 30; David A. Stallman, *A History of Camp Davis* (Hampstead, N.C.: Hampstead Services, Inc., 1990), 3; *Census Population, 1980*, 24-25; *Census of Population and Housing, 1990*, 19; William S. Powell, ed., *The North Carolina Gazetteer* (Chapel Hill: University of North Carolina Press, 1968), 98; *Session Laws of North Carolina, 1989*, c. 10; R. G. Leary, County Manager, Onslow County, telephone conversation with author, August 16, 1993; *Answer Book*, 70.

8. Cheney, *North Carolina Government*, 1335, 1337, 1339, 1341, 1343, 1363, 1365, 1367, 1369, 1371, 1407, 1409, 1411, 1413, 1415.

9. Cheney, *North Carolina Government*, 1343, 1345, 1371, 1415; Richard H. Scammon and Alice V. McGillivray, eds. and comps., *America Votes: A Handbook of Contemporary American Elections Statistics*, 20 vols. to date (Washington, D.C.: Election Research Center, 1956—), 14:294, 298; 16:325, 327, 329; 18:342, 344; 19:337; *Raleigh News and Observer*, November 5, 1992.

10. Cheney, *North Carolina Government*, 1224-1225; *North Carolina Manual* (Raleigh: Secretary of State, n.d.), *1975*, 389; *1977*, 403-404; *1979*, 287, 348; *1981*, 199, 273-274; *1983*, 199, 287, 289; *1985*, 265, 357-358; *1987*, 279, 365, 367; *1989*, 325, 304, 414; *1991-1992*, 227, 298.

11. Bellamy, "Onslow County's Black History," 35.

12. Bellamy, "Onslow County's Black History," 35-38; Mary Boney, Supervisor of the Onslow County Board of Elections, telephone conversation with author, August 24, 1993.

13. County Commission Minutes, 1900-1924 passim; *Public-Local Laws of North Carolina, Extra Session, 1924*, c. 208.

14. County Commission Minutes, January, August, November 1909; *Public Laws of North Carolina, 1909*, c. 376.

15. *Public Laws of North Carolina, 1903*, c. 235; *Public Laws of North Carolina, 1905*, c. 642; *Public-Local Laws of North Carolina, 1911*, c. 284; *Public-Local Laws of North Carolina, 1923*, c. 67; *Public-Local Laws of North Carolina, 1927*, c. 649.

16. *Public-Local Laws of North Carolina, 1911*, c. 261; *Public-Local Laws of North Carolina, 1917*, c. 219.

17. *Public-Local Laws of North Carolina, 1917*, c. 679.

18. County Commission Minutes, August 1908; *Public Laws of North Carolina, 1909*, c. 762; *Public-Local Laws of North Carolina, 1911*, c. 394; *Public-Local Laws of North Carolina, 1929*, c. 3.

19. County Commission Minutes, March 1904, September 1904, February 1905, May 1905; *Public Laws of North Carolina, 1905*, c. 642; R. G. Leary, County Manager, Onslow County, telephone conversation with author, August 16, 1993.

20. County Commission Minutes, May 1903, June 1903, August 1915, October 1915; Report of the Grand Jury, Spring Term, 1904, Onslow Superior Court, County Accounts and Reports, Onslow County, Miscellaneous Records; "100 Milestones of 1972," *The State*, January 1973, 52; R. G. Leary, County Manager, Onslow County, telephone conversation with author, August 16, 1993.

21. County Commission Minutes, 1902-1903 passim, January 1904, June 1909, March 1909, February 1911; Report of the Grand Jury, Spring 1904, Onslow Superior Court, County Accounts and Reports, Onslow County, Miscellaneous Records; *Public Laws of North Carolina, Extra Session, 1908*, c. 15, 60; *Public-Local Laws of North Carolina, 1923*, c. 67; Brown, *Commonwealth of Onslow*, 196.

22. W. B. Wright, "100 Milestones of 1969," *The State*, January 1, 1970, 51; *Report on a Survey of the Organization and Administration of County Government in North Carolina* (Washington, D.C.: Institute for Government Research, 1930), 80-83; "Onslow County Government Working for You," prepared by the county manager for 1992-1993 (n.p., n.d.).

23. *Fourteenth Census of the United States Taken in the Year 1920*, vol. 6, pt. 2, *Agriculture* (Washington, D.C.: Government Printing Office, 1922), 257, hereafter cited as *Agriculture, Fourteenth Census*; "Historic and Architectural Resources of Onslow County," Section E, 22-23.

24. "Historic and Architectural Resources of Onslow County," Section E, 23; Cross, "Onslow County," 19; *Agriculture, Fourteenth Census*, 257; R. C. Jurney et al., *Soil Survey of Onslow County, North Carolina* (Washington, D.C.: Government Printing Office, 1928), 104.

25. Charles P. Loomis, "The Rise and Decline of the North Carolina Farmers' Union," *North Carolina Historical Review* 7 (July 1930): 305-325.

26. Cross, "Onslow County," 10; County Commission Minutes, September 1917, March 1918, April 1918; Brown, *Commonwealth of Onslow*, 211-218; *Answer Book*, 38.

27. *Agriculture, Fourteenth Census*, 238, 507; Harden F. Taylor et al., *Survey of Marine Fisheries of North Carolina* (Chapel Hill: University of North Carolina Press, 1951), 296.

28. *Census of Agriculture, 1978*, vol. 1, pt. 33, *North Carolina* (Washington, D.C.: Bureau of the Census, n.d.), 118-119; *Census of Agriculture, 1987*, vol. 1, pt. 33, *North Carolina* (Washington, D.C.: Bureau of the Census, n.d.), 150, 163, 176, 215.

29. *Census of Agriculture, 1987*, 385; *Answer Book*, 38.

30. Joseph Hyde Pratt, ed., *Report of the Fisheries Convention Held at New Bern, North Carolina, December 13, 1911* (Raleigh: Edwards & Broughton, 1912), 208-238.

31. Pratt, *Report of the Fisheries Convention*, 208-238.

32. *Public Laws of North Carolina, 1902*, cc. 250, 370; *Public Laws of North Carolina, 1907*, c. 949; *Public Laws of North Carolina, 1909*, c. 514; *Public Laws of North Carolina, 1915*, c. 130.

33. *Public Laws of North Carolina, 1907*, c. 977; *Public Laws of North Carolina, 1903*, c. 724; *Public-Local Laws of North Carolina, 1913*, c. 707; *Public Laws of North Carolina, 1915*, cc. 133, 184; *Public-Local Laws of North Carolina, 1923*, c. 130.

34. Taylor, *Survey of Marine Fisheries*, 298, 506.

35. *Data Book, 1979, Region P. Socio-Economic Base Study* (New Bern, N.C.: Neuse River Council of Governments, 1979), 76; *Answer Book*, 35.

36. Perry, "Naval Stores Industry in Onslow County," 37-38; "Historic and Architectural Resources of Onslow County," Section E, 14.

37. Cross, "Onslow County," 20; "Historic and Architectural Resources of Onslow County," Section E, 18.

38. "Historic and Architectural Resources of Onslow County," Section E, 18-19; *Census of Manufactures, 1977*, vol. 3, pt. 2 (Washington, D.C.: Department of Commerce, n.d.), 34; *Census of Manufactures, 1987, North Carolina* (Washington, D.C.: Department of Commerce, 1990), 76.

39. Brown, *Commonwealth of Onslow*, 364-365.

40. ———, Captain, U.S. Army Corps of Engineers, to Brigadier General A. Mackenzie, Chief of Engineers, February 10, 1906, Littleton Papers.

41. Angley, "An Historical Overview of Bogue Inlet," 13-14.

42. S. F. Gray, USCG, to George A. Merrit, USCG Ret., February 28, 1950, Littleton Papers.

43. *Intracoastal Waterway, Beaufort, N.C. to Key West, Fla., Station* (Washington, D.C.: Government Printing Office, 1913), 45.

44. Hartzer, *Great and Useful Purpose*, 62; Loftfield, "Testing and Excavations at 31 on 196," 21.

45. *Fourteenth Census of the United States Taken in the Year 1920*, vol. 9. *Manufactures, 1919* (Washington, D.C.: Government Printing Office, 1923), 1103; Taylor, *Survey of Marine Fisheries*, 508.

46. This and the following two paragraphs are based on Still, "Shipbuilding in Onslow."

47. S. Huntington Hobbs Jr., *North Carolina: An Economic and Social Profile* (Chapel Hill: University of North Carolina Press, 1958), 311, table 51; *Census of Manufactures, 1977*, 34-38; *Census of Manufactures, 1987*, 76; *Answer Book*, 33.

48. *Public Laws of North Carolina, 1903*, c. 712; *Public Laws of North Carolina, 1907*, cc. 95, 772; Loftfield and Littleton, *Reconnaissance*, 162-163.

49. *Public-Local Laws of North Carolina, 1911*, c. 394; County Commission Minutes, October 1913.

50. County Commission Minutes, March 1915, August 1916, November 1916, April 1922, June 1922; *Public-Local Laws of North Carolina, 1911*, c. 394; *Public-Local Laws of North Carolina, 1913*, c. 221; *Public-Local Laws of North Carolina, Extra-Session, 1913*, cc. 126, 194, 196, 214, 216; *Public-Local Laws of North Carolina, 1915*, c. 59; *Public-Local Laws of North Carolina, 1919*, c. 68; *Public-Local Laws of North Carolina Extra Session, 1920*, c. 146.

51. *Public-Local Laws of North Carolina, 1923*, c. 568; *Public-Local Laws of North Carolina, Extra Session, 1924*, c. 104. See also *Public-Local Laws of North Carolina, 1929*, c. 139.

52. County Commission Minutes, July 1918; Brown, *Commonwealth of Onslow*, 204-205.

53. Brown, *Commonwealth of Onslow*, 206.

54. County Commission Minutes, January 1903, February 1905, April 1907, October 1915, January 1917; *Public Laws of North Carolina, 1901*, c. 265; *Public Laws of North Carolina, 1905*, c. 595; *Public Laws of North Carolina, 1907*, c. 525.

55. County Commission Minutes, June 1906, November 1906, January 1907, September 1907, April 1918; Wayne Harp, Bridge Division, North Carolina Department of Transportation, telephone conversation with author, August 26, 1993.

56. County Commission Minutes, January 1903, August 1906, May 1907; Brown, *Commonwealth of Onslow*, 360.

57. *Public-Local Laws of North Carolina, 1913*, c. 779; *Public-Local Laws of North Carolina, Extra-Session, 1913*, c. 189; *Public Laws of North Carolina, 1917*, c. 64; County Commission Minutes, April 1917, October 1917, November 1917, December 1917, February 1918.

58. *Private Laws of North Carolina, 1901*, cc. 196, 385.

59. *Private Laws of North Carolina, 1905*, c. 67; Jurney, *Soil Survey of Onslow County*, 102; Brown, *Commonwealth of Onslow*, 199; *Wilmington Sunday Star News*, January 22, 1984; August 25, 1985.

60. "Albert J. Ellis Airport, 1971-1991," Brochure (n.p., n.d.); Douglas B. Barrett, Director of Aviation, Albert J. Ellis Airport, letter to the author, August 23, 1993.

61. Taylor, *Survey of Marine Fisheries*, 296, 509, quote on 300.

62. *Public Laws of North Carolina, 1901*, c. 554; *Private Laws of North Carolina, 1913*, c. 387; *Public-Local Laws of North Carolina, 1917*, c. 441; County Commission Minutes, December 1903; R. D. W. Connor, ed., *A Manual of North Carolina* (Raleigh: E. M. Uzzell & Co., 1913), 1020.

63. *Public Laws of North Carolina, 1927*, c. 42; *Public Laws of North Carolina, 1937*, c. 49; *Session Laws of North Carolina, 1945*, c. 32; *Session Laws of North Carolina, 1947*, c. 1030.

64. Loftfield and Littleton, *Reconnaissance*, 164-165; Bill Sharpe, "Onslow . . . The Big Change," *The State*, March 26, 1955, 23; John Clements, ed., *North Carolina Facts* (Dallas: Clements Research, Inc., 1988), 202; *Answer Book*, 18-19, 21.

65. County Commission Minutes, April 1914, September 1916.

66. Brown, *Commonwealth of Onslow*, 200-203.

67. County Commission Minutes, April 1909; *Public-Local Laws of North Carolina, 1913*, c. 705; Brown, *Commonwealth of Onslow*, 203-204.

68. *Biennial Report of the Superintendent of Public Instruction of North Carolina for the Scholastic Years 1900-1901 and 1901-1902* (Raleigh: Edwards & Broughton, 1902), 82-83, 88-89, 94-95, 102-103, 126-127, hereafter cited as *Superintendent's Report, Public Instruction, 1900-1901 and 1901-1902*.

69. *Heritage of Onslow*, 17-28; *Answer Book*, 58. Onslow High was later added to offer an alternative high school curriculum in the evening at various campuses. *Superintendent Report, Public Instruction, 1900-1901 and 1901-1902*, 82-83, 88-89, 94-95, 102-103, 126-127.

70. County Commission Minutes, September 1904, January 1905, April 1905, July 1905, July 1911.

71. Samuel Huntington Hobbs Jr., *North Carolina: Economic and Social* (Chapel Hill: University of North Carolina Press, 1930), table 53; *Fourteenth Census of the United States Taken in the Year 1920*, vol. 3, *Population* (Washington, D.C.: Government Printing Office, 1922), 741.

72. *Heritage of Onslow*, 29-30; Brown, *Commonwealth of Onslow*, 177.

73. Bellamy, "Onslow County's Black History," 29-30.

74. Bellamy, "Onslow County's Black History," 31-33.

75. Cheney, *North Carolina Government*, 1225; *Heritage of Onslow*, 31.

76. *North Carolina State Government Statistical Abstract*, 154, 176-177.

77. Coastal Carolina Community College. *Yesterday and Today. "Years of Success"* (n.p., n.d.); *Answer Book*, 60.

78. Brown, *Commonwealth of Onslow*, 136-137.

79. Brown, *Commonwealth of Onslow*, 137-138; *Answer Book*, 22.

80. Brown, *Commonwealth of Onslow*, 208; *Answer Book*, 46.

81. William A. Link, " 'The Harvest is Ripe, but the Laborers are Few': The Hookworm Crusade in North Carolina, 1909-1915," *North Carolina Historical Review* 67 (January 1990): 1-27.

82. Link, "The Harvest is Ripe," 20-27; County Commission Minutes, August, September, December 1911.

83. County Commission Minutes, December 1902, January 1903, February 1903, March 1903, May 1903, June 1903, July 1903, November 1903, January 1904, February 1904, March 1904, August 1904, October 1904, December 1904, February 1905, March 1905.

84. County Commission Minutes, March, June 1905; *Public Laws of North Carolina, 1903*, c. 235; *Public Laws of North Carolina, 1905*, c. 642.

85. Brown, *Commonwealth of Onslow*, 190-191; "100 Milestones of 1974," *The State*, January 1975, 46.

86. *Answer Book*, 24, 28-29.

87. Loftfield and Littleton, *Reconnaissance*, 166.

88. Commission Minutes, June 1905; *Public Laws of North Carolina, 1905*, cc. 838, 839; *Public-Local Laws of North Carolina, 1939*, c. 593.

89. *Public Laws of North Carolina, 1909*, c. 840; *Public-Local Laws of North Carolina, 1913*, c. 591; *Public-Local Laws of North Carolina, 1923*, c. 539; *Public-Local Laws of North Carolina, 1925*, cc. 488, 555.

90. *Answer Book*, 56.

91. Brown, *Commonwealth of Onslow*, 175-176.

92. Brown, *Commonwealth of Onslow*, 177.

93. Brown, *Commonwealth of Onslow*, 177-179.

94. Brown, *Commonwealth of Onslow*, 224-225; Clippings related to the library in Onslow County in an untitled scrapbook, Onslow Public Library, Jacksonville, N.C.

95. Brown, *Commonwealth of Onslow*, 183; Stallman, *History of Camp Davis*, 3-16.

96. Edward F. Turberg, "U.S. Naval Ordnance Testing Facility, Topsail Island," National Register of Historic Places Nomination Form, Division of Archives and History, Raleigh; Stallman, *History of Camp Davis*, 17-20.

97. Loftfield and Littleton, *Reconnaissance*, 168.

98. Gertrude S. Carraway, *Camp Lejeune Leathernecks* (New Bern, N.C.: Owen G. Dunn Company, 1946), 5-16.

99. Carraway, *Camp Lejeune Leathernecks*, 42-58: Brown, *Commonwealth of Onslow*, 186.

100. Brown, *Commonwealth of Onslow*, 188–190; Loftfield and Littleton, *Reconnaissance*, 168–169.

101. Mrs. Tyre Moore to Hon. Graham H. Barden, April 8, 1954; Graham A. Barden to Colonel H. C. Rowland Jr., August 30, 1956; A. Turner Shaw to Hon. Graham A. Barden, December 20, 1952, and enclosed petition dated December 1952, David Henderson Papers, Special Collections Department, Duke University Library, Durham.

102. *Answer Book*, 43.

103. *Data Book, 1979*, 4; *County Business Patterns, 1981. North Carolina* (Washington, D.C.: Government Printing Office, 1982), A-1; *Answer Book*, 39.

104. Bill Sharpe, "Onslow . . . The Big Change," *The State*, March 26, 1955, 22; *North Carolina State Government Statistical Abstract*, 484–485, 488–489; *Answer Book*, 33.

105. *North Carolina State Government Statistical Abstract*, 446–451, 457–459; *Wilmington Sunday Star News*, August 1, 1993; *Answer Book*, 17; *Census of Population and Housing, 1990*, 165, 174.

BIBLIOGRAPHY

PRIMARY SOURCES

A. Manuscripts

Duffy, Charles. Papers. Special Collections Department. Duke University Library, Durham.

French, Joseph M. Papers. East Carolina Manuscript Collection. J. Y. Joyner Library. East Carolina University, Greenville.

Hayes Collection. Southern Historical Collection. University of North Carolina Library, Chapel Hill.

Henderson, David. Papers. Special Collections Department. Duke University Library, Durham.

Littleton, Tucker. Papers. Private Collections. State Archives. Division of Archives and History, Raleigh.

Redd, Marcus Lafayette. Papers. Private Collections. State Archives. Division of Archives and History, Raleigh.

Williams, John Wesley. Papers. Special Collections Department. Duke University Library, Durham.

B. Government and Official Records

1. Unpublished (State Archives. Division of Archives and History, Raleigh.)

Anglican Church Records, microfilm

Legislative Papers

Minutes of the Carteret Court of Pleas and Quarter Sessions

Minutes of the Craven Court of Pleas and Quarter Sessions

Minutes of the Hyde Court of Pleas and Quarter Sessions

Minutes of the Tyrrell Court of Pleas and Quarter Sessions

Onslow County

    Deed Books

    Estates Records

    Minutes, County Commissioners

    Minutes of the Onslow County Court of Pleas and Quarter Sessions

    Miscellaneous Records

Secretary of State Papers

Treasurers' and Comptrollers' Papers

2. Published

Biennial Report of the Superintendent of Public Instruction of North Carolina for the Scholastic Years 1896-'97 and 1897-'98. Raleigh: Guy V. Barnes, 1898.

Biennial Report of the Superintendent of Public Instruction of North Carolina for the ScholasticYears 1900-1901 and 1901-1902. Raleigh: Edwards & Broughton, 1902.

*Census of Agriculture, 1978.*Vol. 1. Pt. 33. *North Carolina.* Washington, D.C.: Bureau of the Census, n.d.

*Census of Agriculture, 1987.*Vol. 1. Pt. 33. *North Carolina.* Washington, D.C.: Bureau of the Census, n.d.

Census of Manufactures, 1977. Vol. 3. Pt. 2.Washington: Department of Commerce, n.d.

Census of Manufactures, 1987. North Carolina. Washington, D.C.: Department of Commerce, 1990.

*Census of Population, 1980. North Carolina.*Vol. 1. Pt. 35. Washington, D.C.: Department of Commerce, 1982.

Census of Population and Housing, 1990. North Carolina. Washington, D.C.: Department of Commerce, 1991.

Cheney, John L., Jr., ed. *North Carolina Government, 1585-1979: A Narrative and Statistical History.* Raleigh: Department of the Secretary of State, 1981.

Compendium of the Tenth Census. Pt. 1. New York: Arno Press, 1976.

Congressional Record. 47th Cong., 1st sess., March 1881–March 1882; 2nd sess., December 1882–February 1883.

Connor, R. D. W., ed. *A Manual of North Carolina.* Raleigh: E. M. Uzzell & Co., 1913.

*County Business Patterns, 1981. North Carolina.*Washington, D.C.: Government Printing Office, 1982.

Data Book 1979. Region P. Socio-Economic Base Study. New Bern, N.C.: Neuse River Council of Governments, 1979.

DeBow, J. E. B., comp. *The Seventh Census of the United States. 1850.* Washington, D.C.: Robert Armstrong, 1853.

*Fifteenth Census of the United States, 1930.*Vol. 1. *Population.*Washington, D.C.: Government Printing Office, 1931.

*Fourteenth Census of the United States Taken in the Year 1920.*Vol. 3. *Population.* Washington, D.C.: Government Printing Office, 1922.

Fourteenth Census of the United States Taken in the Year 1920. Vol. 6. Pt. 2. *Agriculture.* Washington, D.C.: Government Printing Office, 1922.

*Fourteenth Census of the United States Taken in the Year 1920.*Vol. 9. *Manufactures. 1919.* Washington, D.C.: Government Printing Office, 1923.

Intracoastal Waterways, Beaufort, N.C. to Key West, Fla., Station. Washington, D.C.: Government Printing Office, 1913.

Jurney, R. C., et al. *Soil Survey of Onslow County, North Carolina.* Washington, D.C.: Government Printing Office, 1928.

Kennedy, Joseph P., comp. *Agriculture of the United States in 1860. . . .* Washington, D.C.: Government Printing Office, 1864.

————. *Population of the United States in 1860.* Washington, D.C.: Government Printing Office, 1864.

Manufactures of the United States in 1860. . . . Washington, D.C.: Government Printing Office, 1865.

North Carolina Manual, 1977, 1979, 1981, 1983, 1985, 1987, 1989, 1991, 1992. Raleigh: Secretary of State. Appropriate dates.

North Carolina State Government Statistical Abstract. 5th ed., 1984. Raleigh: State Data Center, n.d.

Official Records of the Union and Confederate Navies in the War of the Rebellion. 28 vols. Washington, D.C.: Government Printing Office, 1894-1922.

"Onslow County Government Working for You." N.p., n.d.

Population of the United States . . . as Returned at the Twelfth Census, 1900. Washington, D.C.: Government Printing Office, 1901.

Report on a Survey of the Organization and Administration of County Government in North Carolina. Washington, D.C.: Institute for County Government, 1930.

Scammon, Richard, and Alice V. McGillivray, eds. and comps. *America Votes: A Handbook of Contemporary American Election Statistics.* 20 vols. to date. Washington, D.C.: Election Research Center, 1956—.

Walker, Francis A., comp. *A Compendium of the Ninth Census. . . .* Washington, D.C.: Government Printing Office, 1872.

The War of the Rebellion: A Compilation of the Official Records of the Union and Confederate Armies. 70 vols. in 127. Washington, D.C.: Government Printing Office, 1880-1901.

C. Newspapers

Beaufort Weekly Record

Kinston Daily Free Press

New Bern Atlantic

New Bern Carolina Sentinel (Sentinel)

New Bern Chronicle

New Bern Daily Journal

New Bern Martin's North-Carolina Gazette

New Bern New Era

New Bern North-Carolina Gazette

New Bern State Gazette of North-Carolina

New Bern Weekly Union

Newbern Weekly Progress

Newbernian

North-Carolina Chronicle, or *Fayetteville Gazette*

People's Press. and Wilmington Advertiser

Philadelphia Pennsylvania Gazette

Raleigh Minerva

Raleigh News and Observer

Raleigh North Carolina Standard

Raleigh Register

Wilmington Daily Journal

Wilmington Gazette

Wilmington Journal

Wilmington Morning Star

Wilmington People's Press

Wilmington Sunday Star-News

Wilmington Weekly Star

D. Miscellaneous

Avirett, James Battle. *The Old Plantation: How We Lived in the Great House and Cabin Before the War.* New York: F. Tennyson Neely Co., 1901.

Branson, Levi, ed. *Branson's North Carolina Business Directory for 1867-8.* Raleigh: Branson & Jones, n.d.

————. *Branson's North Carolina Business Directory, 1877 and 1878.* Raleigh: L. Branson, 1878.

————. *Branson's North Carolina Business Directory for 1884.* Raleigh: Levi Branson, 1884.

————. *Branson's North Carolina Business Directory, 1896.* Raleigh: Levi Branson, 1896.

Carroll, Grady, ed. *Francis Asbury in North Carolina.* Nashville, Tenn.: Parthenon Press, n.d.

Clark, Walter, ed. *Histories of the Several Regiments and Battalions from North Carolina in the Great War, 1861-'65.* 5 vols. Raleigh: State of North Carolina, 1901.

————. *The State Records of North Carolina.* 16 vols., numbered 11-26. Winston and Goldsboro, N.C.: State of North Carolina, 1895-1907.

Davis, James. *The Office and Authority of a Justice of the Peace.* Newburn, N.C.: James Davis, 1774.

Grimes, J. Bryan, ed. *North Carolina Wills and Inventories.* Raleigh: Edwards & Broughton, 1912.

Heads of Families at the First Census of the United States Taken in the Year 1790. Baltimore: Genealogical Publishing Company, 1966.

Hoyt, William H., ed. *The Papers of Archibald D. Murphey.* Vol. 2. Raleigh: E. M. Uzzell & Co., 1914.

Jackson, Donald and Dorothy Twohig, ed. *The Diaries of George Washington.* Vol. 6. Charlottesville: University of Virginia Press, 1979.

Johnston, Hugh B., ed. "The Journal of Ebenezer Hazard in North Carolina, 1777 and 1778." *North Carolina Historical Review* 36 (July 1959): 358-381.

Laws and Resolutions of the State of North Carolina.

"William Logan's Journal of a Journey to Georgia, 1745." *Pennsylvania Magazine of History and Biography* 36 (1912): 1-16.

McEachern, Leora H., and Isabel M. Williams, eds. *Wilmington-New Hanover Safety Committee Minutes, 1774-1776.* Wilmington, N.C.: Wilmington-New Hanover County American Bi-Centennial Association, 1974.

Manarin, Louis H., and Weymouth T. Jordan Jr., comps. *North Carolina Troops, 1861-1865: A Roster.* 13 vols. to date. Raleigh: Division of Archives and History, Department of Cultural Resources, 1966—.

Powell, William S., ed. *The Correspondence of William Tryon and Other Selected Papers.* Vol. 2. Raleigh: Division of Archives and History, Department of Cultural Resources, 1981.

Pratt, Joseph Hyde, ed. *Report of the Fisheries Convention Held at New Bern, North Carolina, December 13, 1911.* Raleigh: Edwards & Broughton, 1912.

Proceedings and Debates of the Convention of North Carolina, Called to Amend the Constitution of the State, Which Assembled at Raleigh, June 4, 1835. Raleigh: Joseph Gales and Son, 1836.

Saunders, William L., ed. *The Colonial Records of North Carolina.* 10 vols. Raleigh: State of North Carolina, 1886-1890.

Schoepf, Johann David. *Travels in the Confederation (1783-1784).* Vol. 2. Translated and edited by Alfred J. Morrison. Philadelphia: William J. Campbell, 1911.

Wright, Louis B., and Marion Tinling, eds. *Quebec to Carolina in 1785-1786: Being the Travel Diary and Observations of Robert Hunter, Jr., a Young Merchant of London.* San Marino, Calif.: The Huntington Library, 1943.

SECONDARY SOURCES

A. Articles

Bellamy, Donnie D. "Slavery in Microcosm: Onslow County, North Carolina." *Journal of Negro History* 62 (October 1977): 339-350.

Counihan, Harold J. "The North Carolina Constitutional Convention of 1835: A Study in Jacksonian Democracy." *North Carolina Historical Review* 46 (autumn 1969): 335-364.

De Van Massey, Gregory. "The British Expedition to Wilmington, January-November 1781." *North Carolina Historical Review* 66 (October 1989): 387-411.

Dill, Alonzo Thomas, Jr. "Eighteenth Century New Bern: A History of the Town and Craven County, 1700-1800. Part VIII." *North Carolina Historical Review* 23 (October 1946): 495-535.

Greene, Jack P. "The North Carolina Lower House and the Power to Appoint Public Treasurers, 1711-1775." *North Carolina Historical Review* 40 (winter 1963): 37-53.

Hinshaw, Clifford Reginald, Jr. "North Carolina Canals Before 1860." *North Carolina Historical Review* 25 (January 1948): 1-57.

Kay, Marvin L. Michael. "The Payment of Provincial and Local Taxes in North Carolina, 1748-1771." *William and Mary Quarterly*, 3rd ser., 26 (April 1969): 218-240.

Link, William A. " 'The Harvest is Ripe, but the Laborers are Few': The Hookworm Crusade in North Carolina, 1909-1915." *North Carolina Historical Review* 67 (January 1990): 1-27.

Loomis, Charles P. "The Rise and Decline of the North Carolina Farmers' Union." *North Carolina Historical Review* 7 (July 1930): 305-325.

Pool, William C. "An Economic Interpretation of the Ratification of the Federal Constitution in North Carolina." Parts 1-3. *North Carolina Historical Review* 27 (April/July/October 1950): 119-141, 289-313, 437-461.

Schweninger, Loren. "John Carruthers Stanly and the Anomaly of Black Slaveholding." *North Carolina Historical Review* 67 (April 1990): 159-192.

Simpson, Marcus B., Jr., and Sallie M. Simpson. "The Pursuit of Leviathan: A History of Whaling on the North Carolina Coast." *North Carolina Historical Review* 65 (January 1988): 1-51.

Starling, Roger B. "The Plank Road Movement in North Carolina." Parts 1 and 2. *North Carolina Historical Review* 16 (January/April 1939): 1-22, 147-173.

Watson, Alan D. "Regulation and Administration of Roads and Bridges in Colonial Eastern North Carolina." *North Carolina Historical Review* 45 (autumn 1968): 399-417.

————. "The Ferry in Colonial North Carolina: A Vital Link in Transportation." *North Carolina Historical Review* 51 (summer 1974): 247-260.

————. "The Appointment of Sheriffs in Colonial North Carolina: A Reexamination." *North Carolina Historical Review* 53 (autumn 1976): 385-398.

————. "County Fiscal Policy in North Carolina." *North Carolina Historical Review* 55 (summer 1978): 284-305.

————. "Household Size and Composition in Pre-Revolutionary North Carolina." *Mississippi Quarterly* 31 (fall 1978): 551-569.

B. Monographs

Blassingame, John W. *The Slave Community: Plantation Life in the Antebellum South.* New York: Oxford University Press, 1972.

Brown, Joseph Parsons. *The Commonwealth of Onslow: A History.* New Bern, N.C.: Owen G. Dunn, 1960.

Carraway, Gertrude S. *Camp Lejeune Leathernecks.* New Bern, N.C.: Owen G. Dunn, 1946.

Crittenden, Charles Christopher. *The Commerce of North Carolina, 1763-1789.* New Haven: Yale University Press, 1936.

Crow, Jeffrey J., and Robert R. Durden. *Maverick Republican in the Old North State: A Political Biography of Daniel L. Russell.* Baton Rouge: Louisiana State University Press, 1977.

Franklin, John Hope. *The Free Negro in North Carolina, 1790-1860.* Chapel Hill: University of North Carolina Press, 1943.

Greene, Jack P. *The Quest for Power: The Lower Houses of Assembly in the Southern Royal Colonies, 1689-1776.* Chapel Hill: University of North Carolina Press, 1963.

Hartzer, Ronald B. *To Great and Useful Purpose: A History of the Wilmington District U.S. Army Corps of Engineers.* N.p., n.d.

Hobbs, Samuel Huntington, Jr. *North Carolina: Economic and Social.* Chapel Hill: University of North Carolina Press, 1930.

————. *North Carolina: An Economic and Social Profile.* Chapel Hill: University of North Carolina Press, 1958.

Hoffmann, William S. *Andrew Jackson and North Carolina Politics.* The James Sprunt Studies in History and Political Science, vol. 40. Chapel Hill: University of North Carolina Press, 1958.

Jeffrey, Thomas E. *State Parties and National Politics: North Carolina, 1815-1861.* Athens, Ga.: University of Georgia Press, 1989.

Johnson, Guion Griffis. *Ante-Bellum North Carolina: A Social History.* Chapel Hill: University of North Carolina Press, 1937.

Kruman, Marc W. *Parties and Politics in North Carolina, 1836-1865.* Baton Rouge: Louisiana State University Press, 1983.

Lee, Lawrence. *The Lower Cape Fear in Colonial Days.* Chapel Hill: University of North Carolina Press, 1965.

Ludlum, David M. *Early American Hurricanes, 1472-1870.* Boston: American Meteorological Society, 1963.

McCain, Paul. *The County Court in North Carolina before 1750.* Durham, N.C.: Duke University Press, 1954.

Merrens, H. Roy. *Colonial North Carolina in the Eighteenth Century: A Study in Historical Geography.* Chapel Hill: University of North Carolina Press, 1964.

Newsome, Albert Ray. *The Presidential Election of 1824 in North Carolina.* The James Sprunt Studies in History and Political Science, vol. 23, no. 1. Chapel Hill: University of North Carolina Press, 1939.

Perdue, Theda. *Native Carolinians: The Indians of North Carolina.* Raleigh: Division of Archives and History, North Carolina Department of Cultural Resources, 1985.

Prince, Richard E. *Atlantic Coast Line Railroad: Steam Locomotives, Ships, and History.* Green River, Wyo.: Richard E. Prince, 1966.

Sitterson, Joseph Carlyle. *The Secession Movement in North Carolina.* The James Sprunt Series in History and Political Science, vol. 23, no. 2. Chapel Hill: University of North Carolina Press, 1939.

Smith, Daniel Blake. *Inside the Great House: Planter Family Life in Eighteenth-Century Chesapeake Society.* Ithaca, N.Y.: Cornell University Press, 1980.

Sprunt, James. *Chronicle of the Lower Cape Fear River, 1660-1916.* 2nd ed. Raleigh: Edwards & Broughton Printing Company, 1916.

Stallman, David A. *A History of Camp Davis.* Hampstead, N.C.: Hampstead Services, Inc., 1990.

Wager, Paul. *County Government and Administration in North Carolina.* Chapel Hill: University of North Carolina Press, 1928.

Wroth, Lawrence C. *The Voyages of Giovanni Da Verrazzano, 1524-1528.* New Haven: Yale University Press, 1970.

C. Miscellaneous

"Albert J. Ellis Airport, 1791-1991." Brochure. N.p., n.d.

"Alum Spring." National Register of Historic Places Nomination Form. Division of Archives and History, Raleigh.

Angley, Wilson. "An Historical Overview of Bogue Inlet." October 16, 1984, Research Branch Report. In Historical Research Reports, ser. 2, compiled and edited by Wilson Angley. Research Branch, North Carolina Division of Archives and History, Department of Cultural Resources, 1990. Microfilm.

The Answer Book. Published by the *Jacksonville (N.C.) Daily News.* August 30, 1992.

Ashe, Samuel A. *Biographical History of North Carolina*. Vol. 5. Greensboro, N.C.: C. L. Van Noppen, 1906.

Clements, John. *North Carolina Facts*. Dallas: Clements Research, Inc., 1988.

Clippings related to the Public Library in Onslow County in an untitled scrapbook. Onslow Public Library, Jacksonville, N.C.

Coastal Carolina Community College. Yesterday and Today. "Years of Success." N.p., n.d.

Corbitt, David Leroy. *The Formation of the North Carolina Counties, 1663-1943.* Raleigh: State Department of Archives and History, 1950.

Ferrell, Joseph S., ed. *County Government in North Carolina.* 2d ed. Chapel Hill: Institute of Government, 1979.

The Heritage of Onslow County. Winston-Salem, N.C.: Hunter Publishing Company, n.d.

"Historic and Architectural Resources of Onslow County, North Carolina." National Register of Historic Places Multiple Property Documentary Form. Division of Archives and History, Raleigh.

Loftfield, Thomas C. "Excavations at 31 on v 33, A Late Woodland Seasonal Village." Typescript. Marine Science Fund. University of North Carolina at Wilmington.

————. "Testing and Excavation at 31 on 82." Typescript. Department of Anthropology. University of North Carolina at Wilmington.

————. "Testing and Excavation at 31 on 196 Permuda Island." Typescript. Department of Anthropology, University of North Carolina at Wilmington, 1985.

Loftfield, Thomas C., principal investigator, and Tucker R. Littleton, comp. *An Archaeological and Historical Reconnaissance of U.S. Marine Corps Base, Camp Lejeune. Part 2. The Historic Record.* N.p., 1981.

"100 Milestones of 1972." *The State*, January 1973.

"100 Milestones of 1974." *The State*, January 1975.

Phelps, David Sutton. "Archaeology of the North Carolina Coast and Coastal Plain: Problems and Hypotheses." In *The Prehistory of North Carolina: An Archaeological Symposium*, edited by Mark A. Mathis and Jeffrey J. Crow, 18-26. Raleigh: Division of Archives and History, North Carolina Department of Cultural Resources, 1983.

Powell, William S., ed. *The North Carolina Gazetteer.* Chapel Hill: University of North Carolina Press, 1968.

————. *Dictionary of North Carolina Biography.* Vol. 2. Chapel Hill: University of North Carolina Press, 1986.

Sharpe, Bill. "The Clam that Began to Build an Airstrip." *The State*, March 26, 1955.

————. "Onslow . . . The Big Change." *The State*, March 26, 1955.

Taylor, Harden F. et al. *Survey of Marine Fisheries of North Carolina.* Chapel Hill: University of North Carolina Press, 1951.

Turberg, Edward F. "U.S. Naval Ordnance Testing Facility, Topsail Island." National Register of Historic Places Nomination Form. Division of Archives and History, Raleigh.

Watson, Alan D., Dennis R. Lawson, and Donald R. Lennon. *Harnett, Hooper & Howe.* Wilmington, N.C.: Louis T. Moore Memorial Commission, 1979.

Wright, W. B. "100 Milestones of 1969." *The State*, January 1, 1970.

D. Unpublished Papers (Seminar on Onslow County History, Swansboro, N.C., 1982)

Bellamy, Donnie D. "Onslow County's Black History."

Cross, Jerry L. "Onslow County, 1865–1920: Transition, Change, and Continuity."

Johnson, Guion Griffis. "Antebellum Onslow County: A Social History."

Lemmon, Sarah McCulloh. "Onslow County During the War of 1812."

Manarin, Louis. "Onslow County During the Civil War."

Mathews, Alice E. "The Social History of Onslow County."

Perry, Percival. "The Naval Stores Industry in Onslow County, North Carolina, 1735–1920."

Still, William N., Jr. "Shipbuilding in Onslow County."

Watson, Alan D. "Colonial Onslow County."

INDEX

A

Adams, John Quincy, 60

Adams, Samuel, 24

Agriculture: depressed conditions of, in late nineteenth century, 99; during antebellum period, 47-49; during colonial era, 13, 22; effects of Civil War on, 86-87; in late nineteenth century, 88; and politics in late nineteenth century, 78-79; in twentieth century, 111-113

Albemarle, 2, 6, 61, 68

Albemarle County, 14

Albert J. Ellis Airport, 122-123

Alice Webb (schooner), 71

Allen, Eleazar, 7

Alum Spring, 35, 85, 104

Aman, Dennis, 49

Aman's Store, 32

Ambrose, James, 22

Ambrose, Nancy, 35

AME churches, 102

American Missionary Association, 100

American Missionary Society, 97

American Party, 107

AME Zion churches, 102, 123

Anglican Church, 22-23, 35

Antifederalists, 29

Appeal (antislavery tract), 40

Archdale Precinct, 2

Asbury, Francis, 46

Ashe, John, 4, 18, 26

Atlantic and North Carolina Railroad, 93

Atlantic Coast Line Railroad, 94, 122

Atlantic Coast Railway Company, 94

Atlantic Missionary Baptist Church, 102

Averitt, James, 43

Averitt, John A.: alters public road, 52; employs poor whites, 34; helps lead New River Canal Company, 54; owns Rich Lands plantation, 33-34, slaves, 37-38, 47-48, turpentine distilleries, 49-50; sends daughter to St. Mary's school, 43; serves as delegate to 1835 convention, 61-62, in house of commons, 63

Averitt family, 40, 44

Avery, Lewis A., 92

B

Ballard, Lot, 46

Bank of Onslow, 109

Baptists, 23, 45-46, 102, 123

Barker, Dr. (phrenologist), 45

Barker, Thomas, 7

Barkersville, 92. *See also* Stella

Barnum, Z. B., 56

Barrage Balloon Training Center (Camp Davis), 132; pictured, 133

Bath County, 2, 14

Bay View, 98

Bay View Railroad, 95

Bear Banks, 50

Bear Creek, 3, 50, 71, 73

Bear Inlet: becomes commodities inspection site, 14; during Civil War, 68-69, 71; as entrance to county, 17; funds appropriated to build fort at, 6; shipwrecks at, 18

Beasleys Creek, 6

Bedford (schooner), 17

Belgrade, 121, 127

Belgrade Courier, 127

Bell, John C., 64-65

Bell, Ronnie J., 108

Ben (slave belonging to Benjamin Jarman), 37

Bennett, John, 20

Beulaville, 127

"Big August" picnic, 104

Bixby, William H., 96

172

173

Hammocks, 129
Hammocks Beach State Park, 2
Harding, Warren G., 107
Hardison, Paul, 108
Hargett, F. W., 121
Harman, H. A., 101
Harrell, Peter, 30
Harrison, Benjamin, 80
Harrison, Luther, 88
Harvey, Benjamin, 26
Harvey, John, 26
Harvey, Seth, 27-28
Hatch Fork, 91
Hawkins, Bazel, 55
Hawkins, Catherine, 35
Hawkins, William, 59
Hazard, Ebenezer, 24
Health care: during antebellum period, 40; during Civil War, 73; during colonial era, 20; during late nineteenth century, 85-86, 102-103; during twentieth century, 111, 128-129
Heidelberg, Christian, 9
Henderson, Fred C., 127
Henderson, Isaac N., 88
Heritage, Sarah, 85
Hermitage, Caleb, 20
Hill, Edward, 87
Hill, Monte, 119; pictured, 118
Hill, William L., 39
Hill family, 119
Hitch Logging Company, 115
Hodges, William, 9
Hofmann, J. V., 116
Hofmann Forest, 116
Hogg, Robert, 18
Hoke, Robert F., 67
Holden, William W., 74-77
Holly Ridge: establishment of Camp Davis at, 132-133; health clinic in, 129; incorporation of, 107; Thomas A. McIntyre buys land around, 99; transportation links to, 94, 121
Holly Shelter, 27
Hoover, Herbert, 107
Howard, Edward, 23
Howard, James, 8, 17-18, 41
Howard, Joseph, 9-11, 16
Howard, Josiah, 39
Howards Bay, 17
Howquah (Union ship), 71
Huggins, A. C., 83, 98

Huggins, Owen: chairs meeting to respond to Lincoln's election, 65; heads county court, 74; helps lead New River Canal Company, 54; loses race for house of commons, 63; storms damage property of, 48
Huggins Island, 69-70
Humphrey, Lott, 58
Humphrey, Lott W., 36, 54, 63, 68
Humphrey, White D., 30, 74
Humphrey Troop, 68
Hunter, Ezekiel, 7-8, 23
Hurley, Ann, 20
Hurst, Gerald B., 108
Hurst, Wilda H., 108

I

Intracoastal Waterway, 117
Ireland, Miss O. J., 99
Isaac (slave), 19

J

Jackson, Andrew, 33, 60
Jacksonville, 47, 57, 64, 80, 122, 136; banking in, during depression, 131; black candidates for political office in, 108; bridges at, 93, 121; churches in, 45, 102; civil rights convention held in, 77; courthouse at, 86; during Civil War, 70-71; education in, 42, 125-127; electrification of, 124; growth of, after World War II, 105-106, in late nineteenth century, 98; hosts Onslow Agricultural Fair, 49; incorporation of, 33; influence of Camp Lejeune on, 132; meeting held in, in response to Lincoln's election, 65; name changed to, 29; naval stores in, 115; newspapers in, 101, 127; occupied by Union troops, 70; phrenologist visits, 45; physician in, 129; proposed as site for county home, 111; public library headquarters in, 131; Sons of Temperance in, 47; telephone service in, 124; transportation links to, 93-95, 98, 117, 121; Van Buren supporters meet in, 62; votes in favor of prohibition, 123; White Government Union organized in, 80. *See also* Onslow Court House; Wantland's Ferry

Petersburg and Weldon Railroad, 67
Peterson, Andrew, 101
Pevensey (blockade-runner), 71
Pickett, George E., 67
Piney Green, 102
Pitts, Mary, 20
Planters Railroad Company, 93
Pollard, Tommy, 108
Pool, John, 64
Population: during antebellum period, 30-31; during colonial era, 18; in late nineteenth century, 97-98; in twentieth century, 105
Populism, 78-81, 101
Porter, E., 102
Pounds, Mary, 20
Presbyterians, 23, 123
Prittyman, J. F., 115
Prohibition, 123
Prometheus (steamboat), 50-51; pictured, 51
Public Library of Onslow County, 131

Q

Quaker Bridge Road, 91
Quakers, 23
Queens Creek, 114

R

Ragan, Sam, 127
Ragsdale, Hugh, 108
Railroads: during antebellum period, 54-55; following Civil War, 93-94; in late nineteenth century, 94-95, 98-99; and lumbering interests, 115-116; in twentieth century, 122
Raleigh, Walter, 2
Raleigh North Carolina Standard, 74
Randolph-Macon College, 42
Ransom, Jack, 19
Rebecca (slave belonging to Benjamin Jarman), 37
Redd, Marcus L. F.: advises daughter at boarding school, 35; operates saltworks, 69; serves as captain of Onslow Greys, 47, 66, 68
Regulator movement, 6, 9, 25
Republican Party: during Reconstruction, 75, 77; during twentieth century, 107-108; in 1860 presidential election, 64; inception of, 64; in late nineteenth century, 78-81; and public education, 100

Revolutionary War, 25-28, 34
Rhodes, A. H., 85
Rhodes, Edward H., 66
Rhodes, Henry, 7-8, 18, 26-28
Rice, Nathaniel, 4, 18
Rich Lands, 76, 78, 98; area of, raided by British, 28; origins of, 155; and Richlands, 155
Richlands, 88, 122; attempt to establish racetrack in, 130; banking in, during depression, 131; connected to Dover and South Bound Railroad, 122; education in, 41-43; 125; electrification of, 124; growth of, in twentieth century, 106; health clinic in, 129; incorporation of, 98; incorporation of, reaffirmed by legislature, 106; medical demonstrations in, 128; Onslow County Museum located in, 128; opening of mercantile store in, 56; opposition to free blacks in, 36; origins of, 155; physician in, 103; prohibition in, 102; public library in, 131; railroad subscription effort in, 94; religion in, 45-46; and Rich Lands, 155; Sons of Temperance in, 47; telephone service in, 124
Richlands Academy, 42-43, 47, 73, 76
Richlands and New River Plank Road Company, 53
Richlands District, 34-35
Rich Lands plantation, 34, 37, 43, 61; livestock at, 22; management of slaves on, 47-48; size and location of, 34; slave cabins on, 39; slave wedding on, 38
Richlands Township, 77; creates road board, 120; established, 81; home schooling in, 100; promotion of tobacco in, 88; votes to subscribe to railroad stock, 122; voting district established, 109
Roads: during antebellum period, 29, 51-53; during colonial era, 3, 14, 16; in late nineteenth century, 91-92; in twentieth century, 119-121
Roberts, Edward, 21
Rockefeller Sanitary Commission, 128
Roman Catholics, 123
Roosevelt, Franklin D., 131, 135
Roosevelt, Theodore, 107
Rough and Readys, 67

180

Stump Sound (community), 98
Stump Sound Banks, 56
Stump Sound District, 63, 77
Stump Sound Township, 81, 101, 109, 120
Summersill, Edward W., 108
Swann, Samuel, 6-7, 32
Swansboro, 35, 49, 53, 56, 100; church in, 102; creation of lifeboat station near, 117; creation of port district of, 55; during Civil War, 68-71; during first half of nineteenth century, 32; education in, 42-43, 100, 125; fishing near, 89; Front Street in, pictured 106; growth of, in twentieth century, 106-107; impact of Camp Lejeune on, 135; incorporation of, 32, renewed, 98; lumbering in, 98; maritime trade involving, 56, 96; newspaper in, 127; opposition to free blacks in, 36; prohibition in, 102; public library in, 131; recreation in, 44-45, 103; religion in, 45-46; shipbuilding at, 50, 87, 118; Swansboro Academy, 32, 42; telephone service in, 124; transportation links to, 54, 95, 121
Swansboro District, 31, 63
Swansboro Graded School: students at, pictured, 125
Swansboro Land and Lumber Company, 107, 115; store and office of, pictured, 116; Swansboro Lumber Company, 96-97
Swansboro Tideland News, 127
Swansboro Township: established, 81; established as voting district, 109; literacy rates in, 101; votes to subscribe to railroad stock, 122

T

Taft, William Howard, 107
Tarboro (steamer), 96-97
Tar Landing, 91
Tatham, William, 50
Taverns, 20, 23-24, 46
Telephone service, 124
Tenth Regiment N.C. Troops, 68
Terry, Hilery, 97
Third Regiment N.C. State Troops, 66-67
Thirty-fifth Regiment N.C. Troops, 67

Thirty-sixth Regiment N.C. Troops, 68
Thompson, Cyrus, 78-79, 85, 102; pictured, 79
Thompson, Frank, 80, 101
Thompson, Franklin, Sr., 78, 87
Thompson, Walter M., 125-126
Thorne Apple Valley, 119
Thurrell's Bluff, 16
Tide Water Power Company, 124
Tilden, Samuel J., 76
Titus (slave), 19
Todd's Landing, 14
Topsail Banks, 22
Topsail Island, 107, 132-133
Town Point plantation, 99
Trent River Oakey Grove Collegiate and Industrial Training School, 126
Trent River Oakey Grove Missionary Baptist Association, 126
Tryon, William, 6
Turner, Nat, 40
Tuscarora Indians, 2
Tuscarora War, 2
Twenty-fourth Regiment N.C. Troops, 67-68
Twenty-seventh Regiment N.C. Troops, 68
Two Sisters (merchant ship), 55
Tyndall, J. Paul, 127

U

Uncle Philip (slave belonging to John A. Averitt), 48, 50
Underwood, U. A., 111
Union Chapel (Union Chapel Christian Church), 45
Upper Richlands, 155
Upper Richlands District, 63
Upper South West District, 63
U.S. 17 (highway), 121
U.S. Army Corps of Engineers, 96

V

Van Buren, Martin, 60, 62
Vance, Zebulon B., 70, 74, 76
Venters, Carl V., 108
Verona, 94, 121
Verrazzano, Giovanni da, 2

W

Walker, David, 40